Land without Nightingales

Land without Nightingales:

Music in the Making of German-America

Edited by

Philip V. Bohlman and Otto Holzapfel

Studies of the
Max Kade Institute for German American Studies
University of Wisconsin–Madison

901 University Bay Drive, Madison, WI

Library of Congress Cataloging-in-Publication Data

Bohlman, Philip Vilas.
Land without nightingales: music in the making of German-America / Edited by Philip V. Bohlman & Otto Holzapfel.
p. cm. —
(Studies of the Max Kade Institute for German-American Studies)
Includes bibliographical references (p.) and index.
ISBN 0-924119-04-7 (hardcover)
1. German Americans—Music—History and criticism. 2. Folk music—United States—History and criticism. I. Holzapfel, Otto. II. Title. III. Series.
ML3555 .B56 2002
780'.89'31073--dc21 2002005904
CIP

For the generation that follows,
Andrea, Ben, Birgit, and Kirsten,
who so richly make tradition their own.

Contents

Acknowledgments

The transformations accompanying the separation wrought by immigration, the emergence of ethnic differences, and the shaping of multicultural societies are anything but simple. Such transformations are active processes, and they become possible only through the contributions of many different individuals and communities at each stage of a long transformative process. So, too, have the transformations that led to the publication of *Land without Nightingales* been possible only because of the contributions of many individuals and communities, and we take this opportunity to express our gratitude for the engagement and hard work that accompanied this book from the earliest stages to its final publication.

From the very beginning *Land without Nightingales* benefited from discussions that crossed the Atlantic, both acknowledging hyphenized identities and blurring the dichotomies that separate rather than embrace historical and cultural difference. The idea for the conference emerged from years of discussion and collaboration between the editors, whose journeys between Freiburg im Breisgau and Chicago were supported by the Deutsches Volksliedarchiv and the University of Chicago. We are grateful to both institutions for fostering and financing the journeys that brought us together. The University of Chicago, moreover, provided funding for the Centennial conference in April 1992 that at once celebrated the one hundredth anniversary of the founding of the University of Chicago and brought the scholars and musicians together, whose contributions would ultimately form the basis for this book. We owe special thanks to Philip Gossett, Dean of the Humanities, and Kineret Jaffe, chair of the Centennial committee at the University of Chciago. At the first stage we also received generous financial support from the Goethe Institute of Chicago, which hosted several conference events and offered a generous financial subvention that spurred us to undertake the transformation of conference events into a book. We are very grateful to those at the Goethe Institute who worked with us at the time of the conference, particularly to its director Hans Georg Knopp and to Angela Greiner and Hartmut Karottki.

Early financial support also came from the Wieboldt-Rosenwald Collection of German Folk Songs in Special Collections of the Regenstein Library at the University of Chicago, through gifts from Anita S. Darrow and her family. The Wieboldt-Rosenwald Collection also made it possible to engage research and editorial assistants from the remarkable graduate assistants in the Department of Music, notably

Gregory F. Barz, Jerry Cadden, Catherine Cole, and Brian Currid. In the final stages of preparing the manuscript, the labors of Billy K. Vaughn were particularly indispensable. We should also like to express our thanks to the Mills Music Library of the University of Wisconsin-Madison, which made its collection of early sound recordings of German- and Austrian-American music available for the CD appearing together with this volume. As the book began to take shape, the Alexander von Humboldt Foundation supported the ongoing discussions and editorial work in Freiburg im Breisgau and Chicago with a Trans-Atlantic Cooperation Grant (1993-96), for which we are indeed very thankful.

We could not imagine a better home for *Land without Nightingales* than the monograph series of the Max Kade Institute for German-American Studies at the University of Wisconsin-Madison. We are indebted to the Director of the Max Kade Institute, Joseph Salmons, and to the series editor, Mark L. Louden, for their willingness to give this volume such a fine home. Those with a keen eye for book design will already have noticed the elegant touches of A-R Editions of Middleton, Wisconsin, and we are fortunate indeed that James L. Zychowicz was willing to take this project under his wing. The CD owes its existence to the magical sound engineering of Emil H. Lubej, ethnomusicologist extraordinaire at the University of Vienna. The patience and persistence of our editorial assistant, Eric Platt, deserves special recognition, for it was Eric who transformed a manuscript bristling with a sometimes unruly welter of musical examples, photographs, and sound recordings into a book.

A book about music is at its best when it mixes sound and discourse from the beginning. The authors and musicians—and many of our authors are musicians—whose musical and intellectual performances constituted the earliest stage of this book about Central European musics and musical practices were willing to share their talents and experiences in such ways that voices long silenced and those singing new songs in a land no longer strange could be heard. Heartfelt thanks to all of you for raising such crucial questions about the assumptions that would lead anyone to claim that any nation could be a land without nightingales.

Chicago, Illinois
Freiburg im Breisgau

Contributors

Philip V. Bohlman is Professor of Music and Jewish Studies at the University of Chicago.

Alan R. Burdette is Executive Director of the Society for Ethnomusicology.

Kathleen Neils Conzen is Professor of History and Chair of the History Department at the University of Chicago.

Otto Holzapfel is Professor of Folklore and Scandinavian Studies at the University of Freiburg im Breisgau and is Head of the Textual Division of the Deutsches Volksliedarchiv, Freiburg.

James P. Leary is Director of the Folklore Program at the University of Wisconsin-Madison.

Laurence Libin is the Frederick P. Rose Curator of Musical Instruments at the Metropolitan Museum of Art.

Rudolf Pietsch is Professor of Folk-Music Research at the University of Music and Performing Arts in Vienna, Austria.

A. Gregg Roeber is Professor of History and Chair of the History Department at the Pennsylvania State University, where he is also Director of the Max Kade Institute for German-American Studies.

Leo Schelbert is Professor of History at the University of Illinois at Chicago.

Helmut Wulz is Director Emeritus of Folklore at Austrian Radio (ORF) in Klagenfurt.

CD Notes and Commentary

A sound portrait of music from German America contains a remarkable array of sounds, styles, and symbols that together represent German-American identity in a fantastic number of ways. There are individual repertories—some of them, for example, in the sections grouping the examples on this CD—but these are likely to reveal even more diversity than continuity. There are distinctive styles, too, but the historical examples on the CD make it clear that they are shaped by the time, place, and contexts of performance. In some ways, the cornucopia of German-American musics that this sound portrait makes available is particularly distinctive for what it does not document: we witness no leveling or abandonment of style, and German music loses none of its vitality as it becomes American music. The sections on the CD should function inclusively rather than exclusively. In other words, the examples in one section might very well illustrate the unifying characteristics of another section. Several sections may take their shape from related repertories or ensemble structures. Three of the sections provide opportunities to connect musical examples with specific essays: "Choral Singing and Social Music Making" (Alan R. Burdette, Chapt. 9); "Concertina Traditions" (James P. Leary, Chapt. 8); and "Burgenland Music from the Polka Belt" (Rudolf Pietsch, Chapt. 10). Each soundprint on the CD, moreover, gives voice to several themes in the book, making them more vivid and connecting them to the abundant ways music has been crucial to the making of German America.

Traditional Soundprints

1 – Frau Müller & Herr Niemsee: "I bin ja ka Steirer" ("I'm No Styrian"). One of the most striking early examples of Austrian music recorded by Columbia in Austria for distribution to Central Europeans in North America. Little is known about Frau Müller and Herr Niemsee, but the Viennese style of yodeling and shifting Ländler tempi only support the assertion of this song's text that the singers do not come from rural, alpine Styria in Austria.

2 – Irving DeWitz: "Ländler." Born in 1896, Irving DeWitz reigned for decades as one of the most influential concertinists in the Dodge County region of eastern Wisconsin. In this performance he translates the alpine character of the Ländler

from the European button box to its American cousin, the concertina. (Recorded 1985 in Hustisford, Wisconsin, and originally released on *Ach Ya!*, 3, 3)

3 – Fritz Koch and Orchestra: "Neue Schnadahüpferl" ("New Schnadahüpferl"). A European recording made for distribution in North America at the beginning of the twentieth century, this Schnadahüpferl becomes "new" in several ways. For example, the more traditional alpine imagery of the genre's string of quatrains follows the cosmopolitan gamut of modern Germany by comparing the culture and geography of Berlin and Frankfurt am Main. (Recorded 1912 in New York City)

4 – Elinor Navarry and Julia Kübler: "Och Moder, ich will en Din han" ("Oh Mother, I Want That Thing"). Recorded in 1916, this traditional song in dialogue between mother and daughter most often appears in numerous dialects, as well as in Swiss German and Yiddish. Elinor Navarry and Julia Kübler unravel the riddle in the song—the daughter eventually asks her mother for a husband—in the dialect of the Cologne area of western Germany. (Recorded 1916 in New York City)

5 – Ella Mittelstadt Fischer (1875–1963): "In des Gartens dunkler Laube" ("In the Shadows of the Garden"). A well-known German ballad or narrative strophic genre, related to the English-language "Lord Lovell," here sung by a singer who had performed as a child in the late nineteenth century at the Schlitz Palmgarten in Milwaukee. (Recorded 1946 in Mayville, Wisconsin, and originally released on *Ach Ya!,* 1, 4)

Choral Singing and Social Music Making

6 – Franz Schubert Männerchor: "An die Heimat" ("To the Homeland"). The next two recorded examples, both made in 1916 on the eve of the American entry into World War II, reflect the two sides of the hyphen in early twentieth-century German-American identity. The Franz Schubert Männerchor, one of the best known singing societies of New York City, maintained a large repertory of *Heimatlieder* or "homeland songs," and this one was recorded as a benefit for war veterans.

7 – Germania Männerchor: "Bundesgruß/Introduction/Zwei Blümchen." The three parts of this example reflect the traditionalization of German choral music in distinctive ways. In the fieldnotes accompanying this example, Alan Burdette remarks that the Germania Männerchor of Evansville, Indiana, traditionalizes "Zwei

Blümchen," which "is only performed by the Männerchor at their annual Stiftungsfest" (cf. Alan Burdette's essay).

8 – The Rhein Valley Brass: "Helena Polka." Choral and dance traditions intersect in regions where German social organizations continue to flourish. A field recording by Alan Burdette at the Germania Männerchor's Christmas dance in 1994, this performance reveals the extent to which German-American communities cultivate dance music to bolster the public activities of German social organizations.

> The Rhein Valley Brass: Bill Haas, tuba; Jim Allison, tuba; Charlie Haas, trombone; Al Wilbur, trumpet; Dan Kieffer, trumpet; Larry Miller, euphonium; Dana Meyer, clarinet; Janet Gascoigne-Vogles, clarinet; Bob Klaus, drums.

Viennese Urban Traditions

9 – Henry Schuckert and Henry Schepp: Johann Strauss, Jr., "Wiener Bürgerwalzer" ("Viennese Citizens' Waltz"). In the popular music disseminated to German-speaking Americans on early twentieth-century ethnic recordings, diverse Viennese urban traditions enjoyed a noticeable presence. The American concertina duo of Schuckert and Schepp performed and recorded a particularly eclectic repertory, in this case a domesticated, if rather untamed, version of Johann Strauss's well-known "Wiener Bürgerwalzer." (Recorded 1926 in Chicago)

10 – Adolf Engel and Elsbet Nolte: Robert Stolz, "Im Prater blühen wieder die Bäume" ("The Trees in the Prater Are Again in Blossom"). The famous Viennese amusement park, the Prater, was home to entertainment of all kinds, much of it suited to the multicultural districts between the Prater and the Danube River. The Prater served also as a symbol of fantasy and leisure, as in Robert Stolz's song for the popular stage. (Recorded 1928 in New York City)

11 – Richard Waldemar: "Wiener Praterleben" ("Life in the Prater of Vienna"). The full cultural diversity of the Vienna Prater emerges in the declamatory style of Richard Waldemar, written in the manner of a street hawker drawing attention to the attractions of the entertainment district. Popular song recordings such as "Wiener Praterleben" engendered nostalgia for an Old World that most of the immigrant and ethnic consumers had probably never sampled themselves.

Sacred Traditions

12 – Jeremiah Dencke: "Meine Seele erhebet dem Herrn" ("My Soul Lifts up to the Lord"). Born in Silesia, Jeremiah Dencke (1725–1795) immigrated to the American colonies in 1761, where he played a crucial role in the establishment of the Protestant, German-language musical tradition of the Moravians. Performed here by Cynthia Clarey, soprano, and the New World String Orchestra, "Meine Seele erhebet dem Herrn" was composed in 1767 for a "Mägden-Fest," a celebration for young women, who would also have been capable of singing the song. Used with permission of New World Records, which released the recording on *The Flowering of Vocal Music in America, 1767–1823* (New World 80467-2).

13 – Zanvel (Zewulon) Kwartin: "Le-David Mizmor" ("Remember David"). Raised and trained for the cantorate in Eastern Europe, Zanvel Kwartin (1874–1952) took a position as one of the chief cantors in the Orthodox community in Vienna, where he wove the elaborate improvisatory style of Eastern European liturgy into a Central European fabric. After World War I, Kwartin immigrated to Philadelphia, where he played a major role in establishing the role of the star cantor in Jewish-American sacred music.

14 – Clara Stuewer and Meta Brusewitz: "Wo findet die Seele die Heimat der Ruh'?" ("Where Does the Soul Rest in Its Home?"). Members of the Wisconsin Synod Lutheran choir of Bonduel, Wisconsin, these sisters-in-law maintained a large repertory of hymns in German until the last decade of the twentieth century. In public, they preferred to sing together, using the harmonization of hymnals designed for the Lutheran home and school. (Recorded 1978 in Bonduel, Wisconsin, and originally released on *Ach Ya!,* 2, 11)

Mixed Languages/Mixed Traditions

15 – Friends of Jewish Music: Max Janowski, "Vos vet zein az Moschiach vet kumen?" ("What Will Happen When the Messiah Comes?"). This song about the coming of the Messiah circulates among Ashkenazic Jewish communities in two and three languages: Hebrew, Yiddish, and German. As in this example, arranged by the distinguished German-American cantor and composer, Max Janowski, the three languages spread questions and answers around different generations and Jewish experiences before the Diaspora comes to its end. Used with permission of the Friends of Jewish Music.

16 – Albert Kolberg: "Lauterbach and Mein Hut Medley." The two German folksongs that combine with the blues-yodeling style of performance made famous by Jimmie Rodgers seem to travel together wherever they appear in German America. Al Kolberg (bn. 1912) of Howards Grove, Wisconsin, sang the medley on local radio programs, but it is also known in Burgenland versions from Pennsylvania and even in Amish versions from Indiana.

17 – Kosatka Concertina Quartet: "Gate City March." A mixture of Stephen Foster tunes and German folk-music standards, the German in this potpourri cannot be separated from the American. In this arrangement, which skillfully employs quodlibet, "Gate City March" was no doubt used for concert performances that became distinctly American, rather than dances. (Recorded 1926 in Chicago)

Polka and Dance

18 – Whoopee John Wilfahrt: "Holz-Auktion" ("Wood Auction"). Of the two examples from early Whoopee John Wilfahrt recordings included in this CD, "Holz-Auktion" bears more direct witness to European roots. A standard in the Czech and Austrian dance repertory, this polka exploits the contrasting sounds of brass and woodwind sections, accented by the novelty of the percussion section. (Recorded 1933 in Chicago)

19 – Henry Schuckert and Henry Schepp: "Czy pamietasz cóś mowiła?" ("Do You Remember What You Were Saying?"). The eclectic repertory of the concertina duo, Schuckert and Schepp, ranged across Central and East-central Europe. The Czechs and, in this case, Poles to whom such examples were directed, however, surely interacted with Germans and Austrians in many parts of the Polka Belt. (Recorded 1924 in Chicago)

20 – Whoopee John Wilfahrt: "Aunt Ella's Polka." A fully "American arrangement" in a Whoopee John Wilfahrt performance, with the heavy brass and percussion sound distinctive of "Dutchman" style, nonetheless does not obscure Whoopee John's own concertina playing that provides the core of the arrangement. (Recorded 1930 in Chicago)

Concertina Traditions

21 – Kosatka Concertina Quartet: "Repasz Band March." The "Repasz Band March" enjoyed a double life, first as a standard in the dance repertory played by concertina ensembles, and then as the subject of many of the Silberhorn concertina jokes (cf. James P. Leary's article). Together with "Gate City March" (ex. 17), the "Repasz Band March" gives a sense of the remarkable flexibility and range of styles for which the Kosatka Concertina Quartet was known. (Recorded 1926 in Chicago)

22 – Bruno Rudzinski: "Francuska polka" ("Polka française"). Concertina styles negotiated the stylistic borders between German, Austrian, Czech, and Polish dance musics in the United States. Here, we hear Bruno Rudzinski not only singing in Polish, but also imitating instrumental dance styles, some of which were at the time might well have been generated by African-American musics, that reflect the frequent transformation of the *polka française* into a novelty piece. (Recorded 1928 in Chicago)

23 – Rudy Patek and Charles Blim: "W noc letnia – waltz" ("On a Summer Night"). Czech and Austrian Americans exchanged polkas and waltzes across their stylistic and ethnic borders, creating an instrumental dance repertory that was at once international and ethnic American. In this lovely recording the borders disappear, producing a performance that satisfies in both concert and dance settings. (Recorded 1924 in Chicago)

Burgenland Music from the Polka Belt

24 – Eddie Kemeter: "She's Too Fat for Me" and two variants. Eddie Kemeter is one of the towering figures of the Burgenland dance tradition from the Lehigh Valley of Pennsylvania. Burgenland Americans emigrated from one of the most ethnically diverse regions of Central Europe, where Croat, Hungarian, Jewish, and Roma minorities lived together, and it is thus not uncommon to find diverse musical and textual strands woven together, as in this stand by the Slovenian-American Frankie Yankovich.

25 – Eddie Kemeter: "Golden Slippers Hoedown." The American side of Eddie Kemeter's repertory asserts itself in this example, but it does not overwhelm the ethnic diversity that defines the Polka Belt. The performance transforms the well

known "Oh, Them Golden Slippers" into an ethnic dance style, in which "hoedown" symbolizes the same processes of change as "polka" (cf. Rudolf Pietsch's essay).

26 – The Shanta Band: "Krumpirnsupp'n Lied." As Burgenland bands became popular in the areas of the Polka Belt in which they settled, they borrowed from the repertories and styles of neighboring ethnic groups. Still, they were careful to cultivate a distinctively Burgenland component in their repertories, such as the "Krumpirnsupp'n Lied," played here by the Shanta Band, one of the best known ensembles in the Lehigh Valley.

27 – The Austrian Mixed Chorus of Chicago: "Du weißt genau, ich wart' auf dich" ("You Know Exactly, I'm Waiting for You"), "Wohl auf der Alm" ("On the Alpine Meadow"), and "Hoam geht's net" ("You Can't Go Home"). The Austrian Mixed Chorus of Chicago includes members with family ties to virtually every linguistic and cultural region of Austria, especially to Burgenland. Crucial to their identity as an ethnically inclusive chorus is their ability to sing in various dialects, as these performances clearly demonstrate.

Recorded Sources

Ach Ya! Traditional German-American Music from Wisconsin. Wisconsin Folklife Center FVF 301, 1985.

The Flowering of Vocal Music in America, 1767–1823. New World 80467-2, 1994.

Acknowledgments

We gratefully acknowledge permission from the Friends of Jewish Music (Chicago), the Max Kade Institute for German-American Studies (Madison), and New World Records (New York City) for permission to include previously released recordings on this CD. The 78-rpm recordings from which the historical examples were taken are housed in the Mills Music Library of the University of Wisconsin-Madison, and we would like to express our gratitude to Geraldine Laudati and Steven Sundell of the Mills Music Library for making them available. Alan R. Burdette, James P. Leary, and Rudolf Pietsch generously made recordings available for this CD.

“I guess I give up the hyphen, Hans. I don’t care if they drop a thousand bombs on the Kaiser’s head. I don’t feel so German now. My children, they’re born here, this is their country. . . .”

Beutle hawked and spit at this perfidy, ordered four new gramophone records from Columbia’s Patriotic German Music selection: “*Hipp, Hipp, Hurrah,*” “*Die Watcht am Rhein,*” “*Wir müssen siegen,*” and “*Deutschland, Deutschland über Alles,*” sung by a rich-toned male quartet. But this was not enough. . . . Two evenings a week, after supper, he took his accordion down to the saloons in Prank and tried to explain reasonably to the men he knew that as a person of German extraction he was loyal both to his motherland, Germany, and to his bride, America. He tried to persuade them with German music.

E. Annie Proulx, *Accordion Crimes*

1

THE MUSICAL CULTURE OF GERMAN-AMERICANS: VIEWS FROM DIFFERENT SIDES OF THE HYPHEN

Otto Holzapfel and Philip V. Bohlman

Music in a "Land ohne Nachtigall"

Only eight days after he had disembarked on the East Coast of the United States in 1832, underway to farm the land he had purchased in Ohio, Nikolaus Lenau wrote to his brother-in-law of his impressions of the new land and its culture. Westward-bound, Lenau stopped with his traveling companions to benefit from the hospitality of a pioneer settlement, but encountered there a cultural gulf between his own European German culture and that of the New World to which he had journeyed (letter from Nikolaus Lenau to Anton Schurz, 16 October 1832; in Weber 1981:78):

> The inhabitant's large family received us quite pleasantly. The women and the children had really been scrubbed up. I found the luxury in this lonely, God-forsaken farmhouse quite remarkable, though rather less remarkable than the shocking, gaudy, tasteless apparel, particularly that of the children. I suppose that when one cleans oneself in an isolated world, one does so tastelessly. Taste is a child of society, if indeed the last-born. . . . The Americans have no wine, no nightingale! Perhaps they hear their mockingbird in a glass of apple cider, their dollars jingling in their pockets. For me, I'd rather sit next to a German and hear, as he drinks his wine, the song of the lovely nightingale, if in fact my pockets are emptier. Dear brother, these Americans are petty little shopkeepers, who stink to high heaven. When it comes to any sort of spiritual life, they're totally oblivious. The nightingale was very wise never to appear among these miserable wretches. To my way of thinking, it is of profound, symbolic importance that there are no nightingales in America. This has occurred to me almost as a poetic truth.

It will hardly surprise any of us who, of course, know Nikolaus Lenau better as a member of the Romantic circle of Swabian poets, that he lasted less than a year in the "land without nightingales." He returned to Central Europe, where the spiritual life might not have been any more to his liking, but at least it was not dead. His comments decrying an America without arts and culture were, in fact, neither the first nor the last from the German side of the hyphen that revealed an inability to hear a new song, to recognize a new place for music in the culture of the New World.

The image of America as a "land without nightingales" was so metaphoric for Rolf Weber, that he used the image for the title of his 1981 anthology of observations on the life and culture of German-American immigrants. We find a similar perspective from the German side of the hyphen in Hermann Kriege's 1849 essay on "Music in New York" (Weber 1981:145). "One often hears the opinion expressed that during the last decade the arts, specifically music, have made enormous progress, even giant steps of progress in this Yankeeland, which is obsessed with material well-being. If this is the case, then I am completely incapable—and I say this as a German—of fathoming what the earlier, more primitive stage of music must have been." Alexis de Tocqueville, although not a German immigrant, but nevertheless one of the most trenchant European observers of the potential for the arts on the American side of the hyphen, wrote a more sympathetic account of the future for poetry in democratic America, albeit not after equivocating on the contemporary situation (Tocqueville 1966, vol. 2:78, 80–81):

> I readily admit that the Americans have no poets; I cannot allow that they have no poetic ideas. In Europe people talk a great deal of the wilds of America, but the Americans themselves never think about them: they are insensible to the wonders of inanimate nature, and they may be said not to perceive the mighty forests which surround them till they fall beneath the hatchet. . . . Amongst a democratic people poetry will not be fed with legendary lays or the memorials of old traditions. The poet will not attempt to people the universe with supernatural beings in whom his readers and his own fancy have ceased to believe. . . . Such are the poems of democracy. The principle of equality does not then destroy all the subjects of poetry: it renders them less numerous, but more vast.

Lenau, Kriege, and de Tocqueville viewed America from a privileged perspective, and their remarks reflect their uneasiness about losing that privilege. Most of those who contributed to the musical culture of German-Americans did not share the same privileges, and it is hardly surprising that their observations conveyed a very different set of expectations of encounters with and contributions to North America. Laborers without work, the culturally disenfranchised, and the religiously persecuted, these immigrants to North America approached it with hope and creativity. Their musical chronicles, therefore, overlook the loss and draw our attention to the gain. We witness this already in one of the most widespread of all German emigrant's songs (cf. Hauer 1992:31), which appears in Figure 1 in a variant from Lorraine in eastern France. Leaving the Old World behind and turning to the New, the so-called "Elsässer Auswandererlied" ("Alsatian Emigrant's Song") musically problematizes the hyphen in complex ways, which appear again and again throughout this book.

We introduce the present volume with these observations on music and the arts to give a sense of the long tradition of situating a hyphen between the European and American perspectives on the musical life of German-Americans. That hyphen, as we wish to suggest, has symbolized a certain amount of insecurity, even irreconcilability between the ways of one world and those of another. It represents the greater ease with which one hears one's own music and responds with confusion to that of someone else. But it also symbolizes processes of change, the transformation and proliferation of musics and the identities associated with them.

As the editors of the volume we should also say from the outset that it is a hyphen that has served as a catalyst in many of our own discussions over the years. Clearly, Otto Holzapfel has mustered his perspectives from one side of the hyphen, Philip Bohlman from the other. Together, we have worked on American projects and on German projects. Our shared experiences, moreover, are not unique, but are rather similar to the other scholars contributing to this volume. It is safe to say that no one has remained on only one side of the hyphen. Just as we have shared these perspectives, however, they have changed, and this book represents some of the directions in which these changing perspectives have taken us. Quite unlike de Tocqueville, who found the subjects of poetry less numerous in America (1966, vol. 2:81), we have found the German-American musics far more numerous than when we first began reckoning with the hyphen.

German-American Music: Variables and Complex Identities

Folk music, religious music, art music, popular music. *Hochdeutsch*, *Plattdeutsch*, dialect, German with an American accent so heavy many of us strain to understand it. Traditional, almost frozen, European styles; changing, chameleon-like American styles. Ethnic identities historicized and recovered from the past; identities adapted to a transformed, modern society. The musics that represent the musical culture of German-Americans—the musics that appear in transcriptions and illus-

Ich verkauf mein Gut

Schnell. ♩ = 96.

Ich ver - kauf mein Gut und Häus-chen Wohl um ein ge - rin - ges

Geld, Wir wol - len aus Frank - reich rei - sen In ein

an - dern Teil der Welt.

Und wie wir auf Metz sein kommen,
Auf Metz wohl in die Stadt,
So gingen wir zum Prefet
Und liefern unsere Schriften ab.

„Herr Prefet, ach, Herr Prefet,
Wir haben eine Bitt an Euch!
Ihr sollet unsern Pass unterschreiben,
Wir wollen aus Frankreich."

‚Was ist denn die Ursach,
Dass ihr aus Frankreich geht,
Euer Leben zu riskieren,
In Amerika zu gehn?'

Figure 1. "Ich verkauf mein Gut" (I Sell My Possessions), reprinted from pp. 159–161 in Pinck 1926.

„Hier können wir nicht mehr bleiben,
Hier können wir nicht mehr sein,
Die Hissje und Notare,
Die haben den grössten Teil.“

Und wie wir auf Havre sein kommen,
So schreiben wir gleich zurück:
„Wir haben schon erfahren,
Wir machen unser Glück.“

trations throughout this book—defy simple, singular classification. They cross stylistic and cultural boundaries so readily as to render these useless as means of categorizing and classifying. The music history represented in this book is hardly that of a monolithic ethnic group. Nor does it embody strictly the experiences of immigration and acculturation, the culture of a German *Volksliedlandschaft* (folksong landscape) or an American region, the unity of a music culture. Each piece or style, examined by itself, offers different traits that we could describe as German, American, or some combination thereof. Together, however, they seem more unrelated than unified. Together, they pose a fundamental question challenging the scholars who have contributed the following essays: Just what is "German-American music"?

To seek out possible answers to this question requires that we examine at least two components of the concept, "German-American music," itself. It is clear from the title that this introduction explores different relations implicit in the coupling of "German" with "American," but before presenting views from the different sides of the hyphen, we would first like to question the other fundamental component, namely "music." Our aim will not be to cobble together a convenient definition, rather to illustrate that the precise nature of music in an ethnic culture cannot be so easily pinned down. In fact, it is the whole notion that there is a "precise nature" of German-American music that we wish to problematize in the introduction.

It is obvious that we need to consider music at some point as a *product*, that is a sonic product that we can represent with notation, song texts, or even through dancing. Much of the scholarship devoted to German-American music treats it primarily as a product: songs about the emigrant's tribulations; the publication of hymnbooks; texts that retain the German language; the choral traditions of American *Gesangvereine* (singing societies). The very ontology of a German song text in a culture where the language has a largely symbolic role conveys a sense of German-Americanness. The musical product also signifies; in other words, it is about some experience, whether the narrative of the ballad or emigrant song, or the physical *communitas* of the dancers performing to Dutchman music at a Fasching (pre-Lenten) ball.

The musical product, however, often contrasts in its German-Americanness with the *producer*, the musician, dancer, or composer. If a singer is of German-American descent, does she sing German-American music? She might, of course, if she is a member of an ethnic chorus, but then would we or would she consider the music sung in her church choir or danced at a polka festival still German-American? A somewhat different situation has arisen in the past two decades, during a period of growing ethnic revival in the United States. Many Americans have creatively chosen their own ethnicity, ascribing it to themselves and their lives, including their musical lives. Some of these identities reflect European history and politics, for example a Polish-Pomeranian-Prussian-German identity, which is the predominant heritage in the "most German-American" state, Wisconsin. Other identities reflect the encounter with regional and ethnic identities in the United States, for example the North German-South German mixture in Milwaukee. Religion and class further confuse these identities, complicating still more the notion of "German-American."

In the essays of this book it is not simply a matter of blurring the boundaries within a Croatian-Burgenland-Austrian-Bavarian-German nest of identities (see, for example, Pietsch below), but also adapting an identity for which there is no familial background whatsoever. Historically, the producers of German-American musical traditions have often not been German-American, whether the Moravians of colonial America, Hungarian operetta composers of the nineteenth century, or Bohemian and Polish polka bands of the twentieth century. Do we understand these as German-American musicians?

Between the producer and the products of music there is also a process of *production*. The identity of the product depends also on the transformations that take place during performance. Many German-American choruses perform standard German works, but they juxtapose repertories and functions that would be unimaginable in Europe, for example, a potpourri of dialects from every province in Austria. The role of dance in the polka belt might well be considered postmodern in its impact on German-American popular traditions, for musicians must move fluidly from style to style as they move from town to town, and the dancers must reformulate the fluid styles played on successive Friday nights by Dutchman, Polish, Slovenian, or Czech bands. Vital for the process of production is the *context of performance*, the cultural reasons a community chooses to use music as a form of ethnic identity. Religion offers one context of performance, the "Germania Hall" in a Chicago neighborhood another.

Finally, the *means of production* play a salient role in mediating the nature of German-American music. Songbooks with German repertories were mass-produced in the nineteenth century, undergirding the diverse nature of German organizational life, or *Vereinswesen*. Music presses commodified identities, giving Pomeranian immigrants in northern Wisconsin an opportunity to share in the *Hochdeutsch* repertories of Saxon immigrants in Missouri, their co-denominationalists in the Missouri Synod of the Lutheran Church (Bohlman 1985). German-American ethnic recordings in the twentieth century stimulated the sales of concertinas and saxophones alike to German-Americans, but also became a tool for instrument hawkers peddling accordions to Cajun musicians in Louisiana. Ethnic identities rose and fell, retreated and reappeared, all on the heels of changing recording trends or the availability of sheet and choral music.

The various interactions among producer, product, production, and means of production did not level differences, thereby leading to a shared corpus of musical traits characteristic of German-American music. If anything, their interrelations combined musics in new ways, forged new repertories and areas of musical activity, and particularized even more extensively the nature of German-American music. We dare say that they do not bring us any closer to specifying that nature, much less defining what German-American music is, but they considerably broaden the discourse of German-American music history.

Traditional Topoi in German-American Musical Scholarship

Though not abundant in quantity, German-American musical scholarship has a fairly extensive history. Several approaches, growing from several disciplines, characterize this scholarship, and we would like to turn to these. If there is one dominant theme that especially characterizes the study of music in German-American culture, it is that music-making takes place at several social levels, designated usually by the concepts folk music, religious music, and art music. We would normally expect to find the category of popular music filling out these levels, but, in fact, it is only recently that scholars have begun to investigate the presence of popular dance traditions or the influence of mass-produced sheet music on German-American musical culture. The reasons for such neglect result both from a general neglect of class as a social determinant in German-American society and the more specific problem of understanding music without texts in German or without text at all (e.g., popular dance forms) as signifying ethnicity.

The different levels sketched here have provided scholars of German-American music with rather distinctive fields, further making music one of the most significant parameters for studying German-American history and ethnicity. Studies of folk music have taken many different forms. At one fundamental level, folk-music scholars and ethnomusicologists have taken to the field urged on by salvage ethnology, tracking down and preserving the last vestiges of tradition. Bohlman's early forays into the study of folk music in rural Wisconsin (1980) were aimed at gathering up songs lest they be forgotten, but like many other scholars he found that the initial search for folksongs seduced him further into the complexity of German-American rural societies. It was, of course, possible to collect several tape-reels of folksongs, but these were not to be separated from other types of music-making, particularly in religious contexts. The point is that if German folksongs were going to disappear from Wisconsin, they would have done so long before Bohlman had arrived on the scene. They had not disappeared, but survived, not as vestiges, rather as components of vaster, more complex repertories with entirely new functions (cf. Bohlman 1985).

Classical or art music has also been a privileged area in German-American musical scholarship. Musicologists are wont to provide statistics for American orchestras that drew their players almost entirely from waves of German immigrants. Beginning with the German-speaking Moravians in colonial Pennsylvania, American chamber music has owed no less a debt to Central Europe. American students, too, flocked to Germany in the nineteenth century, there to learn the great masterworks and take their degrees, returning to the United States to establish musical life and conservatory training along the lines of what we simply call "the German model."

Religious music has benefited, too, from several scholarly traditions. At one level, numerous studies of music as a component of German denominationalism and sectarianism result from the labors of scholars working within theological frameworks. At another level, religious musics of groups like the Amish, the Mennonites, and the Hutterites have become the paradigms for "marginal survival," the retention of German music in the New World environment, despite the disappearance of those traditions in the Old World. At still another level, German-American religious music offers itself to scholars as a social core or cultural-aesthetic glue, that is as tradition that centripetalizes language, community, and value system and then encodes them in music and ritual. Religious music has a striking way of being unavoidably German-American.

These levels of music-making, of course, take on the appearance of repertories. Other themes in German-American musical scholarship, however, are more contextually grounded. Moreover, these themes have less to do with the ways in which German texts assert themselves and encourage survival than with the impact of the New World on American elements in music. Among the most common themes of German-American historiography is, therefore, the local or regional study, which documents festival life in Cincinnati, symphony life in Milwaukee, or the pioneer composer in Kentucky. Informing these studies are motifs ranging from boosterism to Turnerism (cf. Luebke 1990:138–56). Scholarship devoted to Pennsylvania German music is, therefore, abundant, much of it produced by Pennsylvania Germans and intended for both scholarly and popular consumption (cf. Boyer, Buffington, and Yoder 1964; and Yoder 1975). Not infrequently, an additional motivation informs local studies, namely filiopietism, the celebration of musical German forefathers and foremothers, who brought great music to the frontier and ensured its survival through the erection of lasting musical institutions.

Music has also been studied as a component or reflection of profound historical events affecting German-American culture. The 1848 Revolution in Central Europe, in fact, did enter the narratives of many songs and did precede one of the first major waves of German immigration, whose impact on the musical culture of the Midwest in particular was considerable (see Meier 1917). Some scholars traditionally trace the decline in folksong per se to the effects of the First and Second World Wars on German language retention. Whether, in fact, people stopped singing in German simply as a result of the wars is difficult to prove, but there can be no doubt that the organizational life of the *Gesangverein* underwent radical transformations during the wars and emerged thereafter in quite different forms.

These various themes in musical scholarship tended not only to cross disciplinary boundaries but also to pop up on both sides of the hyphen. In some cases, say, in studies of the music of religious sectarianism, American and German scholars proceeded in relative isolation, but it is safe to say that similar themes captured their imaginations. What they did with those themes, nevertheless, differed. Europeans and Americans, with views from opposite sides of the hyphen, constructed very distinct notions of what these New World musical cultures were—or were not.

From the German Side of the Hyphen

Ethnic music and folk music—the musics that ascribe identity and form distinctive music cultures—look very different from and on the German side of the hyphen. The traits and conditions that are most important on the German side often seem absent on the American side. To some extent, this results from different histories of migration and cultural distinctiveness. German musicology and folk-music research, with their particular histories, also contribute substantially to such differences.

More than any other concept, the language of an ethnic music seems the determining factor when viewed from the German side of the hyphen. German-American music, if nothing else, should utilize the German language. When German disappears and another language supplants it, a folksong is no longer German; after all, it would not represent a German identity for a German. The importance of language in German folklore is evident in the concept of a *Sprachinsel* (speech island), a bounded community of German speakers outside of Germany, historically occurring most frequently in Eastern Europe (cf. Schenk 1988). Just from the designation itself, it becomes clear that language is privileged as the core of identity, and the maintenance of the speech island itself (e.g., the Transylvania Saxons in Romania or Gottschee Colonies in Slovenia) has depended on persistent use of the language and on an unbroken tradition of songs in German (for the classic case study, see Brednich, Kumer, and Suppan 1969–1984).

Language functions to hinder change, and it therefore symbolizes another trait that is often essential from the German side of the hyphen: conservation. Conservation means far more than simply the failure to change; it reveals that music can possess power and authority, and by extension that it provides historical glue. To conserve German songs in North America, therefore, means to cling to what is special about the past and to use the past to ascribe identity to the present. Conservation extends to institutional structures. From the German side of the hyphen, therefore, it has always seemed especially significant that German churches and men's choruses have survived and thrived in North America. These are the conserving links to the canon of German music.

German musical scholarship relies extensively on a cultural geography of music, called "musical landscapes" or "folksong landscapes" (*Musiklandschaften, Volksliedlandschaften*). Music has a connection to place in Central European thought—to the local village, to the dialect region, or to the nation. Music (especially folk music) tells us something about a place, and it evokes a sense of an entire landscape, its culture, and the ways in which individuals identify themselves with place. The concept of musical landscape founders when applied to the other side of the hyphen. Simply stated, North America does not provide the same musical landscapes. It is not, however, simple, for even more difficult to understand is the dynamic nature of American landscapes, a sense of expansive space where distance undoes the social meaning of music.

Whereas landscape provides a fundamental category of context, genre offers the thematically unifying category of text for German scholars. Genre is inseparable from cultural identity. Ballads, for example, have High German texts only, and they rely on a centripetalizing music history. *Vierzeiler* (quatrains) are primarily alpine and therefore rely on dialect, which by extension localizes them. Genre bounds German Protestant hymns and Austrian popular dance alike, weaving them into complex webs of identity. These genres, however, cease to exist in the New World. Even those that survive do so because they have undergone and withstood change and hybridization. Whatever else, the genre does not translate, and there is, from the perspective of the German side, no equivalent concept to take its place.

Translatability poses other problems. For many European scholars, it seems as if the rural folk culture that forms local and regional style characteristics simply does not and cannot exist in North America. The problem is not the absence of rural culture in North America, but rather that entire repertories specific to a rural region, such as that for Burgenland (see Pietsch in this volume), have no place to go. Music is dependent on fundamental socioeconomic conditions, and these exist only in Europe. Indeed, American collections of Central European dances contain only urban forms with rural forms, even the widespread Ländler, absent or at best exceptional.

The concepts on the German side of the hyphen, therefore, derive from notions of core or canon, and accordingly they acquire a musical value that makes it even harder to look across the musical and cultural space occupied by the hyphen. European folk-music researchers struggle with the music they encounter in North America. Folk music sounds worse, as verses are forgotten and shared knowledge falters; stylistic authenticity is unknown, and hybrid styles are normative. No one seems to care what repertories are mixed together. And so, from the German side of the hyphen, the American side is beyond the pale, as if an historical aporia intervenes, creating a new but terribly foreign world of musical practices.

From the American Side of the Hyphen

The role of language as a determinant of German-American music emerges initially through ethnographic encounter. During fieldwork, consultants asked to sing "German songs" often perform wildly diverse repertories, in which German as a language has a very confusing function. Even in regions with an extensive history of German settlement, repertories contain a mixture of High German texts, dialect songs, and many songs in English. Language rarely seems to be a factor in the decision to sing a "German song." Language in a heavily German region such as northern Wisconsin may be a factor, though it is a factor because it has been bound to the different processes of history, acculturation, and musical life that characterized the transition of groups of dialect-speaking immigrants into communities of hymn-singing American Lutherans into class and occupational groupings that enjoyed polkas and other interethnic forms of American popular music (see Bohlman 1985). The languages of "German-American" songs bore witness to these historical trajectories, indeed were inseparable from them. From the American perspective, it seems historically justified that German-Americans should sing in English.

Just as the *Volksliedlandschaft* and the *Sprachinsel* undergird German perspectives of folk-music repertory, so too does cultural geography cause us to recognize patterns in German-American music. At the most general level, regionalism exerts a very important influence. The regions at issue, however, are those in North America, where immigrants from different European regions have gathered, consolidating their musical traditions and adapting them to the American cultural environment. Again, language, dialect, and song often play less important roles in the formation of an American ethnic region than urbanization and modernization, or acculturation and class. The Polka Belt, stretching from upstate New York and eastern Pennsylvania to New Ulm, Minnesota, exemplifies one form of a modern musical re-

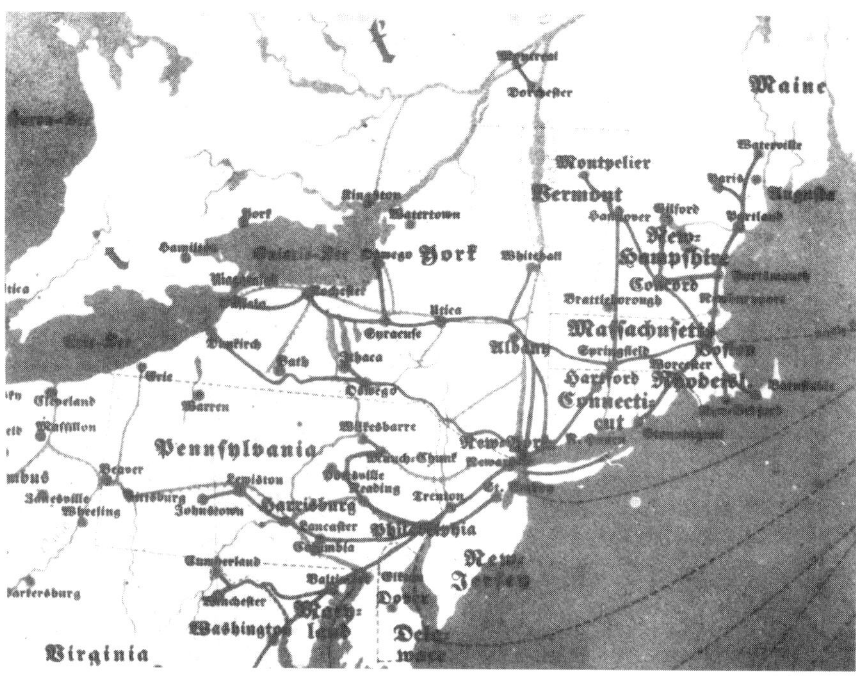

Figure 2. Map of German Immigration to North America (1850s). Source: Library of Congress

gion, to which German-American musicians have made notable contributions, particularly at the eastern and western ends (see Pietsch in this volume). A musical region may also be constructed for reasons that, in part, result from the performative nature of music. In Chicago, Central European choruses and bands often perform in those neighborhoods in which the greatest critical mass can assemble for the concert itself, often when that critical mass does not exist among the neighborhood's residents.

It follows, then, that the musical institutions that characterize these American musical regions differ markedly from their European counterparts. Ethnic churches, for example, were the most important locus for maintaining German-American musical traditions in the rural Midwest during the nineteenth century and early twentieth century (see Conzen in this volume). For Chicagoans of Central European ethnicity, whether or not they speak German or the same variety of German, the *Gesangverein* is itself an institution that concentrates all aspects of musical life. In many rural areas and working-class neighborhoods of American cities, the bar, social club, or veteran's hall functions as the center of musical life, suggesting, moreover, the need to investigate much more extensively the presence of music in the institutions of workers' culture and occupational groups (see Ensslen 1988).

Assumptions about the nature of tradition also differ dramatically from the American perspective. The privileging of oral tradition as fundamental to the transmission of folk music no longer addresses the conditions of a musical culture in which literacy is widespread, in which people regularly sing ethnic music from books, and in which, each week, many inscribe ethnic dance with their bodies. If tradition itself undergoes radical reformulation, we would then expect very different musical genres to characterize repertories in North America. In many of the following essays the reader will observe a contrast, if not clash, between the formation of genre in Central Europe and in North America. The emigrant song, with its narratives of shipwrecks hawked as broadsides, has no comparable genre in North America. American genres often represent completely different narratives, for example the historicization of community identity through the juxtaposition of different European styles by American singing societies. American genres conflate past, present, and future, proliferating as new forms of ethnic identity become appropriate and older forms lose their functions.

Ethnicity itself, and particularly ethnicity as a symbolic form of expressive performance, has emerged as a powerful motif in the American perspectives on German-American music. The differences between emigrant and immigrant, *Auswanderung* and *Einwanderung*, are no longer simply semantic. One focuses on what one takes from the Old World; the other recognizes what happens in the New World. They represent different forms and choices of identity. The shift from immigrant culture to ethnic culture further blurs the sharp cultural divisions of German-Americans from any other group. When we begin to speak of ethnicity, then, we also recognize the patterns of exchange that bring about this form of ascribed identity. Isolating German music from other American musics is far less fruitful than trying to understand the complex contributions of German-American popular musics to the ethnic mainstream, with its shifting patterns of identities and concomitantly shifting musical sounds. From the European side of the hyphen it may seem as if recognizing the many musical identities possible within a society where ethnicity continually acquires new meanings is a hopeless move away from the German, even a wanton discarding of the German altogether. In fact, we do not intend to be quite so radical or irresponsible, but rather to use music to refocus our perspectives —all our perspectives—on the hyphen, that is to say, on the processes of change that occur in the cultural space it has come to symbolize.

The Hyphen Reconsidered

> There are many ways to read the role of the hyphen; however, all those who think critically about this punctuation mark agree that the hyphen *performs*—it is never neutral or natural (Brody 1995:149).

Thus far, it seems almost as if the hyphen is the problem. The hyphen has symbolized separation, abandonment, loss. The hyphen provides an excuse for an identity where wholeness is no longer possible. The hyphen unleashes a teleological move toward assimilation and Americanization. The longer the hyphen is present, the greater the distance between German and American. The hyphen places cultural identity in a struggle for survival.

The authors of the essays in this book, however, do not describe the sense of separation and dissolution of cultural identity that the hyphen so often symbolizes. The hyphen has come, instead, to represent quite different processes, indeed, a constellation of processes that themselves allow for a more complex interpretation of German-American music and music history. Rather than a border between German and American cultural identities, the hyphen emerges from these essays as a symbol of dynamic transformation. Rather than indicating change in a single direction, from the German to the American, the hyphen comes to represent exchange that flows in several directions. Rather than drawing attention to assimilation and Americanization as if they were the end results of deterioration, the hyphen can serve to facilitate revival and renewal. Most significant, however, is the hyphen's capacity to draw our attention to processes that resituate German and American musics in new contexts, ranging from the individual and local to the most global. After three centuries, the hyphen persists.

In the most recent studies of ethnicity and ethnic music, especially in folklore and folk-music studies, the hyphen's power to separate allows for the construction of two different historical periods in the transformations of ethnic music. In the first, music and musical practices in North America remain those of the old country, reshaped and adapted, but retained nonetheless, at least to the extent this is possible. Generally, these traditions fall under the rubric of "immigrant music," signifying that they consist primarily of what an immigrant group has brought with it. In contrast, "ethnic music" is that music that results when immigrant music has been adapted to new contexts. Although adaptation may be creative, for example, through the creation of new festivals, institutions, or musical organizations, it more often results from the consolidation of resources or the response to potential impoverishment. Immigrant music, it follows, is more likely to employ the language and instruments of the old country, whereas ethnic music may introduce song texts in English and instruments from a mainstream instrumentarium.

One of the most striking characteristics of the approaches taken by the authors in this volume is that, by and large, they do not sketch a simple passage from one side of the hyphen to the other. Or rather, they do not start and stop with the hyphen. Quite the contrary, taken as a whole the processes that the authors of the following essays examine are much more complex, and they fully empower the hyphen to serve as a metonym for a wider range of historical and cultural processes. We should like to turn briefly and schematically to seven processes that emerge in the book, which in turn are meant to represent seven ways in which the hyphen functions to make German-American cultural identity and music history dynamic and creative.

The first process most often appears in connection with discussions of *emigrant songs*. Emigrant songs, for example, in Leo Schelbert's essay, are not simply the songs brought with those leaving the old country, called "emigrant" rather than "immigrant" from the European side of the hyphen. Emigrant songs are far more historically engaged than this, for their authors and singers are attempting to address political, religious, and socioeconomic conditions in Europe. They represent activist agendas; they engage themselves with—indeed, they describe the conditions of—an emigrant culture, one in which the exchange between the Old World and the New is already in play (e.g., Figure 1).

The music of *immigration* differs from that of emigration because it already responds to the conditions of the immigrant culture in North America. Its products—repertory, language, religious functions—may be those of Europe, but the processes that bring about their adaptation to the New World are necessarily at work. In this sense, immigrant music is not already trapped in a spiral of loss and abandonment. New products, such as songbooks from Central Europe, may arrive in massive numbers, only to fuel the processes of adaptation. These same products may bolster the historical (i.e., pre-hyphen) traditions, as in the case of religious repertories that retain hymns in High German when those who sing them—Amish, Hutterites, Lutheran denominations—maintain other repertories in dialect or English. Immigrant music is not, therefore, simply the music of the first generation, but may undergird repertories for many generations.

Ethnic music, it follows, is not simply the music of a second, assimilating generation. Again, ethnic music arises from creative responses to the changing contexts of ethnic culture and identity. Music, moreover, acquires heightened functions as ethnic music, for example, at intraethnic holiday celebrations or interethnic festivals. In the former, ethnic music must compress and consolidate a set of symbols so that their meanings connect one community event to the next. For this reason, ethnic music often involves dance, especially dance forms such as polka that allow the community to perform its own identity. Contrasting with the function of dance at a community holiday celebration, dance at interethnic festivals situates the community in a different web of connections. Ethnic identity intensifies because of competitive settings among these connections, especially because it acquires a new power and justification through spectacle occurring in the public sphere.

It is with the fourth function of the hyphen that the essays in this book open up new theoretical domains in the interpretation of musics on both sides of the hyphen. Because ethnic musics do undergo processes of assimilation and they do enter the mainstream, we use the term *mainstream music* to refer to the fourth function. If Lutheran hymnals substitute English hymns for German, if Lawrence Welk allows the mediated performance of music stripped of ethnicity, and if Dutchman polka bands play wherever they acquire paying gigs, this does not mean they have sold out to assimilation and thrown out the hyphen. Mainstream music in these essays, whether in the Polka Belt sketched by Rudolf Pietsch or the myriad bands whose traces Kathleen Neils Conzen identifies in southern Minnesota, does not form a black hole of abandonment, but rather responds to an unexpected creativity.

If the essays in this volume free us from a notion that assimilation is to be avoided as something negative, they also free us to formulate new questions about translating and recoding the music of German-Americans. No longer must this music be in German; no longer must its functions be those of German music. This liberation of German-American music might be called *translated music*, though translation extends beyond the text into the contexts and the ascription of cultural identity. Most important is that the issue is not English versus German. The fundamental issue, rather, is just how music empowers and performs translation. Again, dance is an obvious case for such acts of translation, making polka or Ländler German, Czech, or Burgenländer—or some combination thereof. Religion provides other musical contexts for the translation of culture. Translated music may, indeed, be a site for re-ethnification; whereas language in immigrant traditions located ethnicity only at the surface, cultural identity may be translated so that it coheres as a core accessible to all.

Revival occupies a category of its own, although there are few conditions of modernity and postmodernity more evident in the international musical landscape occupied by German and German-American musics. On one hand, revival arrests the processes of abandonment and therefore interrupts the teleological change accompanying modernity. On the other, revival introduces a remarkably diverse set of conditions for new creativity. Revival, therefore, crosses the gulf between modernity and postmodernity and makes possible new combinations and hybrids from German and American repertories. In the musical culture of German-Americans, revival operates at local and regional levels, especially in Pennsylvania German areas, where revived repertories now thrive long after the traditions they revive have effectively become impossible. Revival also depends on an international network of traveling ensembles and the distribution of recordings and CDs. The music that fills CD bins marked "Germany" or "Switzerland" in American record stores consists entirely of revived repertories, in many ways, quite distinct from the national bins surrounding them. Folk musics and old hit songs (*Schlager*) alike fill these bins, providing a stable flow of past identities for the present.

Finally, the hyphen between German and American often extends beyond the historical boundaries of those terms: German-American music is also a *transnational* if not *global music*. The same processes that make African and South Asian musics available throughout the world also expand the international currency of the musics juxtaposed by the hyphen between German and American. The broadcasting of "folklike" (*volkstümlich*) music around the world plays not only to massive audiences when, say, the massively popular television program "Musikantenstadel" is staged outside of Europe, but also when folklike groups play in the taverns and restaurants of Chicago and Milwaukee each weekend. Still, even in global musics, we witness processes of change and reception that are present in other functions of the hyphen. Again, despite the fear of abandonment, the hyphen is invested with remarkable creativity. For those who desire it, access to German-American music is facilitated by the hyphen, which is multivalent in the performance possibilities it not only tolerates but also expedites. When one wants to participate in German-American music at the beginning of the twenty-first century, one needs only to identify and then tune into the hyphen.

German-America/German-American Musical Culture/German-American Music

The hyphen, considered for its performative potential, unleashes a torrent of new meanings for what German-America might be and has been at various historical moments and in various regions of North America. The essays in this book participate in the unleashing of this torrent of meanings, and in so doing they function in a way that will make some historians of ethnicity, folk-music scholars, and ethnomusicologists uneasy. If a book on German-American music is "long overdue," it is because there has long been an expectation that there has been a failure to pin down exactly what German-American music really is.

Scholars on both sides of the hyphen have concerned themselves with this problem. On one side, European folk-music scholars have been disturbed that German-American music has deteriorated—the language ceases to have meaning; German *Schlager*, or popular hits, have more currency than "authentic" traditions; German-Americans creating art music have composed nothing at the high level of their European cousins. German-American music, thus considered, just doesn't cut it.

On the other side, American scholars have searched for the ways German-American music might have clung to the German side. This search, however, was largely in vain, for far more common—one could say predominant, or even normative—was the wanton disregard or rejection of the European. The American side of the hyphen was by far the more important, so much so that the hyphen's meaning seems immaterial.

The essays in this book muster an entirely different set of approaches. They break rank with the tradition enforced by the hyphen. It would be appropriate to start at the beginning. The "German" in German-American is decidedly not Germany, either in a modern sense or in any historical senses. The essays by Schelbert, Helmut Wulz, Laurence Libin, and Pietsch do not address music histories of ethnic groups whose ancestors came from Germany; the essays by A. Gregg Roeber, Bohlman, and James Leary address issues suggesting that musicians with German ancestry freely mixed with those of other ancestries. Broadening the designation "German" to "Central European" helps relatively little, because it suggests a common history and a cultural cohesion, such as that based on a single language, which also fails to emerge from the essays. In Part II, religion and the networks formed by religious belief systems contribute more to the connections among German-speaking religious sects or denominations than does language; more than anything, these groups rejected Central Europe and took whatever path was available to them to escape it.

The designation "German," moreover, does not specify a language. Many of the songs cited in the book may have German texts, but the more important issue—one repeatedly overlooked in studies of ethnic music—is *which* German texts? High German, dialect, archaic, bowdlerized, hybrid, parody, misunderstood, not understood at all? It does make a difference, and it does create difference. It undermines the signification of the term "German." If language is a determining factor, there are at least two other questions that further heighten our uneasiness. First, what about the music without language? Dance music, instrumental music, organs in the church or synagogue, concertinas on the prairies. Second, what about music in which another language has replaced German? We do not only mean English; Polish and Czech may supplant German in songs woven into polkas. It is too convenient to say that the music ceases being German. And we believe it is inaccurate. German-Americans hear and sing many songs in English. Take those songs away, and you have removed the core of the tradition itself.

Germanness in music is also a question of immigration history. It is not only a question that the "Germany" from which immigrants to North America were departing was itself constantly changing, but also that each generation historicized its

German past or that of its ancestors in very different ways. The Germany of the first generations of immigration, beginning with the settlement of Germantown, Pennsylvania, in 1683, was very different from the Germany abandoned by the "Forty-Eighters" for political or economic reasons after the failed Revolution of 1848. German immigrants to the Upper Midwest from approximately 1880 until the 1910s, the period that saw a truly mass immigration from Central Europe, had many of the same economic motivations as immigrants from the Austro-Hungarian Empire in the 1920s, the period of most extensive Austrian immigration. If their immigrant hyphen has been framed by similar motivations, their ethnic responses to it were anything but similar.

The historical issues from which the German side of the hyphen emerged were extraordinarily unstable, indeed, from 1683 until the present. At every stage of immigration history, economic conditions and the concomitant competition for scarce agricultural or labor resources made it necessary for Germans to leave a situation that was untenable for their families (cf. Wokeck 1985; Moltmann 1985; Bretting 1985). The economic conditions, however, were rarely the sole motivation. The "Old Lutherans" first settling the Midwest in the 1830s and 1840s, for example, brought with them a desire to found a new communal life based on pietism, but they left the northeastern provinces of Germany because the Prussian Empire increasingly made it impossible for peasants and small landholders to retain their fields. German Jews who arrived in substantial numbers during the height of German settlement in the second half of nineteenth century were inspired by a land of relative religious tolerance, where Reform Judaism could and would flourish, but the major difference between Germany and the United States was often that an entrepreneur had full access to the acquisition of land and the building of new businesses.

The Germanness of each historical moment in immigrant history is also called into question by those who reject it. Studies of ethnicity and ethnic music traditionally privilege the pride that songs project, hence a celebration of and nostalgia for the past. Organizations that foster ethnic music performances, as Alan Burdette and Pietsch demonstrate in their essays, create environments where music embodies the sense of well-being that connects one to a common past. We ask ourselves, however, just which Germany is celebrated by ethnic music in the present. Is this the Germany of the twentieth century? Is this the nation that succumbed to fascism and that devoted enormous economic and cultural resources to world wars, mass destruction, and the Holocaust? The essays in this volume make it impossible to assume that such questions are simply rhetorical, and that the answer to them is simply, "of course not." What Germany is in German-American music and in the processes whereby music makes German-America is always changing and invariably contested.

If the essays in this book destabilize the German side of the hyphen, it follows that they change the American side as well. But how? First of all, most of the authors have been quite willing to admit to a historical trajectory of growing Americanization. It is only honest to admit this. Conzen opens the volume with a detailed history of an Americanization that has developed over the course of a century and a half. Pietsch closes the volume by situating Burgenland-American music in a mainstream, essentially arguing a case for acculturation. Burdette focuses on the way in which broader trends of American ethnicity actually provide a framework for localized performances of Germanness; real tradition is abstract, not German. The religious traditions examined by Roeber, Bohlman, and Wulz resist or capitulate to the influences of North America, witnessing to the fact that Americanization is ever present (cf. Holzapfel 1998).

If Americanization is accepted, it is also acceptable. No author fights against it or explains it away; no author bemoans it or makes a case for the good old days. Instead, the essays recognize the potential for Americanization to provide a creative context for the German-American musical culture. By reformulating this recognition into a focused discussion on change and on modern historical transformations, the essays go considerably beyond most attempts to theorize ethnic music. The musics examined in this volume are far more American than German. This fact is fundamental to an understanding of the creativity undergirding the musical culture of German-Americans.

We do not wish to dwell long on what will soon be obvious to the reader: just who German-Americans are is open to question at all historical moments in the following essays. Obviously, Burgenland and Swiss immigrants (Pietsch and Schelbert) may or may not choose to be German-Americans; surely few would have chosen to be German prior to emigration. Hutterites and German Jews (Wulz and Bohlman) concern themselves primarily with other forms of identity, above all religious. Concertina players and factory workers (Leary) identify with occupational groups that extend far beyond the borders of ethnicity, German-American or otherwise. The political and mercantile interests reflected in immigrant musical practices (Libin) also cross the borders of ethnic community. German-Americans identify themselves with small groups and large communities; they step into and out of German-American identities; they pick and choose from the ethnic and economic resources available to them; there are moments when it is important to use music to lay claim to a German-American identity, and other moments when it is irrelevant. German-American identity is approached creatively and imaginatively, and music facilitates the myriad ways in which German-Americans construct their identities.

If the essays draw our attention to ethnic border crossing, class structure and struggle, and the intensification of religious communities, they do so by identifying music in these dynamic social and historical strategies (cf. Slobin 1993). It is not altogether clear whether there is any point in referring to this music as "German-American." We have come, in fact, to think not. At the very least, one would be hard-pressed to claim that most of the music in the musical culture of German-Americans is German-American. Religious musical traditions have always borrowed from sacred and secular sources outside the canonic repertories. Popular musics flood unabated across the dance floors of ethnic social organizations, and hidden radios open the doors of Hutterite tradition to country and western. The St. Cloud bicycle band offers more to young German-Americans than mixed choruses. Perhaps it is so obvious that no ethnic music historian ever admits to the fact that no member of an ethnic community devotes most or even much musical energy to ethnic music. There are too many other interesting musics in the world.

That is, moreover, the point. Turning to ethnic music, whether once a week in church or twice a year at the Christmas and Fasching dances, is a matter of choice. Reproducing a religious sect's history through daily singing practices or building a collection of polka CDs depends on a series of choices, communal and personal, spiritual and financial. Indeed, any musical culture results from the sum and interaction of such choices. The musical culture of German-Americans certainly does, and it has been doing so for three centuries. Identifying with the musical culture of German-Americans is only one choice or set of choices, but it has, nonetheless, historically persisted. The music history that results from such choices, therefore, is not monolithic or hegemonic, as claimed by filiopietism. It is local and individual; it is made musically by those who choose to identify some part of themselves with it.

The Silence of an Other German-America

There are other German-Americas whose topoi and placements of the hyphen are silent or at least not heard. These are the German-Americas that German-American studies does not study; the musics of these German-Americas remain unclaimed because their presence in the study of immigration and ethnicity would be to sully German-American history with implications of racism and genocide, of an ethnicity where ethnic pride and racial exclusion have too often been versions of the same forms of identity. This is the German-America of Germans who immigrated to North America in the aftermath of World War II and the Holocaust. Its silence notwithstanding, this is a first-generation German-America.

The silence of the post-Holocaust German-America is both understandable and troubling. The silence is understandable because many German-Americans who immigrated during and after World War II were not motivated directly by the Holocaust, the murder of six million Jews and millions of others whose non-German identity provided Germans sufficient reason to murder them. The silence is troubling because, in reality, it is anything but silent; or rather, the silence of the post-Holocaust generation of German-Americans about the Holocaust has not erased it from memory. The German-American silence about the Holocaust permeates the larger mentality of German-Americanness at the beginning of the twenty-first century. We ask ourselves; Just how might we listen into the silence? Just how might we rethink the history and music culture of that other German-America?

The mentality of the post-Holocaust German-America is indeed very amorphous and extraordinarily difficult to define. It is a mentality that yields little to traditional ethnography. Its presence, nonetheless, is very palpable, which in turn is suggestive of alternative forms of ethnography. In preparing the present introduction, we undertook an ethnographic approach that would map the traces of that mentality and give them some identity in the midst of silence. We examined American mass culture for the ways in which Germanness, music, and the Holocaust were triangulated; in fact, we had little difficult locating such ways.

If one searches under the subject heading "Germany" in just about any library, research or public, urban or suburban, one turns up a remarkable number of listings. The American interest in Germany is, and was throughout the Cold War, quite remarkable. The only country for which there are more subject listings than Germany is the United States. Under the main subject listing "Germany" there are several sublistings that are distinctive, and in some cases unique, to Germany, for example, "Reformation." As much as these sublistings reflect some aspects of the American perception of Germany, the two that predominate in the American libraries we surveyed were, not surprisingly, "Music" and "The Holocaust."

Not surprisingly? We expect to find "Music" and "Germany" coupled, and the long list of additional sublistings under "Music" confirms just why: composer biographies abound; the Austro-German tradition forms the core of a library's collection of scores and recordings; German historiography and German letters rarely excludes music in one form or another. Not surprisingly? Americans are passionate readers about the Holocaust, and it would be impossible to uncouple books on modern Germany from the Holocaust. Germany, music, the Holocaust. Together, they instantiate and represent the most pervasive American perceptions of modern Germany.

In her recent volume of oral histories, *Tearing the Silence: On Being German in America* (1997), Ursula Hegi gathered one of the most trenchant and moving critiques of post-Holocaust German-America. An immigrant German-American herself, Hegi interrogates the very silence of her generation of Germans in America. The individuals whose stories fill *Tearing the Silence* are all plagued, in one way or another, by the impossibility of separating their identity from the history of twentieth-century Germany and specifically from the Holocaust. Most of those willing to tell their stories to and through Hegi—she solicited volunteers through the media—did so as part of a lifelong process of distancing themselves from their German pasts, and yet their willingness to tear the silence also grew from their own sense of an identity that was German as well as American.

Music, too, appears in the stories as a cultural symbol more German than American, and we find ourselves wondering just whether music assists or resists in the processes of tearing the silence. In the story of "Ulrich," for example, the German-American choruses conducted by his authoritarian father remained trapped in a stifling bastion against Americanness, and they came to symbolize what it was he needed to escape (Hegi 1997:80). Ultimately, then, tearing the silence was the act of confirming the shift from a German to a German-American identity, even when that shift did not free one from the German side of the hyphen.

The other German-America is present in many of the essays in this volume, both directly and indirectly. It is present in the ways immigrant communities endeavored to escape from Central Europe and the ethnic and religious repression that have rarely not characterized German history. It is present in the ways Austrian- and Swiss-Americans have rejected attempts to remake them into German-Americans. It is present in the aporia that results when German-Jewish music is placed in historical essays but then it fails to appear in essays about German-American music in the past fifty years. The other German-America, too, is present because the silence that would obscure it must still be addressed.

Toward a New Music Historiography: The Multicultural Basis of German-American Music

The hyphen's presence challenges us to be inclusive, to broaden the entire field of German-American musical studies. Many previous motivations underlying such studies were, in contrast, exclusive, driven by filiopietistic fervor or focused on only one genre or region. This exclusivity meant that many German-American musics were neglected and that the music histories of many German-American groups went undocumented; it meant that the diverse voices of many German-American musicians were never heard.

It is then another challenge of the present book to turn and tune our ears to those musics that have been excluded from previous German-American musical studies. In our historical examinations, we must turn our ears to music histories that were brief and ephemeral, as well as those that may have unfolded over centuries, but thrive in social structures and with musical repertories that no longer have parallels in Europe. We must formulate entirely new historical frameworks, particularly those that do not rely teleologically on cause and effect, the growth of musical traditions from German seeds planted in American soil. We must reformulate our constructs of the groups and communities in which German-American musical practices are to be found. When we survey musical scholarship for studies of music of German Jews in America, of German Free Thinkers, or of Austrian working-class neighborhoods in Chicago, we find shockingly little. But these groups—and many, many others—had active musical cultures, and their musical practices formed histories, indeed a multitude of music histories that together constitute the broad subject of this volume.

Yet another challenge of the book is, then, to seek out the relationships among the different historical streams, different musical styles, and different cultural meanings. In the introductory essay we have begun by recognizing these differences, our differences, perhaps the basic differences in views from opposite sides of the hyphen. We also recognize the disciplinary differences that the essayists bring as scholars working in diverse fields: in history, folklore, historical musicology, folk-*music* research and folk*song* research, ethnomusicology, organology, and linguistics. With the differences brought together in this volume as a starting point, the book introduces a moment to begin searching for new similarities and common themes and to represent these. We believe that the essays make a clear case that the moment is right to begin formulating a new discourse that will allow us to understand the vast polyphony of voices arising from German-American musics and musical cultures. Unlike Nikolaus Lenau, we feel it is increasingly imperative not to remain deaf to any of these voices.

Bibliography

Bachmann-Geiser, Brigitte, and Eugen Bachmann. *Amische: Die Lebensweise der Amischen in Berne, Indiana*. Berne: Benteli Verlag, 1988.

Bohlman, Philip V. "Music in the Culture of German-Americans in North Central Wisconsin." Master's thesis, University of Illinois, 1980.

________. "Deutsch-amerikanische Musik in Wisconsin—Überleben im Melting Pot." *Jahrbuch für Volksliedforschung* 30 (1985): 99–116.

________. "Religious Music/Secular Music: The Press of the German-American Church and Aesthetic Mediation." In Geitz, ed., 69–90, 1992.

Boyer, Walter E., Albert F. Buffington, and Don Yoder, eds. *Songs along the Mahantongo*. Hatboro, PA: Folklore Associates, 1964.

Brednich, Rolf Wilhelm, Zmaga Kumer, and Wolfgang Suppan, eds. *Gottscheer Volkslieder*. 3 vols. Mainz: B. Schott's Söhne, 1969–1984.

Bretting, Agnes. "Organizing German Immigration: The Role of State Authorities in Germany and the United States." In Trommler and McVeigh, eds., 25–38, 1985.

Brody, Jennifer DeVere. "Hyphen-Nations." In *Cruising the Performative: Interventions into the Representation of Ethnicity, Nationality, and Sexuality*, edited by Sue-Ellen Case, Philip Brett, and Susan Leigh Foster, 149–162. Bloomington: Indiana University Press, 1995.

Ensslen, Klaus. "German-American Working-Class Saloons in Chicago: Their Social Function in an Ethnic and Class-Specific Cultural Context." In *German Workers' Culture in the United States, 1850 to 1920*, edited by Hartmut Keil, 157–180. Washington, DC: Smithsonian Institution Press, 1988.

Geitz, Henry, ed. *The German-American Press*. Madison: Max Kade Institute for German-American Studies, University of Wisconsin–Madison, 1992.

Greene, Victor. *A Passion for Polka: Old-Time Ethnic Music in America*. Berkeley: University of California Press, 1992.

Hauer, Norbert, ed. *". . . in fremde Land dahin": Lieder vom Auswandern, Abschiednehmen, Wegmüssen*. Motzen, Austria: Arbeitsgemeinschaft "Singen und Musizieren in Niederösterreich," Niederösterreichische Liederhefte, 9, 1992.

Hegi, Ursula. *Tearing the Silence: On Being German in America*. New York: Simon and Schuster, 1997.

Holzapfel, Otto. *Religiöse Identität und Gesangbuch: Zur Ideologiegeschichte deutschsprachiger Einwanderer in den USA und die Auseinandersetzung um das 'richtige' Gesangbuch*. Berne: Peter Lang, 1998.

Keil, Charles, Angeliki V. Keil, and Dick Blau. *Polka Happiness*. Philadelphia: Temple University Press, 1992.

Keil, Hartmut, and John B. Jentz. *German Workers in Chicago: A Documentary History of Working-Class Culture from 1850 to World War I*. Urbana: University of Illinois Press, 1988.

Leary, James P. "Old Time Music in Northern Wisconsin." *American Music* 2 (1984): 71–87.

Luebke, Frederick C. *Germans in the New World: Essays in the History of Immigration*. Urbana: University of Illinois Press, 1990.

Meier, John. "Lieder auf Friedrich Hecker." In *Volksliedstudien*, edited by John Meier, 214–246. Strasbourg: Karl J. Trübner, 1917.

Moltmann, Günter. "The Pattern of German Emigration to the United States in the Nineteenth Century." In Trommler and McVeigh, eds., 14–24, 1985.

Pinck, Louis. *Verklingende Weisen: Lothringer Volkslieder*. Vol. 1. Metz: Lothringer Verlags- und Hilfsverein, 1926.

Proulx, E. Annie. *Accordion Crimes*. New York: Scribner, 1996.

Schenk, Annemarie. "Interethnische Forschung." In *Grundriß der Volkskunde: Einführung in die Forschungsfelder der Europäischen Ethnologie*, edited by Rolf W. Brednich, 273–289. Berlin: Dietrich Reimer, 1988.

Slobin, Mark. *Subcultural Sounds: Micromusics of the West*. Hanover, NH: Wesleyan University Press, 1993.

Tocqueville, Alexis de. *Democracy in America*. Vol. 2. Trans. by Henry Reeve. New Rochelle, NY: Arlington House, 1966.

Trommler, Frank, and Joseph McVeigh, eds. *America and the Germans: An Assessment of a Three-Hundred-Year History*. Vol. 1: *Immigration, Language, Ethnicity*. Philadelphia: University of Pennsylvania Press, 1985.

Weber, Rolf, ed. *Land ohne Nachtigall: Deutsche Emigranten in Amerika, 1777–1886*. Berlin: Buchverlag Der Morgen, 1981.

Wokeck, Marianne. "German Immigration to Colonial America: Prototype of a Transatlantic Mass Migration." In Trommler and McVeigh, eds., 3–13, 1985.

Yoder, Don. "Die Volkslieder der Pennsylvanien-Deutschen." In *Handbuch des Volksliedes*, edited by Rolf Wilhelm Brednich, Lutz Röhrich, and Wolfgang Suppan, Vol. 2, 221–270. Munich: Wilhelm Fink, 1975.

________. "Palatine, Hessian, Dutchman: Drei Bezeichnungen für Deutsche in Amerika." *Hessische Blätter für Volks- und Kulturforschung* 17 (1985): 191–212.

I

Making German America

2

ETHNICITY AND MUSICAL CULTURE AMONG THE GERMAN CATHOLICS OF THE SAUK, 1854–1920

Kathleen Neils Conzen

On a Sunday afternoon in early November 1866, several German-Catholic families gathered in Mathias Hemmesch's central Minnesota log cabin to make music. With the season's hard work behind them, they were clearly ready for a little relaxation before the sober weeks of Advent and the snows of winter set in. Their prairie farms on the south bank of the Sauk River were no longer quite so isolated on the outermost edge of the settlement frontier as when they had first staked their claims eight or nine years earlier. But these settlers were still almost four miles from the nearest hamlet and had to rely upon one another for entertainment. So Hemmesch announced that his bar was open and invited his neighbors for the afternoon. And when the young folks decided that they wanted to dance, he asked John Mehr, one of his guests, if they couldn't borrow his son Mathias' "Cordien"— his accordion. (The nonstandard English is that of the justice of the peace who later attempted to adjudicate the resulting dispute.)

John Mehr was initially dubious. Mathias, he said, owned the accordion for his own "Bleshure"—his pleasure. What if he lent it and it got broken? If it breaks, Hemmesch replied, "I bin good for it." Reassured, Mehr sent another of his sons, Jacob, to fetch the accordion from his daughter's house, where it seemed to be lodged at the moment. Jacob borrowed a horse from Hemmesch and soon returned with the instrument. But, he later recalled, he was soon disturbed to see the vigor with which Hemmesch's son-in-law, Michael Philips, as well as a couple of other young men, played it while the young people danced. Later, after the party broke up, Katherine Mehr, who seems to have been at her sister's when Jacob came by for the instrument, stopped off at the Hemmesch's to pick it up on her way home. When young Marie Hemmesch gave it to her, the two girls discovered that it had a hole in it. Marie told her to leave it, that her family would have it repaired, but Katherine grabbed the instrument and ran home. Mathias Mehr, the "busted" accordion's owner, then went round to settle with Michael Philips, whose vigorous playing was held to have caused the hole. Michael offered ten dollars as the instrument's value, but Mathias demanded fourteen dollars, threatening that if he wasn't paid by morning, "I go and suit you."

When Michael failed to arrive with the money, Mathias indeed went to Richmond, the nearest village, to file his complaint with John Lang, shoemaker and justice of the peace. A week later the suit was heard. Plaintiff and defendant, each with his witnesses and supporters, crowded into what was undoubtedly a makeshift courtroom in Lang's shop, and Lang took down their German testimony in his own limited English on flimsy scraps of paper. When all the shouting was over, he gave his ruling. He found for the plaintiff, ordering Michael Philips and Mathias Hemmesch to pay Mathias Mehr the $14 that was in dispute, as well as $13.29 in court costs. And then he threw in a surprise: he also fined Philips; Matt Hemmesch and his son and daughter; John Mehr and his daughter Katherine; neighbor John Miller, another of the accordion players; and anyone else who danced, two dollars each for dancing on Sundays. The law, he observed, "says so" (*Mehr v. Philips* 1866).[1]

Thanks to the outrage of Philips and his father-in-law—and probably of everyone else present—the case was appealed to Stearns County's district court, and thus the record of this Sunday afternoon gathering of German farm families in a log cabin on the Minnesota frontier survives today. The Mehrs and the Hemmesches were only two of the hundreds of German-Catholic families who settled in the wilderness along the Sauk in the years after 1854, constructing there one of the nation's most extensive, autonomous, and enduring German-Catholic culture regions (Conzen 1985 and 1990; Vogeler 1976). Listening to the testimony in a court case like *Mehr v. Philips*, we can start to eavesdrop on the processes by which that culture was created, the values it sought to embody, and the institutions through which it was perpetuated. In *Mehr v. Philips* itself, we can hear this community making law. We can hear it making love—or at least making an occasion when love might blossom. And, most especially for present purposes, we can hear it making music.

We can immediately read in the case of the busted accordion some of the main contours of the local legal culture, and the ambiguous role it played in the construction and defense of this German-Catholic community. The willingness to sue, the familiarity of peasants with legal forms, their ability to elect one of their own to administer their own ethnic brand of justice, all are laid out beautifully in the case

[1] All quotations are from the report of the case made by the justice of the peace, John Lang, filed in *Mehr v. Philips* 1866; the most common local spellings of names are used.

file in John Lang's almost unintelligible English. So, too, is the ultimate vulnerability of the system. In imposing the dancing fine, Lang called down upon the ethnic community the values of an outside Yankee culture, and those outside values then returned to haunt him when, in the course of the appeal, his docket was examined, and its numerous irregularities laid bare. Indeed, other local Germans, including the town constable, seem to have used the occasion to report him to the district court, initiating a suit against him for misconduct in office. The record is not completely clear on this point. What is clear, however, is that Lang's verdict in favor of Mehr was reversed, his fines were voided, and he soon abandoned the village and his office for a homestead in a neighboring township (*Mehr v. Philips* 1866; for Lang, see Mitchell 1915:688). As long as they were in agreement, immigrants in a situation of local dominance, like the one enjoyed by the German Catholics of the Sauk, could use the instruments of American justice to enforce their own behavioral codes. But the temptation was always there for an aggrieved party to break the implied compact and call upon outside authority. The autonomy of immigrant culture, this reading of *Mehr v. Philips* suggests, was real but highly vulnerable.

Love, too, can be readily decoded in this case. *Mehr v. Philips* offers us a rare vignette of immigrant social life, a frontier genre piece. These families' farms were still primitive. They had probably been burned out by Indians four years earlier during the Dakota uprising and forced to take sanctuary in their hastily fortified Richmond log church.[2] Most of the land they claimed was still unimproved (NAM 1870). But we can nevertheless see here a crude society in the making—a neighborhood where Eifelers from Prussia's border with Luxemburg and Bavarians from Franconia far to the east were together constructing a local community bonded by visits and borrowing and creating family-supervised opportunities for its young people to flirt and court. Was it perhaps at a similar gathering that Bavarian-born Michael Philips had decided to marry his Eifel neighbor's daughter?[3] Hemmesch

---

[2] Mehr witnessed a deposition attesting to the despoliation of his neighbor's crops by Indians during the Dakota Uprising of 1862; see John Ley's deposition in the Sioux Claims Commission files (Ley, n.d.).

[3] The Mehr family came from an Eifel village north of Irrel on the Luxemburg border; they arrived in the United States in 1855, spent three years in Illinois, and then took up their 160-acre claim in Munson township in 1858; John Mehr, who was forty-eight at the time of this incident, had not yet acquired title to his claim in 1860 (Mitchell 1915:1074). See Jacob Mehr death card, in private possession, Jean Didier, St. Cloud, MN, and 1860 ms. censuses of population and agriculture (NAM 1860). Mathias Hemisch, fifty-four in 1866, brought his family to Iowa from Prussia shortly after 1850, then moved to the Sauk in the late 1850s (NAM 1860). Michael Phillipp, twenty-eight, and his parents were part of a larger Bavarian contingent that shared this part of the valley with the Prussians; some of the Bavarians had also come from Illinois (NAM 1860). John Lang was Prussian-born (NAM 1860).

probably did not open his home out of pure generosity; when he says "I have Bar in my Haus an have envided my nevers for a company," he is implying that those "nevers" paid for their drinks (*Mehr v. Philips* 1866). He was providing an institution that even the smallest German farming community needed, the frontier's functional equivalent of the *Spinnstube* of old-country tradition, a setting for the courtships as well as the gossip and storytelling that were vital for the construction of community (Figure 1).[4] As Lang's citation of the law against Sunday dancing reminds us, it was an institution that set the community at odds with its Yankee neighbors and created a need for vigilant legal defense. But such gatherings also faced internal opposition. Even in the old country, the Catholic church had a long history of suspicion about the "occasions of sin" such gatherings could provide; in America, there was an additional concern for the scandal they offered to Sabbatarian Protestants. From these paired worries arose the Sunday afternoon Vespers that priests soon began to sponsor in the country parishes of the Sauk, as well as the Saturday evening Benediction services that shortly joined them as alternative supervised rituals for the enactment of community (Medick 1984 and Hoffmann 1934). But well into the twentieth century, "house parties" like Hemmesch's early exemplar remained central to the courtship process and hence to the reproduction of the local culture itself (*Stones and Hills* 1975:107–108; Voigt 1987:61–63; on the rural Midwestern "house party" tradition, see Martin 1994:43–63).

But what then of the music that reverberates so unmistakably through *Mehr v. Philips* as through so many passages of local immigrant life? Did it, too, have a role in the construction and perpetuation of the region's distinctive way of life? The young Mehrs and Hemmesches, the case of the busted accordion suggests, certainly took for granted the necessity of music and dancing as part of celebration and courtship. A musical instrument like a "Cordien" was no less a vital part of the community stock of necessities, to be lent when called upon, than a fanning mill or a grubbing plow.[5] The community had a cadre of men who could play the instrument, and at least one among their number who had been willing to devote some of his very scarce cash to its acquisition. The instrument had a family character. Fa-

[4] The *Spinnstube*, in its traditional form an evening spinning bee for the young women of a German village, was held in a private home under the oversight of a "house father" who was compensated in cash or kind for his services; attracting the young men of the village for singing, dancing, and courting, its socializing and socialization functions tended to insure its survival despite numerous official efforts to control the institution in the name of morality and public order. See Medick (1984).

[5] For the prevalence of borrowing in this as in so many other frontier communities, see Kulzer (1976).

Figure 1. Twenty-nine years after their log cabin house party, old differences long forgotten, the Mehrs and Hemmesches gathered once more—beer steins in hand—in front of the Mehrs' modern farmhouse to celebrate the wedding of Jacob's daughter. Math Hemmesch, now a Melrose brewer, straddles the beer keg to the right, Jacob (with corsage) stands next to the bearded pastor to the left of the bridal pair, Mathias Mehr—the quondam owner of the accordion—holds his daughter in the center of the photograph, while Katherine Hemmesch, nee Mehr—the young girl who brought the busted accordion home—stands with baby in arms at the far left. Her husband Peter Hemmesch stands next to his father and the beer keg. Photograph courtesy of the Stearns County Historical Society.

ther, brother, sister, all knew where it was and valued its preservation. Mehr Sr. seems to have approved of his son's expenditure of money and time on this "Bleshure," and its repair became a matter of family honor. It was also taken for granted that it could be repaired locally—a not unreasonable assumption, since there happened to be an organ-builder nearby producing instruments for the new frame churches that were beginning to replace the pioneer log chapels along the Sauk (*SCD*, 7 December 1865).[6] We cannot know what kind of music Philips and the others actually played, but the odds are good that it was already a syncretic mixture reflecting not only their varying German regional traditions, but also the years spent in different parts of the American Midwest, where some of the children had grown to adulthood. Their right to sing and dance on Sunday meant enough to the Hemmesch and Mehr families to bring them into the public record in the first place, and there they would reappear twenty-one years later, yoked once more by music, as co-donors of a new bell for their parish church (Ortmann 1958:51).

Such a reading of this admittedly minor case suggests that any historian engaged, as I am, in interpreting the formation and evolution of an immigrant culture in a rural area like the Sauk Valley, can no more afford to ignore the occasions, structures, and meanings of music-making than she could ignore the family or the formal institutions of cultural construction and defense. Music mattered to the people of the Sauk, and so it should matter to their interpreter. But why and how did it matter? When, where, and by whom was music made along the Sauk, and what kinds of music was it? What functions did it play within the local culture, and how did both the music and its functions change with time? Did the significance of music for these rural Germans, as for many other ethnic minorities, lie particularly in its community-constituting role, in its ability to help bound the group, express ethnic identity, subvert assimilation?[7] Or should we see equal significance in the musical paths that, like the busted accordion itself, also pointed them outward toward a broader, non-ethnic world?

II

Such questions take on particular salience in light of the complex adaptive role assigned to music within German-American ethnic thought and urban practice. Music, immigrant commentators insisted, functioned both as an emotive bridge back

---

[6] Mitchell documents the continued presence of the organ-builder as late as September 1868 (1915:1121); there were also, of course, accomplished leather workers in this rural community.

[7] Studies stressing the inward, subversive character of ethnic music, though also acknowledging its interaction with broader cultural currents, include Levine (1977), Slobin (1982), and Tawa (1982).

to the old country and as a bond to fellow countrymen in the new. "Isolated you departed from Germany's distant shores," goes a loose translation of one German-American poem, "now timeless German song unites you once again."[8] Music instantly returns the immigrant to the homeland, Friedrich Kapp argued, presenting anew to one's soul all the lovely impressions of youth, and reawakening in one's breast native tones silenced by the struggles of daily life. "Music and song for us are bridges on which we can hasten back to Germany at any time, and across which its spiritual treasures press back to us . . . the cleansing bath that refreshes the spirit of even the weakest and keeps the baseness from clinging."[9] Just as the reawakening of the German nation after the devastation of the Thirty Years' War found its initial expression in music, to be followed by literature and then philosophy, so, too, Kapp theorized, must each German recapitulate this process in his own intellectual development, beginning with the musical cultivation of the emotions and sensibilities; music for the German was a necessity if he was to be true in America to the best in his character. Only thus could he win respect within his new homeland; even more importantly, only thus could he contribute to its cultural shaping and salvation (Kapp 1865). Participation in singing festivals, Christian Esselen insisted, was not only "a duty towards ourselves, to remind ourselves always that even in America we can be human beings," but also "a duty towards societal conditions here, which definitely demand a humanizing through German art and sociability." The task of the Germans in America, agreed another commentator, was to work for the "victory of the good and the beautiful, even in American *Volksleben*." Theodore Müllenmeister, the editor of a St. Paul Catholic newspaper widely read in the Sauk Valley, put the matter succinctly: "It is a mission of the Germans to teach the Americans what good music is, what it means, and how it should be performed."[10]

---

[8] "Getrennt kamt Ihr gezogen aus Deutschlands fernen Gau'n. . . . Geeinigt hat Euch wieder das ew'ge deutsche Lied" (Risler 1869).

[9] "So sind Musik und Gesang für uns die Brücke, auf welcher wir jeder Zeit nach Deutschland zurückeilen, und auf welcher dessen geistige Schätze in ihrer volksthümlichen Form zu uns dringen; so sind Musik und Gesang das reinigende Bad, welches den Geist selbst des Schwächsten frisch erhält und das Ansetzen von Schmutz verhindert" (Kapp 1865).

[10] ". . . eine Pflicht gegen die hiesigen geselligen Zustände, welche einer Humanisirung durch deutsche Kunst und Geselligkeit gewiss bedürfen, wie auch . . . eine Pflicht gegen uns selbst, um uns immer wieder daran zu erinnern, dass wir auch hier in Amerika Menschen sein können," (Esselen 1856); ". . . den Sieg des Guten und Schönen, auch im amerikanischen Volksleben," (Eberbard 1865); ". . . es ist eine Mission der Deutschen, die Amerikaner zu lehren, was gute Musik ist, was sie bedeutet und wie man sie vorträgt," (*DW* 12 September 1868); see also Esselen (1858) and Hagen (1866).

Music, in short, was not just a necessity and consolation for the individual, a bond for the group, and a token for respect; it was a tool for the Germanic remaking of America itself. Music inevitably involved more than simple folk feeling and resistance in a group with a musical culture as complex and evolved as that of the Germans. Even the most vernacular music of the homeland, as Philip V. Bohlman has observed (1985), approached in its technical traits what had become the classical music standard; its instrumentation was being reshaped by industrialization and its performance by the formal influence of schools, churches, singing societies, and military service, while music itself acquired an explicit nationalizing role in the creation of a German state (cf. Stockmann 1992, Ahrens 1988, Ruhr 1987, and Richter 1990). German immigrants in nineteenth-century American cities quickly replicated the rich array of musical associations, music venues and occasions, and musical embellishments of daily life that characterized the provincial communities of the homeland, and in the process the cultivation of particular kinds of music and particular settings for making music became self-conscious instruments in the construction and projection of German-American ethnicity. Music, later recalled one Wisconsin German, "was the bridge over which a piece of German life moved into the American family" (Hense-Jensen 1900:155).[11]

But the more they succeeded in using music to reshape American culture, the more they undermined their own ethnic project. Thus, to take one telling example, ethnic motives clearly underlay the choice of Albert Lortzing's comic opera, *Zar und Zimmermann*, as the first opera to be performed by Milwaukee's young German-American community in 1853 (Conzen 1976:175). There was, first of all, the choice of the opera itself. This was nothing less than a multivalent act of ethnic assertiveness. Simply performing a musical work of this complexity, only sixteen years after its Leipzig premiere, before a mixed audience of Yankees and Germans, was to lay claim to both ethnic cultural identity and cultural superiority—to spread before the feet of a backwoods urban elite the cultural treasure that Germans were bringing America. But to pluck this particular opera from the German treasure chest was to do still more. On the face of it, there is nothing particularly German in a plot that revolves around Czar Peter the Great's disguised presence as a workman in a Dutch shipyard, nor anything particularly German about music that, though self-consciously folkloristic at times, draws upon Netherlandic and Slavic themes. Yet the opera as a whole conveys superbly both the texture of *kleinbürgerlich* Biedermeier

[11] "Die Musik war die Brücke, über welche ein Stück deutschen Lebens in die amerikanische Familie einzog."

Germany, and the values that Germans were bringing to America.[12] When the opening chorus sings of the joy of hard work leavened by festivity, when wedding guests celebrate the value of song and drink, the message meant for sober, money-grubbing Americans is all too clear. But so, too, is the affirmation of a German claim to a republican tradition to match that of the Americans implied by the quest that brings Peter to the West, by the conception of a responsible ruler that he embodies, by the satire of the bureaucracy that Germans in coming to America had spurned. The opera's use of folkloric elements was itself a celebration of the wholeness of a communal culture that Germans found lacking in America.

But their choice also reflected the fact that this opera performance was more than a weapon of ethnic aggression. It was equally an instrument of ethnic construction. The chorus plays an unusually large role in Lortzing's opera, giving singers a literal opportunity to enact community. In laughing at the richly comic character of Bürgermeister van Bett they were reminding themselves of what they had rejected of Germany, while the Czar's controversially nostalgic song of childhood sentimentalized the homeland memories that were the glue binding them to one another. But it must have been the famous "Kantatenprobe" (cantata rehearsal) scene, with its self-reflexive mocking of their own musical efforts, that above all attracted them to Lortzing's opera. In gently satirizing the struggles of the good burghers of Saardam to achieve musical harmony, they were ruefully celebrating their own ridiculously valiant efforts to come together to make music on the Wisconsin frontier. The music, it almost seems, was its own justification, the organized ethnic community the means necessary to achieve it.

This is a refrain, I have argued elsewhere, that runs through much of the nineteenth-century German-American discourse on ethnic culture and community (Conzen 1989). The standard German-American critique of America stressed its joyless materialism. By contrast, they argued, the German could not live without the warmth of human contact, conviviality, festivity. Or as Lortzing's opera put it, "was soll gelingen, muss man mit Gesang vollbringen." Life required moments of leisure heightened by sociability, ritual, and music for work itself to be effective. If American society could not fulfill these human needs, this ethnic analysis continued, Germans would have to organize to provide for them themselves. Through organization they could preserve the German language within which their celebratory impulses were embedded, through celebration they could create the community necessary to continue celebrating, and by the performance of celebration within

[12]For the libretto, see Lortzing (1985). Commentaries consulted include Pahlen (1981), Schirmag (1982), and Worbs (1979).

American society they could gradually alter America itself to make it more receptive to their needs. There were few commonalities of class, religion, dialect, political ideology, or prejudice to bind Germans in a common ethnic identity; what they shared most fundamentally was a common interest in preserving their right to construct a festive culture.

What was ethnically coded in the urban communities of German America, therefore, was not so much any particular kind of music, any particular substantive content, but the fact of music-making itself, and the institutions that made music and festivity possible. Therein lay its strength. A haze of German ethnicity enveloped everything from symphonic music to barroom ditties, from church anthems to militia marches, while ethnic occasions for music-making ranged from the privacy of the family group around the piano to the public spectacle of national singing-society festivals. But in this catholic breadth lay also the vulnerability of an ethnicity so defined. For as German Americans gradually succeeded in making America a more hospitable place for their music and festivity, as they began to shape a non-ethnically coded American music and popular culture in a process nicely described by Berndt Ostendorf, the logic of ethnic maintenance itself began to fade (Ostendorf 1988). One no longer needed a German-American world to enjoy the values of German America. Some, for whom the means had become the end, continued to argue the necessity of preserving ethnic institutions in order to preserve ethnic culture, but more and more group members were already slipping away from the formal ethnic world by the time of the First World War. What would remain as ethnically coded "German" music, subject to revival by later generations, often would be little more than museumized folksongs or kitschy oom-pah bands.

But could music play a similarly ethnicizing yet integrating role in the rural communities of the Midwest where more than a quarter of the German immigrant population settled (for rural settlement patterns, see Conzen 1984)? Scholars are belatedly acknowledging a German musical heritage in the hymnody and "old-time" dance bands of such settlement areas today, but focusing only on ethnic traditions that have survived and evolved tells us little about the full range of the musical culture that may once have existed, or its role in community life (cf. Bohlman 1985, Leary and March 1991, Leary 1984, Leary 1988, Martin 1994, and Greene 1992). One could certainly argue that these peasant immigrants made music because they had always made music, because it was a cultural habit that they brought from the homeland, and because it served the same complex of aesthetic, emotional, and communal needs that music generally serves. The rare Sauk Valley memoir of life in the old country before emigration, for example, is matter-of-course in its mention of lullabies and play songs, church singing, dances, and tavern jollification as part of the normal round of life (see, for example, the autobiographical statements of Kulzer [1976], Ambrose Lethert in SJAA, and John Katzner in SJAA). The Valley's frontier setting, however, suggests one reason why the simple transfer of a pre-migration musical culture cannot necessarily be assumed. The old social contexts within which music was made could never be completely reconstructed in America, nor would accustomed inventories of instruments and skill necessarily be present. Emigration swept up only a partial cross-section of the old-country population, and brought together strangers as well as relatives and friends in the German colonies of America. Moreover, the same cultural currents that moved urban communities, German and Yankee alike, inevitably found their echo in the small towns of the rural Midwest. The result in some rural areas may have been the formation of an enduring, ethnically coded and ethnicity-defining musical tradition, as seems to have occurred among the German Bohemians of Brown County in southern Minnesota, where the "Dutchman" sound of the big polka bands was born (Rippley 1992; Rippley and Paul 1995). But in Stearns County to the north, as four transects through the first seventy years of its musical life will suggest, rural German-American musical culture took a different course: music echoed, to be sure, through much of county life, but it never seemed to take on a strong ethnic coding, and like its urban counterpart it became a significant bridge to a broader, non-ethnic cultural world.

III

Four factors helped mold the distinctive musical culture of the Sauk. The first was the early German preponderance within much of Stearns County. Germans were among the first to settle in the county beginning in 1854, and within twenty-five years they and their American-born children headed about half of the households in the county of twenty-two thousand people, particularly dominating a contiguous central cluster of twenty-two of the county's thirty-three rural townships, fifteen of which were more than eighty percent German.[13] This demographic concentration lent a real measure of autonomy and assurance to German cultural development, while diminishing though never completely eliminating pressures to both borrow from and impress their Yankee neighbors.

---

[13] Population totals and percentages were calculated from NAM (1880). "German" in this context includes not only those from the various states that became part of Germany, but also small numbers of German-speaking Swiss, Luxemburgers, Austrians, Alsatians, and Bohemians. St. Cloud, the county seat, with a population of not quite 2,500, was more diverse, with Germans heading about a third of the households. Close to two thousand German families lived in the county's rural townships by 1880.

The second factor was the Catholic Church. There were small Lutheran, Evangelical, and German Methodist congregations that clung to the fringes of the Valley, but the vast majority of the county's German settlers were Roman Catholic. The church's musical significance lay in its rituals, in its support for traditional social norms, and in the cultivated leadership it provided in what was otherwise essentially a peasant society with a few *Kleinbürger* for leavening. Particularly significant were the Benedictine monks who established a monastery at the heart of the settlement in 1856, the Benedictine nuns who followed a year later, and the educated teacher-organists who played a central role in German parish life. The combination of a truncated social pyramid and church-linked musical leadership would also help blur the line between vernacular and cultivated musical traditions that was more sharply etched in the cities.

The third factor, the diversity of regional origins from which the German settlers derived, was related to the second. Stearns County was a later-stage German-American settlement, formed not by a predominant migration chain from a single German area, but settled almost simultaneously, in response to publicity in Catholic newspapers, by in-migrants from numerous earlier areas of German-Catholic settlement in America, who derived from virtually every Catholic region of the homeland. Their diverse musical cultures had already been mixed and creolized elsewhere in America; the process would inevitably continue along the Sauk.[14]

The fourth factor, the local settlement structure, was linked as much to the region's Catholicism as to its agricultural economy. The county seat, St. Cloud, lay on the Mississippi at the eastern edge of the county, and served as an entrepot to the rich farmlands of the Sauk Valley and the prairies beyond. Wheat-growing, and then by the 1890s dairying, sustained an increasingly prosperous countryside of owner-operated family farms punctuated by a dozen or so larger market towns regularly spaced along the railroads that penetrated the county in the decades after the Civil War, as well as by church-centered hamlets, each with at least a general store and a saloon, that emerged in the "inland" townships lacking railroad access. The Germans of the Sauk had no interest in replicating the inefficient village-based

[14] Just over half the families in the rural townships were of Prussian origin, from such Catholic areas as Westphalia, the Rhineland, and the Eifel; close to eleven percent were Bavarian, mainly Franconian; Luxemburg and Austria each contributed another six percent; Hannover just over three percent; and Switzerland just over two percent; with those from scattered smaller states amounting to another eight percent while fourteen percent reported only "Germany." About two-thirds of St. Cloud's German households were Prussian, another fourteen percent Bavarian, and eleven percent Badenese (tabulations from NAM 1880). Families arriving in 1854 alone came from older settlements in Pennsylvania, New York, Ohio, Indiana, Illinois, Missouri, Iowa, and Wisconsin.

agriculture of the homeland and resided on their farms. But their parish-centered lives, combined with Catholicism's relative tolerance for their festive culture, insured that their country churches, unlike those of their Protestant compatriots, never remained isolated for long, and the hamlets that grew up around the churches provided important foci for public music-making in the countryside.

The evolving interaction of these factors shaped both the occasions and the genres of music-making in the Sauk Valley. Public music-making began early in its settlement history. Father Francis Pierz, the itinerant Indian missionary who invited German settlers to the Valley and conducted their first religious services, frequently found room for a violin in his minimal knapsack. One of the earliest legal records in the county was generated by a scuffle between Germans and non-Germans at a German dance in St. Cloud, and when a pioneer German shopkeeper wished to attract volunteers for a roof-raising, he offered free music as well as beer. Benedictine nuns were giving music lessons by the summer of 1857, and by early December that year the first church bell was ringing out over the Valley (Loso 1989:4–6; McDonald 1957:33–34; *SCV* 10 December 1857). Two years later, St. Cloud's Germans organized a brass band to play at the festive occasions that the community was beginning to support with great regularity. The band's existence was probably rather precarious in this little city of a few hundred people; two years later it—or a reorganized successor—sponsored the city's Fourth of July picnic to raise the three hundred dollars needed to pay for its brass instruments. Band members, the public appeal noted, had already spent thirty dollars apiece of their own money to pay for instruction in St. Paul.[15]

In the countryside, music was less formally organized but equally in evidence. Grasshoppers devastated the little patches of plowed fields along the Sauk in the summers of 1856 and 1857, and many of the pioneers courted actual starvation, but during the winter of 1857 the settlers in the country parish of St. Joseph held barn dances and a church fair, where homemade goods were auctioned off to benefit the church. Joe Phillipi, an Alsatian from Ohio, played the fiddle while his oldest boy sang, and the parishioners sang and danced to accordion music. Music also found its way less formally into frontier cabins like Matt Hemmesch's and into the country taverns that quickly appeared (Kulzer 1976; SCD 10 May 1866; *State of Minn. v. Anton Edelbrock*, SCD, Criminal Case Files, MHS [1862]).

But it was the church itself that probably provided these German pioneers with their most regular occasions for music-making. Served first by Pierz, then by peri-

[15] The band played at the city's 1859 Fourth of July celebration, and at St. Mary's Catholic Church's 1860 New Year's Fair; in June of 1861 it consisted of ten brass pieces and two drums (Mitchell 1915:1092, 1096; *SCD* 3 January 1860 and 19 June 1862).

patetic Benedictines from the monastery, the four little parishes established by 1860 soon multiplied to some twenty-five within the county alone (Yzermans 1989). On Sundays when there was no priest, the settlers would gather together, German books of worship in hand, in a log chapel if they had one, in a private home if they did not, for singing and common prayer, perhaps accompanied by violin or accordion. When the priest came, they might join him in the celebration of Mass by singing a German *Singmesse* from one or another of the diocesan songbooks that they had brought with them from Germany. Thirty years later, the people of St. Martin still remembered how John Blonigen led the hymns and prayers in the absence of the priest, and "how in Spring Hill in 1860, he almost sang Father Eberhard deaf with his bear's voice during the choruses."[16] A good voice was clearly a route to leadership and status! Already the parishes were beginning the annual cycle of feast days and processions that would prove so characteristic a part of local culture, though perhaps never again quite so dramatically as on July 4, 1857, when all the county's infant parishes met in pilgrimage, reciting the rosary and singing hymns along the way, for a Solemn High Mass on the banks of the Sauk to beseech St. Ulric to intercede to lift the grasshopper plague. The grasshoppers left, and Grasshopper Day, with its pilgrimage, became an annual county event (Reiss n.d.; Kulzer 1976).[17]

By the mid-1870s, when the county's first successful German-language newspaper began regular reporting on local events, the shape of the mature first-generation musical culture was clear. It resembled a truncated version of the musical array of the larger urban German-American communities, resting solidly on three institutional legs—town bands, private bands, and church choirs—and making tentative efforts to construct a fourth, singing societies; there were also the beginnings of a town-based genteel culture of private music-making alongside the fiddlers and accordion-players of the countryside. Each had its own sphere within the life of the community, though there was a fair degree of mutual influence and interpenetration. Except in church and parlor, the music-makers, so far as the public record is concerned, seem to have been almost exclusively male. There remains little record of just what exactly they played or how they played it.

---

[16] ". . . wie er in 1860 mit seiner Baerenstimme im Chor mit Gau und Cordi den P. Eberhard fast taub gesungen in Spring Hill" (P. Ambrose Lethert, memorandum dated 1894, St. Martin Parish File, SJAA). For the link between local reputation and church singing, see also Klein (1930:23, 25, 28).

[17] For later "grasshopper" pilgrimages, see *SCJ* 5 June 1873 and *NS* 23 August 1877. Commenting on the 1871 pilgrimage, one of the local English-language newspapers observed that "it was one of the most beautiful sights we have seen—this society, in regular order with banners flying moving out into the country led by the sweet strains of the Silver Cornet Band" (*SCT* 10 June 1871).

German pioneers by this time were still moving onto wild land in the upper reaches of the Valley and along its outer margins, but life in general was far less precarious than it had been fifteen years earlier. As chances for large-scale speculative profits waned with the passing of the frontier, many of the Yankee pioneers departed for greener pastures, leaving the Germans with unquestioned numerical and growing political and cultural dominance. Their local significance was confirmed when the Catholic Church created a Vicariate of Northern Minnesota in 1875, and the Benedictine abbot was consecrated as the first bishop at St. Cloud.

Volunteer bands remained at the center of secular music-making, taking their raison d'être from the need to provide music to accompany the moments of formal festivity that punctuated the social year (see Figure 2). St. Cloud's Brass Band survived the Civil War though with strains: by 1869 their instruments were in pledge with the local parish priest until the indebtedness on them was paid off, and he seems also to have been similarly holding the instruments of "Professor" Fischer's newly formed rival Silver Cornet Band—nineteen in all, between the two. The following summer the Silver Cornet Band sponsored a benefit shooting match to pay off its debt and soon was regaling citizens with evening concerts from a boat on the little lake at the edge of town (*SCT* 2 March 1867, 6 July 1867; *SCJ* 9 July 1868, 28 November 1868, 4 February 1869, 22 July 1869, 29 July 1869, 23 June 1870); the band boat concerts continued the following summer as well (*SCJ* 15 June 1871). Whether the occasion was a formal parade to celebrate the opening of the railroad, a political rally, a Fourth of July celebration, a church-benefit picnic or fair, the annual pre-Lenten Carnival parade, or a stylish wedding, at least one of the bands was there (*SCJ* 13 September 1866; *SCT* 31 October 1868; *SCT* 11 July 1868; *SCJ* 25 September 1873; 12 February 1874; 9 May 1872). When a Sauk Valley delegation traveled to St. Paul in 1871 to join seven thousand other Catholics in marching in support of Pope Pius IX against Victor Emmanuel, the Silver Cornet Band marched in their van. When the new bishop arrived in town, the band was there to serenade him; when he traveled into the countryside for confirmations, the band traveled with him (*SCJ* 26 January 1871; *NS* 29 June 1876; *SCJ* 26 April 1870). But it could also turn out on more mundane occasions: when Lorenz Enderle, the popular local brewer, was released from jail after being charged with violating federal revenue laws, he was accompanied in triumph back to his brewery by the band "in a sleigh drawn by four horses decorated with flags" (*SCJ* 20 January 1870). The formal band habit also began to spread into the countryside as farmers in the hamlet-centered parishes acquired the edge of financial security necessary to elaborate their own festive culture of picnics, benefits, religious rituals, and serenades of favorite

Figure 2. Kimball's town band, at the new railroad town's first Fourth of July celebration, 1889. Photograph courtesy of the Stearns County Historical Society.

local residents—including, frequently, the priest—often as a surprise on their namedays.[18]

Often sharing leadership and membership with the organized bands were less formal private groups that played for hire at the numerous "balls" and other gatherings frequently sponsored by local saloonkeepers particularly before Lent, after Pentecost, after the harvest, and during the Christmas season (*SCT* 23 October 1869, 22 July 1871, 26 August 1871; *SCP* 10 October 1872; *NS* 1 February 1877).[19] By 1869 St. Cloud saloons were regularly providing Saturday evening music as well; "we are fast approaching the leading cities in the matter of concert saloons," a local editor observed (*SCT* 26 June 1869; see also *SCT* 13 May 1871). In the country the local band might be a father and his sons who hired themselves out to supplement their farm income, risking community censure for neglecting their "real" work (Klein

[18]For evidence of a village band in Spring Hill, see, for example, *NS* 6 July 1876, in Albany, *NS* 23 June 1876. The village of St. Martin organized its band in May 1877; for rural serenades, see *NS* 16 March 1876, 31 May 1877. Meire Grove's band was organized by the local organist and choir director in 1883 (Dominik 1994/95:2).

[19] During the pre-Lenten season in 1871, one group of St. Cloud musicians complained loudly when they were hired to play at a country dance and then were not paid (*SCT* 11 February 1871). In Stearns County, at least, house parties and commercially sponsored dances clearly both developed early and in tandem, rather than the latter emerging from and superseding the former in the early twentieth century, a sequence that scholars have hypothesized elsewhere (cf. Leary 1984 and Martin 1994).

1930:21–22, 25, 40; *Albany* 1991:47, 48). Such groups could appropriate the more grandiose title of "orchestra" if they included strings and might join the volunteer bands at public occasions, as when a "string band" played along with the Silver Cornet Band at a "splendid" church benefit in St. Cloud in 1873 (*SCJ* 25 September 1873; see also Mitchell 1915:1138, 1159). Every summer there was at least one beer garden with regular evening music, and reports of wedding dances—often followed by shivarees—became more frequent. As one delighted guest at such an occasion commented, "things became really lively, with singing and whistling, drinking and eating, dancing and leaping. . . ."[20]

By the early 1870s, St. Cloud Germans were also making other efforts to elaborate an associational life on the urban German-American model, organizing often short-lived militia companies, sharpshooters groups, and a gymnastics club (*SCJ* 27 July 1871, 3 August 1871). Though such efforts included singing societies as well, they never enjoyed the relative longevity of the bands. There was a Liederkranz formed as early as 1866, for example, that provoked the formation of a rival Yankee singing society—whose performances were accompanied by the German band; neither seems to have lasted longer than a season (*SCJ* 15, 22, 29 November 1866).[21] By 1870, there were reports of a Philharmonic Society, by 1871 a Jovial Club, and by 1879 a fifty-member Concordia singing society, and as early as 1876 even isolated rural hamlets like Spring Hill and St. Martin could boast of a Liederkranz, but such efforts always seemed more occasional than regular (*SCJ* 3 March 1870, 9 February 1871; Mitchell 1915:1148; *NS* 21 June 1877).[22] A more genteel private musical culture was also emerging, resting no doubt not only on the greater financial security of a nascent business class, but on the music lessons its daughters enjoyed from the nuns. A German couple advertised music lessons as well as piano

[20] "Nun ging es erst recht fröhlich zu. Gesungen wurde und gepfiffen, getrunken und gegessen, getanzt und gesprungen . . ." (*NS* 14 June 1877). For beer garden music, see, e.g., *NS* 6 July 1876; for "charivariing" or "shivareeing" (both variants were used locally), see, e.g., *SCJ* 14 July 1870, 29 August 1872, 26 June 1873.

[21] By the following spring, however, St. Cloud reportedly had two German musical societies, one of which was giving free concerts in the Montana Saloon, one of the city's grandest, and in 1869 the St. Cloud Gesang-Verein participated in the state Sängerfest in Winona and had "a delightful time" (*SCT* 2 March 1867 and 26 June 1869).

[22] Cold Spring, one of the larger market towns, likewise acquired a German singing society in 1875 (Mitchell 1915:1137).

tuning and repair in 1869 (*SCT* 12 June 1869).[23] A German merchant opened "piano rooms" in St. Cloud in 1871, and by 1877 there were reportedly fifty-two pianos in St. Cloud homes; when county treasurer Mathias Gans's new grand piano arrived the previous year, he invited several musically inclined friends over for a pleasant Sunday evening of music, "Nass" und "Küche"—something "wet" and something "from the kitchen" (*NS* 22 March 1877, 30 November 1876).[24] As early as 1868 a thirteen-year-old prodigy named John Hofbauer won local fame for his superb voice and skills with the violin, piano, trumpet, and horn, while in 1874 Robert Mockenhaupt, one of the leading lights among the county's genteel music-makers, had his "Saint Cloud March" for the piano published in New York; it was "said to be good" (*DW* 4 July 1868; *SCJ* 19 November 1874).

As important as new prosperity to the elaboration of the local musical culture, however, were developments within the Catholic Church. The establishment of stable parishes with resident priests concerned to counter the drunkenness and immorality that seemed the inevitable accompaniment of private balls and parties, encouraged the proliferation not only of liturgical but also of church-sponsored secular festivity in the form of fairs, benefits, children's festivals, and the like, all inevitably accompanied by music.[25] By the mid-1870s, the liturgical year in one parish included weekly Lenten stations of the cross, a procession within the church on Holy Saturday, a Rogation week procession to a neighboring parish, a procession to the cemetery on the feast on the discovery of the true cross, the Corpus Christi procession to four altars placed at various points within the parish, the grasshopper procession, a procession to a neighboring parish whose church was being dedicated, a procession within the church precincts in thanksgiving for a good harvest, a procession to the cemetery on All Souls' Day, and offertory processions within the church whenever a particular association celebrated the feast of its patron—all accompanied by singing and often by a band.[26] The annual fund-raising fair served as the social equivalent of the old-country *Kirmes* (celebration of the church's dedication). Spe-

---

[23] Several months later the music teacher, Professor John M. Broome "from the East," founded St. Cloud's first and short-lived German-language newspaper, the *Anzeiger*; there are no extant copies (*SCT* 4 September 1869).

[24] For similar accounts of genteel private German musical gatherings see *NS* 7 December 1876 (in St. Cloud) and *NS* 19 July 1877 (in the hamlet of St. Augusta).

[25] This logic was made explicit, for example, in Father Simplicius's 1877 effort to replace the village of St. Joseph's secular *Fastnacht* (*Fasching*, or pre-Lenten carnival) celebration with a parish fair in order to keep parish youth from dangerous *Belustigungen* (amusements) (*NS* 18 January 1877).

[26] St. Mary's Parish (St. Cloud) Announcements Book, SJAA.

cial events in the life of the parish were also celebrated processionally, particularly first communions, confirmations, first Masses, and church dedications, in a ritual that included the erection of triumphal arches of greenery along the route—sometimes stretching for miles over the prairie—the decoration of houses and church with greenery, flowers, and ribbons; the accompaniment of band music and rifle shots; the formal marching by group of the different elements of the parish; and frequently a concluding banquet. The high point of the church year was the Corpus Christi procession through the community from one outdoor altar to the next in a public affirmation of the power of Christ incarnate (see Figure 3; *SCJ* 12 June 1873, 30 April 1874; *NS* 27 April 1876, 4 May 1876, 18 May 1876, 1 June 1876, 23 June 1876, 29 June 1876, 7 June 1877).

Even the weekly High Mass became a more professional production. The first organ appeared in the county in 1865. By the early 1870s an organ or harmonium was standard even in small country churches, St. Cloud could boast a twenty-four voice choir, and the newspaper might even announce which Mass was being sung, whether it was Mozart's "Twelfth," for instance—a particular favorite—or "Lambeilotti's grand mass." The significant role of bands for religious ritual—they were even used to accompany choir and organ during particularly important Masses—helps explain the support they received from parish priests.[27] Indeed, in the German-Catholic press, the Silver Cornet Band was referred to as the "St. Cloud Church Band" (*SCD* 7 December 1865; *DW* 27 June 1868; *SCJ* 2 April 1874, 5 June 1873, 24 June 1873, 1 July 1871; *DW* 15 February 1868, 20 June 1868).

One key to this professionalization lay in the de facto Catholic control of the public school system in the church hamlets, which enabled local school districts to hire seminary-educated lay teachers trained in music, whose school district salary could be doubled by their stipend as parish organist, choir director, and sexton, enabling them with some difficulty to support a family and thus remain stable fixtures in their communities. These so-called *Kirchenväter* (church fathers), who were frequently dignified with the local title of "Professor," often were products of Milwaukee's Catholic Normal School at St. Francis Seminary, where they were influenced after 1873 by John B. Singenberger's efforts to restore the church's tradition of liturgical chant. St. John's, the local Benedictine college where increasing

[27] "Lambillotte's Paschal Mass" at the First Communion celebration in St. Cloud's St. Mary's parish in 1873 featured the choir, three principal sopranos, two altos, two tenors, and four bass voices, accompanied by organ, cornet, flute, first violin, second violin, bass viol, and the Silver Band (*SCT* 11 June 1873). The "Twelfth" Mass, incorrectly attributed to Mozart by the English Catholic publisher, Novello, was, Robert L. Grimes notes, "probably the most popular of all the orchestral masses employed in America, both by Catholics and Protestants alike" (Grimes 1996: 83–84).

Figure 3. The outdoor Corpus Christi procession still survives today in St. John's parish in Meire Grove, and the Meire Grove Band, its veteran sousaphone player ensconced in a golf cart, still leads the procession. Photograph of the 1994 Corpus Christi observance courtesy of the Stearns County Historical Society.

numbers of county teachers trained, also placed strong emphasis on music from its inception; it formed its own brass band in 1868 and a string quartet the following year (Luetmer 1970:72–88; Grabrian 1973; Higginson 1982:110–113; Barry 1956:115–116, 150). The presence of the *Kirchenväter* gave many parishes a relatively well-educated, musically aware layman who often held the town clerk's office and became a natural focus for community organization; many later moved into county office and mercantile activities and strengthened the cultural pretensions of the nascent middle class.[28] They generally directed the village bands and singing societies and provided the impetus for the Valley's first tentative ventures into more elaborate musical skits and productions by the mid-1870s, while their school exhibitions brought a wider range of the German musical repertoire into the smallest community (*SCJ* 26 June 1873; *NS* 18 May 1876).[29] As they came to dominate the county's public education, their musical influence inevitably diffused even beyond the German community (Figure 4).[30]

If the forms and occasions of music-making mimicked those of urban German America, however, and their festive focus was similarly evident, the music of the Sauk generally lacked the overt ethnicization of its urban counterpart. Even the local English newspapers made little of its Germanness; it was simply community music. The Valley's Yankee minority, to be sure, cultivated its own distinctive music-making tradition from an early time, expressed here as in other American communities of the period particularly through singing schools, congregational singing, and parlor music. "Of those things which make up a city," inquired one of St. Cloud's Yankee editors, "what is more enjoyable, more refining, or more creditable than music?" There was at least one Yankee band, led by George E. Fuller, active in

---

[28] Both Gans and Mockenhaupt, mentioned earlier, had been schoolteachers (Mitchell 1915:782–783; *SCT* 4 September 1869). Another was Henry Krebs, a graduate of Göttingen, who came to St. Augusta in 1858 after twelve years in St. Louis and West Point, Iowa; in St. Augusta he was school teacher, organist, and choir director for some twenty-five years and served two terms as county school superintendent, two terms in the state legislature, and numerous terms as town clerk (Mitchell 1915:795). Lucas Gertken, *Kirchenvater* for forty-two years in Richmond and Meire Grove, had taught for five years in Germany, before his emigration, in the same school where his father and grandfather before him had taught for half a century each; six of his daughters and four of his sons entered the Benedictine order (Mitchell 1915:1236; *The Scriptorium* 1956:121).

[29] See the review in *The Northwestern Chronicle* by "Minnie Mary Lee" (Julia Sargent Wood, a pioneer newspaper editor and author living in Sauk Rapids, across the river from St. Cloud) of an 1874 concert at St. John's (quoted in Barry 1956:116). The concert, she suggested, made its frontier American listeners realize that they had never really known before how music was supposed to sound.

[30] Six *Kirchenväter* went on to hold the position of Stearns County superintendant of schools (Yzermans 1989:1050).

Figure 4. *Kirchenväter* in convention—members of the German Catholic Teachers' Association of Stearns County assembled at St. Martin for their annual meeting in 1907. Photograph courtesy of the Minnesota Historical Society.

St. Cloud in the late 1860s and 1870s, and by the mid-1870s the Granges in the rural Yankee settlements were also fielding their own brass bands (*SCD* 3 January 1861; *SCT* 7 December 1867, 14 March 1868, 4 January 1868; *SCT* 28 January 1871; Mitchell 1915:1109, 1112, 1138, 1148, 1135; William D. Mitchell and Family Papers, MHS; quotation *SCT* 23 November 1867; cf. Broyles 1992 and Knight 1993). But local Yankee music-makers seem to have felt that they labored under a disadvantage in comparison with their more musical German fellow citizens. Certainly Yankee newspaper editors could seldom resist making denigrating comparisons. It took the formation of the Liederkranz to stimulate St. Cloud Yankees to found their own short-lived singing society in 1866, while a similar effort in 1873, prodded by a new music-store owner from Chicago of suspiciously Welsh-sounding origins, "proved a complete fizzle." "There was no interest taken by the singers in this city," one editor noted. "Prof. Rhys is thoroughly disgusted and we do not blame him in the least." Two weeks later the editor praised "the Catholic society here" for having "the best choir to be found in the northern part of the State" and noted laconically that Rhys was planning a singing school (*SCD* 10 January 1861; *SCT* 2 March 1867, 23 November 1867, 4 September 1869, 5 November 1873, 17 December 1873, 31 December 1873).

Political and religious divisions insured that ethnic lines remained strongly demarcated, and much about the music that was played and sung in the homes, taverns, and churches of the Valley must have sounded extremely alien to Yankee ears.

But German music nevertheless played an ambassador's role. The appeal of the Männerchor's "finely executed" 1872 performance of that "beautiful piece of music," "Jägerlust," for example, was difficult to resist, particularly when performed by twenty of St. Cloud's "well-known German citizens" led by County Treasurer Gans, and such performances encouraged increasing musical cooperation across ethnic and religious lines (*SCT* 3 August 1872). Theodore Müllenmeister, who as a St. Paul editor was so insistent about the mission of German music in America, put his convictions into practice when he accepted the position of *Kirchenvater* in rural St. Martin in late 1868 (Kulas 1996:239–240). The following year, when the first Stearns County teacher's institute was held, the Mockenhaupt brothers joined four members of the Presbyterian choir in performing "a most beautifully rendered piece of music" (*SCT* 4 Sept. 1869), and soon Paul Mockenhaupt's "sweet" rendition of "My Mother's Ring" at the Congregational church concert confirmed his reputation as "one [of] our very best singers" (*SCT* 26 February 1873). The county's leading German and Yankee bandmasters shared a common experience of Civil War service—Peter Hoffmann, whose band played in the western part of the county, was said to be "the best drummer in the United States"—and when Fuller, late of the famed First Minnesota's Regimental Band, organized a new band in St. Cloud, its seven Yankee members were joined by four Germans (*SCT* 24 September 1873, St. Cloud City Records 1882). Similarly, when the Concordia singing society in 1880 decided to incorporate and erect St. Cloud's first opera house (a 40- by 120-foot hall seating eight hundred), two Yankees were numbered among its ten officers.[31] Only in the Centennial celebrations of 1876 was there much hint of local German efforts to link music to a special German identity (*NS* 6 July 1876).

The implications of this relative lack of ethnic coding for the musical culture of the Sauk would become more evident by the turn of the century. By that time, new immigration from Germany was largely a thing of the past, the dairying economy had matured, and the second generation was taking over the farms of its parents. Good roads, fast horses, and frequent trains diminished local isolation, while improved schooling exposed more and more of the rural population both to cultivated German culture and to the English language. And the Catholic Church now had the priests and wealth to staff its numerous parishes and deepen its influence in the local community. Music within this context became one of the main channels through

---

[31] Mathias Gans was the Concordia's initial director; he was now succeeded by Peter Kaiser, a graduate of St. Mary's College in Montreal, who did postgraduate work at the University of Michigan, edited St. Cloud's German newspaper, and served as county superintendent of schools until he resigned in 1880 to become principal of the St. Cloud public school district and organist at its German-Catholic church (Mitchell 1915:652, 1151, 1153).

which outside currents flowed into local life, and the local musical culture, while retaining its basic structural elements, began to change in response.

Four new musical trends were particularly evident. The first was the proliferation and commercialization of the bands for hire, the most popular and market-driven sector of the musical culture (see Figure 5). Prosperity and mobility created a clientele of young people eager to dance and able to travel beyond their community to do so, and the new penetration of the German *Vereinswesen* into the countryside meant that there were increasing numbers of associations ready to sponsor occasions for music-making.[32] The eight youths who formed the Young French Band in Luxemburg in 1897 were thus far from alone in attempting to respond to this market (*NS* 28 January 1897; see also *NS* 31 December 1896, 21 January 1897, 11 May 1899; *Albany* 1991:48, 115).[33] Informal house-party dances continued; on more formal occasions like weddings, farmers rented planks to erect temporary outdoor "bowery" dance floors, while local associations often sponsored benefit dances in schoolhouses and town halls. Saloonkeepers frequently fitted up their second stories as halls, and dance pavilions began to appear at local lakes at least by the mid-1880s (*NS* 24 June 1897, 4 and 11 February 1897, 13 April 1899, 17 November 1898; Thielen 1992:120, 127–128; Voigt 1965:40; Mitchell 1915:1170). Even the town bands became more professional, as local governments began to appropriate several hundred dollars annually for their support, in return for free summer concerts and a guarantee of the band's presence at civic and parochial occasions (*NS* 15 April 1897, 13 May 1897; Dominik 1994/95:2).[34]

The second trend was the expansion of the more genteel sector within German musical culture, its increasing openness to non-German popular music trends and non-German participants, and its diffusion down the urban hierarchy into the smaller towns of the county (cf. Knight 1993, Kreitner 1989). The St. Cloud Union Band in 1895, for example, introduced its bicycle auxiliary whose first appearance "proved

---

[32] Local court cases document the occasions for seduction that these dances also afforded (e.g., *Minn. v. Peter Sallinger* 1888, *Minn. v. Mathias Stebinger* 1912; SCDC Criminal Case Files, MHS).

[33] Many of these were family bands and shared membership with the village bands. When Millerville's family band left for a new colony in Saskatchewan, a new band quickly formed to meet the local need (Klein 1930:82). For examples of rural events where such bands played, see *NS* 17 December 1896, 8 July 1897, 6 January, and 17 November 1898.

[34] The St. Cloud City Council similarly attempted to appropriate three hundred dollars to support open-air concerts by the St. Cloud Union Band in 1887, but the corporation counsel ruled that such expenditures were not authorized under the city charter; the city sought voluntary contributions to achieve the same end in 1899 (St. Cloud City Records 1882; *NS* 25 May 1899).

Figure 5. Members of rural Collegeville's late nineteenth-century Meyer Band, whose members were favorite performers at area house parties, as well as at more formal secular and sacred occasions. Victor Himsl, sitting next to the drum, was a schoolteacher educated at St. John's. Photograph courtesy of the Stearns County Historical Society.

a ten strike" (see Figure 6). The band began with thirteen men who played cornets, clarinets, altos, trombone, tenor, baritone, bass, and bass drum with the assistance of pulleys while riding bicycles in formation; within a month, its membership was up to twenty-two (*SCT* 27 June 1895, 24 July 1895).[35] Equally up-to-date was the St. Martin Union Band, pulled through the hamlet's decorated streets on the Fourth of July in 1897 by a "steam machine"—the first time anywhere, locals wondered (*NS* 5 July 1897)? A year later, a group of young St. Cloud German men formed a Concert Mandolin Club, and by 1908 St. Cloud's young German women demonstrated that they too could keep abreast of national music fashion, forming the St. Cloud Ladies Band, which remained active for at least nine years (*NS* 3 March 1898, 13 February 1908; *SCJP* 9 May 1916; *SCTD* 3 July 1917).[36] Teacher-organists in several of the towns now began organizing so-called "orchestras" with musical ambitions beyond those of the village bands. The star of the Albany orchestra

[35] The bicycle band was organized by John Boobar, a local professional bicycle racer of Yankee descent and was active into the early 1900s; the band's uniforms were provided by the Crimson Rim Bicycle Company (Sherwood 1986a and 1986b).

[36] It was reputedly the only ladies' band in the northwest (*SCJP* 17 May 1916). On turn-of-the-century ladies' bands elsewhere, see Hazen and Hazen (1987:55–57).

Figure 6. The St. Cloud Bicycle Band at the Minnesota State Fair. Photograph courtesy of the Stearns County Historical Society.

was a violin prodigy, its director's eleven-year-old son; another musical family in Albany gave regular Sunday afternoon concerts in the yard in front of their house. Accounts of musical skits and dramatic performances became more common, which might include *Neger Lustspiele* or something like the three-act *Posse mit Gesang, Tante Augusta in Amerika*.[37] And then there was perhaps the most popular piece of the period, the St. Cloud Liederkranz's humorous performance of *Das ländliche Conzertprobe*—fifty years later the Catholic countryside was finally joining Milwaukee in this Lortzing-inspired exercise in self-reflexivity![38] Frequent newspaper items chronicling *gemütlich* evenings at home "bei Gesang und Becherklang" (with singing and the clinking of glasses) in both city and countryside attest to the domestic base upon which this growing genteel sector rested (*NS* 14 October 1897, 16 February 1898, 28 September 1899).

The third trend occurred within the religious sector as church authorities began to constrict the role of congregational singing and enhance that of the well-trained choir, which in the county's German congregations generally included both men and women (Hoffmann 1934:79). In part, this reflected the influence funneled into the Valley through the *Kirchenväter* of Europe's Caecilian movement to rescue sacred music from secular polyphony, concertizing, and sentimentality and return to its roots in Latin chant. While the Caecilians encouraged congregational singing, they disapproved of the vernacular *Singmesse* on both aesthetic and liturgical grounds and disparaged the use of instruments other than the organ during Mass.[39] But changes in local musical practice also reflected the growing success of a campaign within the American hierarchy to recast German popular piety in a more acceptable mold. In comparison with the more private devotionalism that nineteenth-century American Catholicism preferred to stress, the public ritual culture that German Catholics imported to America seemed to provide occasions for socializing and hence poten-

---

[37] *Blackface Comedies or Farce with Singing: Aunt Augusta in America* (*NS* 11 February 1897; *Albany* 1991:55; NS 18 November and 4 March 1897).

[38] *The Country Concert Rehearsal* (*NS* 24 December 1896); it seems highly likely that the piece was a take-off on Lortzing's popular "Kantatenprobe" scene.

[39] Milwaukee's Catholic Normal School was the main center of Caecilian influence in America. The performance of the "Lambeilotti" Mass is one early direct indication of Caecilian influence in Stearns County: Louis Lambillotte, S.J., was an important French advocate of the new music. The feast of St. Caecilia, the patroness of music, was marked at the St. Cloud cathedral in 1896 by a sermon on "true caecilian chuch music" (*NS* 26 November 1896; cf. Grabrian 1973, Grimes 1996: 83–84, Nemmers 1949:171–179, and Fellerer 1961:162–200).

tial scandal, it gave an excessive ritual role to the laity, and it could skirt dangerously close to folk magic. Even in Germany the vernacular *Singmessen* were under attack as uncanonical relics of rationalist reform, and in America the insistence that the Mass be sung in Latin simultaneously satisfied the hierarchy's desires for both ultramontanist orthodoxy and Americanizing uniformity.[40] Parishioners were still permitted to thunder out a rousing "Großer Gott" or "Pabstlied" at the conclusion of every ritual event, they could still sing favorite German hymns at Vespers or during May devotions, but both their processional culture and their formal habits of group singing were being slowly altered.[41]

The fourth trend was a certain feminization of music that occurred not only through the expansion of parlor music, but also through the gradual replacement of the *Kirchenväter* by teaching nuns in the public as well as in the few parochial schools. Though the bishop and parish priests preferred nuns because they were cheaper and had less independent authority, parishioners often remained loyal to the laymen, in part because they believed men were better teachers, in part because they valued the range of services the *Kirchenväter* offered the community, but in significant part also because they wanted to retain a measure of lay authority over church affairs. Bitter controversies marked by interdictions and withdrawals of the sacraments wracked various county parishes over this issue beginning in the 1880s, and it was not always the bishop who won. Nevertheless, as the sisters extended their reach into the village schools, the logic of saving money by employing women in the country schools also took hold, and the teaching of music increasingly passed into female hands. While the male organist-teachers held out well into the twentieth century in some communities, others lost the one educated male anchor that their musical culture had possessed at a much earlier date. Though the Benedictines had a strong interest in music, as nuns they could not offer the same public leadership as their male predecessors. At the same time that opportunities grew for women as

---

[40] The German *Singmessen* were authorized for German dioceses as a result of late eighteenth-century Enlightenment reforms under Joseph II (see Pauly 1957:372–381; for nineteenth-century practice, see Fellerer 1976:262–275). Nineteenth-century American bishops lacked authority to sanction vernacular High Mass singing (whether German or English), and conflicts over German parishioners' insistence on retaining their *Singmesse* were not unknown (Higginson 1982:118–119; for general background on the area's religious culture, see Kleitsch 1958; Yzermans 1989, esp. pp. 439–472; and particularly for this period, Hoffmann 1934). The full history of liturgical change in the Valley remains to be explored.

[41] "Holy God, We Praise Thy Name"—the Te Deum—and "Long Live the Pope" (*NS* 3 December 1890, 1 July 1897, 5 May 1898, 11 May 1899).

Figure 7. St. John the Baptist parish choir, Collegeville, around the turn of the century; both the urban aspirations of this rural choir and its female majority are in evidence. Photograph courtesy of the Stearns County Historical Society.

choir directors, organists, theatrical organizers, and performers, and soon even in family bands, the old link between the cultivated musical tradition of the church and the public world of male music-making progressively weakened.[42]

But at the same time as the distinctiveness of local German music-making was fading, its sentimental ethnicization seems to have intensified. Rural festivities in particular began to be cherished for their folkloric quality. Newspaper accounts of parish rituals, for example, reassured readers that deep in the countryside there were still communities where Corpus Christi processions occurred "according to old German customs . . . in festive fashion out in the open air."[43] One could likewise "still" find country weddings and other celebrations being held "in genuine German fashion" (nach echter deutscher Art) (*NS* 11 November 1896; see also *NS* 17 June 1897, 17 February 1898). "Folklorization" was evident as well in the new tendency to isolate and identify particular German music traditions—Bavarian or Tyrolese, for example—as especially suitable for occasions when the local population wished to indulge in specifically ethnic celebration; parts of the local music tradition were clearly beginning to wear quotation marks.[44] When St. Cloud's new bishop, James Trobec, was serenaded in customary fashion by the Liederkranz in 1897, he confessed to the singers that he himself had founded and directed a singing society in his homeland, and urged that they always remain true to German songs and German customs; that admonition was clearly no longer as superfluous as it would have seemed even a decade earlier (*NS* 14 October 1897).

---

[42] For a suggestive account of the conflict that arose when one country pastor attempted to replace his organist/teacher with nuns, see P. Paulin Wiesner, "Bericht," manuscript, St. Martin Parish File, SJAA (see also Luetmer 1970; and McDonald 1957:78–79, 103, 108–112; on the new role of women in church music, see Klein 1930:59, 71, 105; Yzermans 1989:1094–1095; Hoffmann 1934; and Voigt 1992:88). The relationship that Grimes observed between church reform of liturgical music and the progressive distancing of Irish-American musical culture from art-music traditions thus probably had parallels among the German Catholics of the Sauk (Grimes 1996: 179–182).

[43] "Nach altem deutschen Brauch . . . in feierlicher Weise im Freien" (*NS* 17 June 1897). When a new house was blessed in a country village, the paper noted that "this is a lovely German custom that is unfortunately too often consigned to oblivion, and maintaining this custom shows that Mr. Meyer and his family have remained in every respect German to the core" ("Es ist dies eine schöne, leider vielfach der Vergessenheit anheimgegebene deutsche Sitte, und die Beibehaltung dieser Sitte zeigt, daß Herr Meyer und Familie in jeder Hinsicht kerndeutsch geblieben sind") (*NS* 21 December 1899).

[44] See, for example, *NS* 29 July 1897, commenting on the good Bavarian "Tschon" of a local quartet; note also the Bavarian theme adopted for Arban's 1899 Harvest Festival and Albany's Tyrolese Fourth of July (*NS* 28 September and 27 June 1899).

Finally, from the perspective of ethnic music-making there was another ominous straw that was beginning to flutter in the Valley wind by the turn of the century: the spread of mass culture, and with it not only stronger exposure to outside musical influences, but also the rise of forms of public leisure divorced from music. Touring musical troupes had always found an audience in the Valley, but turn-of-the-century construction of new opera houses in St. Cloud, as well as in other county towns, testified to their growing popularity and influence (Mitchell 1915:1193–1194; *NS* 18 August 1898, 6 January 1897). Baseball had been brought back to the county by Civil War veterans, but it was only now that team sports began to occupy a larger place in community consciousness and leisure-time budgets (*SCJ* 23 April 1868; *NS* 24 November 1898). And then there were the innocuous notices of card parties that began to appear in the county's German newspaper (*NS* 3 and 24 February 1898, 11 and 25 May 1899).[45] It was a development that would have significant consequences, as a final transect through the county's musical culture in the years immediately after the First World War suggests.

Music had predictably accompanied the people of the Sauk into and out of the War. Spring Hill, one of the parishes deep in the countryside, celebrated the Fourth of July in 1915 with a parish benefit fair where two area brass bands earned plaudits for their renditions of "Die Wacht am Rhein," "Heil Dir im Siegerkranz," and "Gott erhalte Franz, den Kaiser" (Miller 1993:103–104).[46] But within two years, those same village bands were piping the local boys off to war against the old Fatherlands, this time to the tune of American patriotic hymns. They played their patriotic repertoires vigorously at Loyalty Meetings and bond rallies, the St. Cloud Military Band gave weekly wartime concerts, and village after village formed community singing societies to "fill the air" in patriotic fashion (*NS* 28 February, 23 May, 15 August, and 1 August 1918). Once again one of the county's *Kirchenväter* was moved to composition, and County Superintendent of Schools William A. Boerger's "Our Absent Boys" won wide acclaim, earning a performance at an Oswego, New York, army camp (*NS* 8 May 1919).

---

[45] Testimony to the newness of the trend is the comment contained in a report on an evening card party at the cathedral school hall that "although such parties have generally not been characteristic among Germans, those present nevertheless appear to have amused themselves in the best possible way" ("Wiewohl eine derartige Partie den Deutschen sonst nicht eigen, amüsirten sich die Anwesenden doch anscheinend auf's Beste") (*NS* 20 January 1898).

[46] "The Watch on the Rhine," "Hail to You in the Victor's Wreath," and "God Save Franz, the Kaiser"—patriotic German and Austrian songs. The parade, significantly, was reviewed by the local notable costumed as the Kaiser, rather than by the Uncle Sam figure who was also present.

Stearns County survived the war with its local culture relatively intact. The increasingly bilingual German community was firmly in control of the county's political, educational, and welfare institutions and its media, and it dominated the local economy. Its rules were the local rules of the game. To the extent that those rules were changing, they were changing largely because the community wanted them to change. Even the heavy outside attacks on critical props of the local culture represented by school-language legislation and Prohibition in the 1920s would be largely accommodated on the community's own terms (cf. Wolkerstorfer 1973 and Cofell 1958). The local culture was evolving, however, and music evolved with it.

The card party, for example, had clearly become the predominant form of local entertaining, not only in private settings, but also in church benefits and other forms of community celebration (*NS* 4 July 1918, 3 October 1918, 6 February 1919; Thielen 1992:124). Music may still have been present, but it was no longer the publicized attraction. Dances seemed far more clearly coded for the young alone, and they were far more obviously commercial. Though the house party and bowery dance tradition continued (see Figure 8), every town seemed to sponsor its own weekly dance, and dance pavilions mushroomed behind saloons and on the shores of the county's numerous lakes (*NS* 16 May, 8 August, and 15 August 1918; Thielen 1992:120, 127–128; Voigt 1987:61–62; *Stones and Hills* 1975:107–113). For those too genteel to patronize a saloon or a dance hall, the private *Tanzkränzchen* now offered a more select alternative (*NS* 23 May 1918, 29 May 1919). Repeated reports of automobile purchases and motor trips, of sporting events and bowling, of motion picture presentations and visiting theater and music troupes, document a new leisure culture in which music was either peripheral or purchased.

Village bands, ably seconded by church choirs, still graced the rites of public celebration, maintaining also the pleasant custom of public serenades to mark private rites of passage (*NS* 6 and 20 June 1918; *NS* 16 January, 1 May, 5 June, 3 July, 18 September, and 20 November 1919). But organized amateur music-making was being steadily marginalized, it seemed, pushed to the semi-professional on the one hand or confined to the home on the other. To the extent that the vacuum was not filled by commercial leisure, the new high schools began to step into the breach. Music was becoming identified with youth culture in a way that had been far less noticeable a generation earlier. The Catholic Church's campaign to bring lay initiative under control had also largely succeeded. Now, noted one critical Benedictine in the 1920s, "you may find churches, many of them, where priests do not scruple to have only Low Masses on Sundays, but have chanted services, devotions in the afternoon or evening, on the plea that it is too hard to get singers. . . . A priest . . . of

Figure 8. A family band around 1920 in front of a house where they had a date to play. Photograph courtesy of the Stearns County Historical Society.

Spring Hill had a 'falling out' with his choir and got a phonograph to play some kind of Masses, or sacred songs, his housekeeper operating the instrument in the choir loft." The Bishop, this critic was pleased to note, drew the line here at least. Pay for the choirs was evidently also creeping in (Hoffmann 1934:81). The Bishop had instituted a strong campaign to remove the German language from church affairs during the First World War, and many parish priests continued this after the war; even the hymns now were unfamiliar to the older people, completing their divorce from their passionate commitment to church singing and its confinement to the choir (Yzermans 1989:242–247, Klein 1930:94).[47]

IV

As the second generation neared retirement, then, the social context of its music-making became increasingly similar to that of the non-German areas that surrounded it. We should not push this argument too far without hearing the music itself, without access to the private world of music-making that the sources simply do not permit, and without systematic comparison with neighboring local cultures. But it seems clear that music along the Sauk never acquired the ethnic freight that it did in the cities or in other rural areas where single-group hegemony was less marked.

[47] The Benedictine nuns also now stressed use of English in their own devotions (McDonald 1957:201).

There was never a strong Yankee culture in place to deny the Germans musical satisfaction, never any question but that any music they made would have to be their own. It grew without much ideological stimulus out of the social structures and needs of the local order, and as that order changed, so too did the music. The early lack of an educated immigrant elite removed an important potential stimulus to the sentimentalization and ethnicization of music; it also meant that when an elite grew up out of the peasant community, it had only limited access to an elevated German music tradition and turned to the non-ethnic music of the popular culture of the day. The Catholic Church encouraged a distinctive musical tradition in the Valley from an early period, but over time its efforts to integrate local practice with national norms probably hastened the decline not only of local musical distinctiveness, but also of music's central role in the local culture. In music as in other areas of life, settlers along the Sauk were able to create a local culture on immigrant roots. It embodied ways of thinking and acting that they brought with them from Germany, and they proved ferociously tenacious in their efforts to embed particular family and religious values in their new way of life. But they had little incentive for conscious ethnicization; little reason to see themselves as part of a broader German-American world; little stimulus to see in any particular aspect of their culture, such as music, an indispensable core. The culture they constructed was essentially local rather than ethnic, encompassing the whole of a local society rather than a part, and thus enduring even as its cultural expressions changed.

In the Little Germanies of the cities, German musical traditions either overflowed into the symphony orchestras and Tin Pan Alley tunes of the broader culture, or they ossified into museumized folk music. In a rural area like southern Minnesota's Brown County, where lower-status Bohemian German Catholics had to contend not only with Yankees but with a free-thinking, cultivated bourgeois German elite, music became linked with identity, and they nurtured a living popular tradition that matured into the ethnically coded Big-Band "Dutchman" sound by the 1920s. Sauk Valley groups like the Moonlight Entertainers, the Six Aces Orchestra, Al Pfannenstein's Blue Jackets, Wolf's Accordion Band, and numerous others undoubtedly developed their own syntheses of traditional and more modern dance music as they played the house parties and pavilions of Prohibition-era Stearns County (Thielen 1992; Yzermans 1987:108–109; Loso 1989:135–137; for Brown County, see Greene 1992; Rippley 1992; and Rippley and Paul 1995). But by that time the area's musical identity was probably better epitomized by its most distinctive product, the St. Cloud Boys Band, three hundred strictly disciplined members strong and claiming to be the largest band in the world, sponsored by the local business community and situating itself squarely in the provincial American mainstream.[48]

The case could be made that a truer expression of the region's musical heritage in that decade and by far its most important contribution to American musical culture in the broader sense was the Liturgical Movement fostered at St. John's Abbey in the heart of the Valley. It was Virgil Michel, monk at St. John's and grandson of a St. Paul *Kirchenväter*, who was most responsible for bringing to America in the 1920s the European movement to envision the church as a corporate body of priests and laity united in the liturgy of worship. This was a vision of Catholic life not so different from that which the early settlers had sought to realize, and it found a ready reception among the Benedictine monks and nuns of the Valley—products, many of them, of local families, and pastors and teachers in local parishes—a vision that would find its ultimate expression in the Vatican II reforms that finally returned vernacular congregational singing to the Valley.[49] But as significant as the appropriateness of the new movement to the Valley's ethnic musical heritage was the skepticism with which it was greeted from the first by local congregations now used to what they saw as the accustomed American way (Barry 1956:259–279, McDonald 1957:201–205, Yzermans 1989:157–159). Like Mathias Hemmesch's busted accordion, the musical culture of the Sauk was an important adjunct to the creation of ethnic community, but it also, and perhaps inevitably, became a broad bridge to a transethnic American world.

---

[48] Band alumni played with Gene Krupa and Tommy Dorsey as well as with the United States Army and the Navy bands (Sherwood 1986a and 1986b). It is also worth noting, however, that out in the countryside Alois Phillips, heir to the *Kirchenvater* tradition and teaching in an inland rural district that prided itself on never having employed a woman, formed his own boys' band in the 1920s from students in the surrounding country schools; the name he gave to it was the Little German Band. The Mehr family provided four of the band's twenty-two members (*Albany* 1991:135, Mitchell 1915:1397, Terres 1991:32). Wisconsin-German communities evidently exhibited similar differences in musical culture that would merit exploration (cf. Leary 1998: 271–272, 276–277).

[49] Three of the local Benedictines most important in cultivating the new musical principles of the Liturgical Movement were Fathers Innocent and Norbert Gertken and Sister Urban Gertken, children of one of Stearns County's most noted *Kirchenväter*.

Bibliography

Ahrens, Christian. "Zur Rezeption der Blechblasinstrumente mit Ventilen im 19. Jahrhundert." *Jahrbuch für musikalische Volks- und Völkerkunde* 13 (1988):9–21.

Albany. Albany: The Heart of Minnesota. Albany, MN: Albany Heritage Society, 1991.

Barry, Coleman J., O.S.B. *Worship and Work: Saint John's Abbey and University 1856–1956*. Collegeville, MN: Saint John's Abbey, 1956.

Bohlman, Philip V. "Prolegomena to the Classification of German-American Music." *Yearbook of German-American Studies* 20 (1985):33–48.

Broyles, Michael. *"Music of the Highest Class": Elitism and Populism in Antebellum Boston*. New Haven: Yale University Press, 1992.

Cofell, William L. "An Analysis of the Formation of Community Attitudes toward Secondary Education in St. Martin." M.S. thesis, University of Minnesota, 1958.

Conzen, Kathleen Neils. *Immigrant Milwaukee, 1836–60: Accommodation and Community in a Frontier City*. Cambridge, MA: Harvard University Press, 1976.

________. "Die deutsche Amerikaeinwanderung im ländlichen Kontext: Problemfelder und Forschungsergebnisse." In *Auswanderer, Wanderarbeiter, Gastarbeiter: Bevölkerung, Arbeitsmarkt und Wanderung in Deutschland seit der Mitte des 19. Jahrhunderts*, edited by Klaus Bade, vol. 1, 350–377. Ostfildern: Scripta Mercaturae Verlag, 1984.

________. "Peasant Pioneers: Generational Succession among German Immigrants in Frontier Minnesota." In *The Countryside in the Age of Capitalist Transformation: Essays in the Social History of Rural America*, edited by Steven Hahn and Jonathan Prude, 259–292. Chapel Hill: University of North Carolina Press, 1985.

________. "Ethnicity as Festive Culture: German-America on Parade." In *The Invention of Ethnicity*, edited by Werner Sollors, 44–76. New York: Oxford University Press, 1989.

________. *Making Their Own America: Assimilation Theory and the German Peasant Pioneer*. Annual Lecture Series. Washington, DC and New York: German Historical Institute, 1990.

DW = *Der Wanderer* (St. Paul, Minn.)

Dominik, John. 1994/95. ". . . And the Band Played On . . . And On . . . And On!" *Crossings: Stearns County Historical Society* 20 (1994/5):6.

Eberbard, J. B. "Festrede am 13. Gesangfeste des 'Ersten deutschen Sängerbundes von Nord-Amerika,' 29. August bis 1. September 1865, in Columbus, O." *Deutsch-Amerikanische Monatshefte* 2, 2 (1865):458–463.

Esselen, Christian. "Vermischtes." *Atlantis* 4 (1856):474–477.

________. "Die deutschen Kulturmittel in Amerika." *Atlantis* 10 (1858):401–409.

Fellerer, Karl Gustav. *The History of Catholic Church Music*. Baltimore: Helicon Press, 1961.

________, ed., *Geschichte der katholischen Kirchenmusik*. Kassel: Bärenreiter, 1976.

Grabrian, Sister Bernadette, O.S.B. "Milwaukee, Wisconsin: America's Nucleus of the St. Cecilia Society." *Sacred Music* 100 (1973):3–12.

Greene, Victor. *A Passion for Polka: Old Time Ethnic Music in America*. Berkeley and Los Angeles: University of California Press, 1992.

Grimes, Robert R. *How Shall We Sing in a Foreign Land? Music of Irish Catholic Immigrants in the Antebellum United States*. Notre Dame, IN: University of Notre Dame Press, 1996.

Hagen, Theodore. "Musikalische Revue." *Deutsch-Amerikanische Monatshefte* 3, 2 (1866):308–312.

Hazen, Margaret Hindle, and Robert M. Hazen. *The Music Men: An Illustrated History of Brass Bands in America, 1800–1920*. Washington, DC: Smithsonian Institution Press, 1987.

Hense-Jensen, Wilhelm. *Wisconsin's Deutsch-Amerikaner bis zum Schluss des neunzehnten Jahrhunderts*. Vol. 1. Milwaukee: Im Verlage der Deutschen Gesellschaft, 1900.

Higginson, J. Vincent. *History of American Catholic Hymnals: Survey and Background*. Springfield, OH: Hymn Society of America, 1982.

Hoffmann, Alexius, O.S.B. "Natural History of Collegeville, Minnesota." Unpublished manuscript, St. John's Abbey Archives (SJAA), Collegeville, MN, 1934.

Kapp, Friedrich. "Rede, gehalten am 19. Juli 1865 in Jones Wood, in New-York, zum Schluss des neunten deutschen Sängerfestes." *Deutsch-Amerikanische Monatshefte* 2, 2 (1865):182–188.

Klein, Karl Matthias. *The History of Millerville, Douglas County, Minnesota 1866 to 1930*. Millerville, MN: By the author, 1930.

Kleitsch, Ronald G. "The Religious Social System of the German-Catholics of the Sauk." M.A. thesis, University of Minnesota, 1958.

Knight, Ellen. "Music in Winchester, Massachusetts: A Community Portrait, 1830–1925." *American Music* 11 (1993):263–282.

Kreitner, Kenneth. *Discoursing Sweet Music: Town Bands and Community Life in Turn-of-the-Century Pennsylvania*. Urbana: University of Illinois Press, 1989.

Kulas, John S. *Der Wanderer of St. Paul, The First Decade, 1867–1877: A Mirror of the German-Catholic Immigrant Experience in Minnesota*. New York: Peter Lang, 1996.

Kulzer, George. "Autobiography." *Stearns-Morrison Enterprise* (Albany, MN). 15 June 1976.

Leary, James P. "Old Time Music in Northern Wisconsin." *American Music* 2 (1984): 71–87.

________. "Czech- and German-American 'Polka' Music." *Journal of American Folklore* 101 (1988):339–345.

________. "Polka Music in a Polka State." In *Wisconsin Folklore*, edited by James P. Leary, 268–283. Madison: University of Wisconsin Press, 1998.

Leary, James P., and Richard March. "Dutchman Bands: Genre, Ethnicity, and Pluralism in the Upper Midwest." In *Creative Ethnicity: Symbols and Strategies of Contemporary Life*, edited by Stephen Stein and John Allan Cicala, 21–43. Logan, UT: Utah State University Press, 1991.

Levine, Lawrence W. *Black Culture and Black Consciousness: Afro-American Folk Thought from Slavery to Freedom*. New York: Oxford University Press, 1977.

Ley, John. Deposition, Sioux County Claims Commission Files, National Archives, Washington, DC, n.d.

Lortzing, Albert. *Zar und Zimmermann oder Die beiden Peter*. Wiesbaden: Breitkopf und Härtel, 1985.

Loso, Idelia. *St. Joseph: Preserving a Heritage*. St. Cloud: Sentinel Printing Co., Inc., 1989.

Luetmer, Sr. Nora. "The History of Catholic Education in the Diocese of St. Cloud, 1855–1965." Ph.D. dissertation, University of Minnesota, 1970.

Martin, Philip. *Farmhouse Fiddlers: Music and Dance Traditions in the Rural Midwest*. Mount Horeb, WI: Midwest Traditions, 1994.

McDonald, Sister M. Grace, O.S.B. *With Lamps Burning*. St. Joseph, MN: St. Benedict's Priory Press, 1957.

Medick, Hans. "Village Spinning Bees: Sexual Culture and Free Time among Rural Youth in Early Modern Germany." In *Interest and Emotion: Essays on the Study of Family and Kinship*, edited by Hans Medick and David Warren Sabean, 317–339. Cambridge: Cambridge University Press, 1984.

Mehr v. Philips. Mathews Mehr v. Michael Philips. Stearns County District Court (SCDC), Civil Case Files, Minnesota Historical Society (MHS). St. Paul, MN, 1866.

MHS = Minnesota Historical Society

Miller, S. Mary Gordian, O.S.B. *St. Michael's on the Hill*. Waite Park, MN: Park Press, 1993.

Minnesota v. Edelbrock. State of Minnesota v. Anton Edelbrock. Stearns County District Court (SCDC), Civil Case Files, Minnesota Historical Society (MHS). St. Paul, MN, 1862.

Mitchell, William Bell. *History of Stearns County Minnesota*. Chicago: H. C. Cooper Jr., & Co., 1915.

NAM=National Archives Microfilm. Manuscript Census of Population, Stearns County, MN, 1860a.

________. Manuscript Census of Agriculture, Stearns County, Minnesota, 1860b.

________. Manuscript Census of Agriculture, Stearns County, Minnesota, 1870.

________. Manuscript Census of Population, Stearns County, Minnesota, 1880.

Nemmers, Erwin Esser. *Twenty Centuries of Catholic Church Music*. Milwaukee, 1949.

NS = *Nordstern* (St. Cloud)

Ortmann, Fr. Cyril, O.S.B. *History of St. Martin's Parish, St. Martin, Minnesota*. St. Cloud, MN: By the author, 1958.

Ostendorf, Berndt. "'The Diluted Second Generation': German-Americans in Music, 1870 to 1920." In *German Workers' Culture in the United States 1850 to 1920*, edited by Hartmut Keil, 261–287. Washington, DC: Smithsonian Institution Press, 1988.

Pahlen, Kurt. *Albert Lortzing, Zar und Zimmermann: Opernführer*. Munich: Wilhelm Goldmann Verlag, 1981.

Pauly, Reinhard G. "The Reforms of Church Music under Joseph II." *The Musical Quarterly* 43 (1957): 372–381.

Reiss, P. Bruno, O.S.B. "The First Beginning of St. John's Abbey." Typescript, SJAA, n.d.

Richter, Gotthard. *Akkordeon: Handbuch für Musiker und Instrumentenbauer*. Wilhelmshaven: F. Noetzel, 1990.

Rippley, LaVern J. *The Whoopee John Wilfahrt Dance Band: His Bohemian-German Roots*. Northfield, MN: St. Olaf College German Department, 1992.

Rippley, LaVern J., and Robert J. Paul. 1995. *German-Bohemians: The Quiet Immigrants*. Northfield, MN: St. Olaf College Press for the German-Bohemian Heritage Society.

Risler, [Dr.]. "Festgedicht." *New-Yorker Belletristischer Journal* (23 July). Reprint of Dr. Risler's "festive poem," on the occasion of the Eleventh General Singing Festival of the Nordöstlicher Sängerbund in Baltimore, July 1869.

Ruhr, Peter. "'Mit klingendem Spiel'—badische Blasmusik zwischen der Revolution 1848 und dem Ersten Weltkrieg." In *Ich will aber gerade vom Leben singen . . . : Über populäre Musik vom ausgehenden 19. Jahrhundert bis zum Ende der Weimarer Republik*, edited by Sabine Schutte,115–133. Reinbek bei Hamburg: Rowohlt, 1987.

St. Cloud City Records. Petitions to the City Council. Minnesota Historical Society, 1882.

________. Correspondence of the City Mayor. Minnesota Historical Society, 1887.

SCD = *St. Cloud Democrat*

SCDT = *St. Cloud Daily Times*

Schirmag, Heinz. *Albert Lortzing: Ein Lebens- und Zeitbild*. Berlin: Henschel Verlag Kunst und Gesellschaft, 1982.

SCJ = *St. Cloud Journal*

SCJP = *St. Cloud Journal-Press*

SCP = *St. Cloud Press*

Scriptorium, The. 1956. *The Scriptorium* (Collegeville, Minn.) 15, 1.

SCT = *St. Cloud Times*

SCV = *St. Cloud Visitor*

Sherwood, Charles. "St. Cloud Municipal Bands." *Escape to Minnesota Good Times Magazine* 6, 2 (1986a):10–13.

________. "St. Cloud Municipal Bands." *Escape to Minnesota Good Times Magazine* 6, 3 (1986b):10–13.

SJAA = St. John's Abbey Archives

Slobin, Mark. *Tenement Songs: The Popular Music of the Jewish Immigrants*. Urbana: University of Illinois Press, 1982.

Stones and Hills, Steine und Huegel: Reflections: St. John the Baptist Parish: 1875–1975. Collegeville, MN: St. John the Baptish Parish, 1975.

Stockmann, Doris, ed. *Volks- und Popularmusik in Europa*. Laaber: Laaber Verlag, 1992.

Tawa, Nicholas. *A Sound of Strangers: Musical Culture, Acculturation, and the Post-Civil War Ethnic American*. Metuchen, NJ: Scarecrow, 1982.

Terres, Bud. *Moments to Remember from St. Martin, Stearns County, Minnesota.* Paynesville, MN: Paynesville Press, 1991.

Thielen, Lois. *Freeport: 100 Years of Family, Faith, and Fortune. Freeport*, MN: Freeport City Centennial Committee, 1992.

Vogeler, Ingolf. "The Roman Catholic Culture Region of Central Minnesota." *Pioneer America* 8 (1976):71–83.

Voigt, Robert J. *Pierzana 1865–1965*. St. Cloud, MN: Mills Creative Printing, 1965.

________. *Opoliana 1887–1987*. St. Cloud, MN: Sentinel Printing Co., Inc., 1987.

________. *The People of St.* Wendel. Waite Park, MN: Park Press, 1992.

Wolkerstorfer, Sister John Christine. "Nativism in Minnesota in World War I: A Comparative Study of Brown, Ramsey, and Stearns Counties, 1914–18." Ph.D. diss., University of Minnesota, 1973.

Worbs, Hans Christoph. *Albert Lortzing*. Reinbek bei Hamburg: Rowohlt Taschenbuch Verlag, 1979.

Yzermans, Vincent A. *The Shores of Pelican Lake*. Waite Park, MN: Park Press, 1987.

________. *The Spirit in Central Minnesota: A Centennial Narrative of the Church of Saint Cloud* 1889–1989. 2 vols. St. Cloud: Diocese of St. Cloud, 1989.

3

GLIMPSES OF AN ETHNIC MENTALITY: SIX GERMAN-SWISS TEXTS OF MIGRATION-RELATED FOLKSONGS

Leo Schelbert

Various disciplines and diverse approaches probe the nature and meanings of folksongs (Baumann 1981:29–43; Schepping 1988:399–410). Although their texts and melodies must be viewed in their organic unity if a full understanding is to be achieved, it may be valid to focus only on the songs' textual messages.[1] These may be interpreted as expressions of *mentalité*, that is of a given group's historically grown and widely shared assumptions and emotive reactions to given phenomena that include responses to migration. A review of six German-Swiss texts may examine this claim. First, three contexts—*mentalité*, German-Swiss ethnicity, and migration—shall be touched upon, and then the texts themselves will be analyzed.

Contexts

Mentalité

The term *mentalité*, henceforth rendered as mentality, is rooted in the historiographical tradition of the French Annales School. Although used differently by individual scholars, the concept may be defined as "the collective mental and psychological structure of a group" that shapes the modes of an individual's thoughts, feelings, and actions (Breisach 1983:372).[2] Mentality is not class-bound: "Everyone is in-

---

[1]Schepping offers a concise sketch of the variety of approaches and the dimensions to be explored.

[2]The scholarly literature on the Annales School and the issues surrounding the concept *mentalité* is extensive; for a useful discussion see Gordon (1993), a review essay of Vovelle (1990), with up-to-date bibliographical references.

deed a *mentalité* case," La Capra claims (1985:93).[3] It remains, furthermore, "more or less unconscious" (Morfaux 1980:213). The widely held beliefs, views, customs, and emotions of a given group may derive either from the anonymous creativity of a collectivity that constantly reshapes them in playful adaptation, or they may result from the interplay between a solitary inventor's creation and a group that adopts it as a normative expression of its own mind. The collectively held beliefs and emotions, Paul Foulquié claims, not only influence, but also "inform and command the thought of an individual or a group" (1969:435). Those collectively held thoughts, beliefs, and emotions find various forms of expression. Among these are also folksongs, which may be viewed as expressive textual and tonal forms of a people's mentality; they are spontaneously activated on social, ritual, or festive occasions and address issues of common concern.

German-Swiss Ethnicity

Yet what defines a group as the carrier of a specific mentality? Is it valid to isolate German-Swiss folksongs as expressions of a unique tradition, or should they be viewed simply as part of German culture? Lutz Röhrich (1985), for instance, unhesitatingly included songs of German-Swiss origin in his collection of German emigrant songs. From the vantage point of elite culture, German-speaking Switzerland belongs indeed to the German form of Western civilization, although it is quite removed from Germany's primary centers such as Berlin, Tübingen, or Marburg. Yet Switzerland's gradual emergence as a separate nation during the fourteenth and fifteenth centuries in a bitter struggle against claims of the nobility and the imperial court also meant the emergence of a separate mentality that distinguishes the German-Swiss from their ethnically similar neighbors to the north. Thomas A. Brady (1985:37, 30) characterized that historical evolution as "sweytzer werden," or "turning Swiss." It meant the successful alliance of "communal federations on the northern slopes of the Alps in Uri, Schwyz, Unterwalden, Zug and Glarus . . . with five valley city states, Zurich, Bern, Lucerne, Fribourg and Solothurn." In the view of the guardians of the established order this union was subversive, as a song about South German peasants observed in 1525:

> The peasants tried to learn
> evil tricks from the Swiss

---

[3]He qualifies this claim however: "but not exactly in the same way"; he differentiates between high, official, popular, and mass culture. Furet (1984:15), in contrast, views *mentalité* as a "wholesale conferral of historical dignity on the lower classes and marginal individuals."

and become their own lords.
(Brady 1985:35)

The alliance of two groups—the emerging bourgeoisie of city states and mountain peasants and stockmen in the form of oath-bound associations (*Eidgenossenschaften*) striving for virtual autonomy—was attempted also in Swabia and the upper Rhine region, but was successful only in what by 1515 had evolved into the Swiss Confederation. The Empire's leadership clearly perceived it as a threat to the nobility's predominance and fought by force as well as ideological means against this mode of "exit from the feudal age." Except for the regions of present-day Switzerland, it successfully suppressed "communalism," that is "sworn associations of adult males formed to get, guard, and exercise rights of self-administration and government," in favor of a dualistic prince-and-estates constitution that gradually was to evolve into the absolutist monarchy of Europe's early modern era (Brady 1985:28-29). The German-Swiss in turn countered the imperial onslaught by a mythopoeic rendition of their past struggles; on the basis of oral tradition, the story of William Tell, the oath on the Rütli, and the destruction of the nobility's castles emerged and was authoritatively presented in the so-called White Book of Sarnen.[4] This separate, over the centuries shifting, yet in its core persistent medieval mentality (Marchal 1990: 310–13) found early expression also in song. One text, for instance, contains these words of praise:

Darumb ist so zu prisen die eidgenossenschaft: von Bern die vil wisen, von Solothurn mit kraft, und was zu in da gehört das haben si dick wohl gewert. Si sind mit fromkeit wol behert, mit trüwen recht behaft.	Thus there is so to be praised the oath-association: of Bern those very wise, of Solothurn with strength, and what to them now belongs that they have strongly defended. They are with piety well endowed with loyalty rightly marked.
Von Zug, von Schwiz, von Luzern, von Glaris feste Lüt, von Uri und von Ursern, die habent herte hüt. die von Unterwalden	Of Zug, of Schwyz, of Lucerne, of Glarus people strong, of Uri and Ursern, these do have tough skins. those of Unterwalden

[4]Marchal (1990) offers a recent and authoritative view; on Tell see especially pp. 320–326, with rich bibliographical references.

türrent's wagen balde	do risk things quickly,
si machent es nit lange,	they do not put off for long
was im herzen lit.	what lies in their heart.
(Tobler 1882:114)	

The separate evolution of a small portion of the Holy Roman Empire of the German Nation that is now Switzerland shaped not only social and political institutions differently from its ethnically related northern neighbors, but conditioned also a separate mentality. As Anthony Seeger (1991:23–24) rightly observed: "Events do not simply happen; they are interpreted and created . . . partly [also] through musical performances . . . , and their realization in the present is a demonstration of certain attitudes about the past and future." What are these attitudes and assumptions in the postulated separate German-Swiss mentality? Otto von Greyerz (1927:37–80) suggested several intertwined features, which may be summarized into four claims. First, the mountain world emerged symbolically as the "innermost *Heimat*" of the German-Swiss. Already the "Old Tellenlied" dating from the mid-fifteenth century contained these words of praise:

Ein edel land, guot recht als der Kern,	A noble land, good truly as the core
Das lit beschlossen zwüschen berg	that lies enclosed between mountains
Vil fester dann mit muren.	much stronger than with walls.
(von Greyerz 1927:38)	

(One is reminded of the first sentence in Tacitus' *De Germania*: "mutuo metu aut montibus separatur". . . [the region] is separated by mutual fear and mountains.)

Second, the separate historical evolution gave the German-Swiss a separate mythopoeically shaped historical memory. Songs of battles, victories, and defeats celebrated federated communities and were "at least as texts tied to Switzerland" (Weiss 1978:238), that is to its unique history of a two-centuries long confrontation with princely armies. Yet only a few individuals emerged in this mythopoeic tradition as subjects of praise;[5] it celebrated the collectivity. The 1584 "Mahnlied," a song of admonition, declared for instance:

Es tregt der schöne Schweitzer Stier	It carries the pretty Switzer Bull
Dreyzehen orth / seins Krantzes zier	thirteen places / his garland's grace

[5]Among the historical figures are Arnold von Winkelried (+1386 at Sempach) and Niklaus von der Flüe (1417–1487).

Inn hörnen eingeflochten:	in horns interwoven:
Lößst auff den Krantz /	untie the garland /
brichst ab die Horn /	break off the horn /
All gmach wird die Freyheit verlorn /	the freedom will all too soon be lost /
Drum wir lang hand gefochten	for which we long have fought.
(Marchal 1990:333, facsimile)	

Third, all the hard-won victories of the collectivity, which were endangered not only by external enemies but also by internal dissension, did not derive from its own strength or merit: "Dis hat getan die Gotes hand: That has done God's hand," proclaims a song which celebrates the confederates' victory over Charles of Burgundy at Grandson in 1476. In 1514 Pamphilius Gengenbach of Basel drew the following idealized image of the "Old Oath-Associate [*Eydgnoss*]":

Gott söllen wir vor augen han,	God we shall have before our eyes,
als unser fordern hand gethan,	as our ancestors have done,
so mögen wir groß eer gewinnen,	so we may gain great honor,
und sond der gerechtigkeit bystan	and will stand by justice,
thuot ein alter eydgnoß singen.	an old oath-associate does sing.
(von Greyerz 1927:55)	

Even songs devoted to individuals such as William Tell, Winkelried, and Niklaus von der Flüe do not celebrate powerful individuals, but view them merely as instruments of God (von Greyerz 1927:45).

Fourth, the German-Swiss mentality as it evolved historically focuses neither on the noble nor the burgher, but the peasant as the epitome of genuine nobility. A 1558 song from the Bernese region, pointedly titled "Der Edel Bumann / The Noble Yeoman," contains these stanzas:

Gesang, das wil ich heben an	A song, that I will now begin,
zue lob und ehren dem buwmann,	in praise and honor of the yeoman
ich mag's nit underwegen lan.	I don't want to leave it undone.
Der edel buwmann hat mir guets getone.	The noble yeoman to me has a good sound.
Ich prys den bumann überlut,	I praise the yeoman overloud,
der uns den wyn und koren buwt,	who grows us the wine and grain,
den böllen, rüeben und das krut,	the onion, carrot, and the cabbage,

die kicher erbsen, linsen, muess und bonen.	the chick-peas, lentils, pap, and beans.
(von Greyerz 1927:50)	

The peasant is praised, of course, also in other traditions. In the German-Swiss case, however, he is honored in context of the "Swiss Bull" who is proclaimed just as noble as the Imperial Eagle, an emblem of the emperor and nobility. The German-Swiss mentality does not celebrate life in the later Romantic mode of idyllization, however, but views the peasant as the main representative of the oath-associations and their successful struggle against the powerful nobility. No claim is made here for the superior moral status or juridical correctness of the stance of those associations in the face of claims of emperor and nobles; nor should the principles those sworn associations embodied be confused with those of the later nation-state composed of individual citizens as first proclaimed by the American and French Revolutions. The Swiss confederation rested on a mythology of a people protected by mountains; tested in wars against princely designs; guided by God; and, at its core, formed by the peasantry of mountain valleys, especially those of the Ur-Schweiz, of primal Switzerland, consisting of Uri, Schwyz, and Unterwalden. It is this mentality that sets the German-Swiss apart from the inhabitants of the regions to their north, although they share tribal pasts, language, texts, and mythopoeic topoi.

Migration

Since the gradual formation of Switzerland at the end of the Middle Ages, its areas were regions of emigration as well as immigration (Bickel 1947:88–108). In the later nineteenth century, emigration from and immigration to Switzerland fluctuated, but overall tended toward balance. Figures for 1880 suggest the following distribution:

Table 1. Swiss Abroad and Foreign-born in Switzerland

Swiss Abroad *Region*	*Number*	*Percent*
Europe	119,707	51.1
Americas	107,780	46.1
Africa	3,456	1.5
Australia	2,300	1.0
Asia	802	0.3
TOTAL	234,045	100.0

Foreign-Born in Switzerland		
Country of Origin	*Number*	*Percent*
Germany	95,253	45.14
France	53,653	25.42
Italy	41,530	19.68
Austria	12,859	6.09
Other	7,740	3.67
TOTAL	211,035	100.00

(Schelbert 1976:182, 184)

For other years proportions are similar and show that numerous Swiss had relatives abroad or came in contact with foreigners residing in Switzerland. Nativism, therefore, was not alien to the German-Swiss mentality, as a folksong about Italians suggests. It is found in the collection of Hanns in der Gand (1882–1947), actually Ladislaus Kruspi, the son of a Polish immigrant to Switzerland, who grew up in Erstfeld, Canton Uri. He was a singer, composer, and avid collector of folksongs, which he published in various books. In 1921–1922 he went to the United States where he visited Swiss communities and tried to revive the tradition of spontaneous singing. On his return, a letter from an Otto Baumgartner, 307 George Street, New Haven, CT, included a folksong, which Baumgartner remembered with unreflected innocence. Two stanzas read as follows:

I der Schwiz un andera Ländera, i jedem Urkanton,
Da find' ma t'Italiener, die schaffet um de Lohn,
So billig als nur müglech, an jedera tät das nit,
Der Italiener aber dä springt a halb Stund wit.

Un wen'd ama n'ort a stinkparagge weist,
Wo's fister is un gar erbärmlich heiss,
Und t'Näster foll a Wäntela, d'r Chuchi foll a dräck,
Da ist der Lazeroni, da bringt na niemer wägg.
(Schweizer Volkslied Archiv)

In literal English translation:

In Switzerland and other lands, in every Ur-Canton,
there one finds Italians who work for a wage
as cheaply as possible and not everyone would do it,
yet the Italian, he will run for it for half an hour.

and if one knows somewhere of a smelly shed,
where it is dark and miserably hot,
and the beds full of bugs, the kitchen full of dirt,
there will live the Lazeroni, there nobody can remove him.

Emigrants from Switzerland to the United States were part of the many European immigrant groups that joined the descendants of earlier settlers in the westward movement across what is now the United States. Between 1820 and 1930 Swiss migration to the United States shows the following proportions:

Table 2. Immigration from Switzerland to the United States 1820–1930

Decade	*Number*	*Percent (of European Immigrants)*
1820–1830	3,226	3.03
1830–1840	4,821	0.98
1841–1850	4,644	0.29
1851–1860	25,011	1.01
1861–1870	23,286	1.13
1871–1880	28,293	1.24
1881–1890	81,988	1.73
1891–1900	31,179	0.88
1901–1910	34,922	0.43
1911–1920	23,091	0.53
1921–1930	29,676	1.02

(U.S. Bureau of the Census, *Statistical Abstract (1920)*, 100; [1940], 101.)

Swiss immigrants came from a tradition of singing, which they also carried to the United States. For instance, the laborer Luise Rüd (1968), born in 1875, when interviewed at age 91, answered the question what she had enjoyed most in her youth with these words: "Singing. When on Sundays after singing practice we strolled through the village, the four or five of us, and sang. People enjoyed it as well as we did" (Rüd 1968). She listed songs that have remained part of the widely known and sung repertoire such as:

Luegit vo Berge und Tal	Look from mountains and valley
Uf dene Berge möcht i lebe	on these mountains I would like to live
Im schönsten Wiesengrunde	in the most beautiful meadow
Von ferne sei herzlich gegrüsset	from afar be heartily greeted
Wo Berge sich erheben	where mountains rise up
Vo Luzern uf Weggis zue	from Lucerne toward Weggis.

Wherever Swiss settled in larger numbers they formed singing societies. In Chicago, for instance, they founded the Schweizer Männerchor on May 11, 1869, "to promote singing, especially of patriotic songs." By 1880 the group counted about one hundred members and was flanked by the Helvetia Damenchor (Steinach 1889:243–244). Steinach's work shows that in the 1880s there was hardly a Swiss community in the United States without one or several associations formed to preserve and further the culture of singing.

During his travels in the United States, Hanns in der Gand had also received a list of "as far as I know generally unknown Swiss songs" that had been collected by a Frau Stortz of Council Bluffs, Iowa, and "listed by Pastor Gruber." The list reflects a mixture of High German and dialect texts that on the one hand celebrate Switzerland's mountains and traditions and on the other reflect on life's shifting moods. One title observes: "A delight in honor, who will forbid it? . . . But the graveyard lies not far away." In a letter Hanns in der Gand had received on October 1, 1938, an Arnold Keller of Portland, Oregon, explained that the Swiss in that state were mainly Bernese, while those in the state of Washington were from Schwyz and Unterwalden; the free time remaining to the immigrants "from the struggle for existence," he claimed, served to deepen "the attachment to the dear fatherland. Their thoughts were directed to the *Heimat's* mountainous world by singing, especially yodeling and dancing." The six texts now to be reviewed belong to the Swiss immigrants' repertoire and reflect that peculiar German-Swiss mentality that had evolved over centuries and shaped also the views on migration.

Texts

The Swiss Folksong Archive, founded in 1906 on the initiative of E. Hoffmann-Kreyer and Otto von Greyerz (Baumann 1981:18) in the City of Basel, contains a wealth of primary, well-ordered materials. The building where the archive is housed (Augustinergasse 19) overlooks the Rhine toward the very place where in earlier times thousands of emigrants left for destinations overseas. The song collection also documents how German-Swiss viewed emigration of compatriots in general and to the United States in particular. The six texts were chosen to show the range of assumptions, views, and emotions evoked by people leaving Switzerland, especially to regions overseas.

1. *The Emigrant as Prodigal Son.* In song collections this song is titled "Amerikanerlied / The American's Song" (Gaßmann 1961:91). Its origin is sketched in a reply given to a query of E. Hoffmann-Kreyer by the painter Emil Breurmann of Basel who declared:

> I am happy to reply to your questions concerning the *Amerikalied* as far as I am able to. I wrote the song anno 1897. . . . The first stanza, however, is not from me, but belongs to an older song, which one, however, I do not know. It was once handed to me together with the melody by Mr. Phillip Trüdinger. . . . I wrote the stanzas for an evening of merry-making in the Artists Association of Basel where the song was then sung every Saturday. From there the song became widely known. I was quite surprised, for instance, when at an evening event in Munich I heard my verses intoned by young Swiss who were totally unknown to me.

By 1906 the text had grown to seven, by 1916 to eleven stanzas. Two belonged to the original song that Breurmann had used; the rest was added by unknown hands.

The text, given here after Gaßmann (1961:91–92), poses several questions to the emigrant: How could he leave the beauty of the valley on the blue lake? How could he refuse to share his own people's good and bad days? How could he coldly turn his back to the country that had nurtured him as a mother nurtures her child? How could anyone contemplate tearing up the citizenship document, that gift of the mountains, and abjure the league forever? Did the forefathers such as Tell and Winkelried ever flee their country in days of misfortune? They will lament the emigrant as a prodigal son. Yet none of these questions seems to matter to the prospective "American." Go then, the song continues with some sarcasm, dig your own grave in the golden sand and perish at the Sacramento River! Those who sing this song, however, will find their rest among their ancestors. The emigrant may leave; they as free Swiss will live and die in the land of their forebears.

The text, it seems, finely interweaves the various themes of the German-Swiss mentality: the sense of a unique history, the praise of the gift of ancient freedom, the remembrance of the heroes of the past as symbols of community, the love of the mountains, the undying attachment to the land whose force pulses in one's blood. It is these very riches the emigrant squanders like the prodigal son of the New Testament story; lured by the faraway phantom of gold, he will find only a premature grave in a distant and alien world.

The text also became a favorite text for Swiss soldiers who transformed it, however, in several ways (Gaßmann 1961:93–94). The citizenship paper was replaced by the *Dienstbüchlein*, a booklet each male Swiss is issued at age 18 that contains the record of his militia service, a duty from which one was released until quite recently only for reasons of health. The stanzas also reveal the soldier's rough-and-tumble humor; rhymes are made up ad hoc, like the following lines of the refrain:

Yes, yes, the land, the land America
is so far from the land Europia.

The verb *wäscht* (one washes) is rhymed with the word *häscht* (one has) and gives the text a humorous, if not sarcastic tone. In the stanza:

Dig your own grave in the desert's sand,
perish at the Sacramento stream!

the polite verb *verdirb* is replaced in some versions with the coarser *verreck* (croak) used in reference to the dying of an animal. The lines of stanza three:

where the alien braids wreaths of
Edelweiss and alpine roses!

introduce an ironic tone by having an "alien," an outsider, make a wreath, whereas stanza four introduces a new theme:

It whistles, the anchor chains groan!
and at the bullhorn stands the captain,
with such terrifying tones
it's hard to go to America.

Yet both versions view the emigrant with disbelief and a touch of scorn. He is a prodigal son, ungrateful toward a caring mother, faithless toward the ancestors; only a misfit could take such an unbelievable step. Frau Stortz of Council Bluffs, Iowa, whose list also included the *Amerikanerlied*, dryly commented: "Melody known to me. If that song had been sung at my departure, I probably would have stayed home."

2. *A Farewell to the Sons of Schams*. The next text also questions the wisdom of leaving, but in a much milder and empathetic form. Its origin is uncertain, and it was supposedly written in the 1880s by an immigrant to the Schams Valley named Jenny from the Glarus Valley. A note to the text preserved in the Volkslied Archiv (SVA 24535) observes that after 1854 numerous Schamser emigrated to California's goldfields, but that most returned after ten to fifteen years. The Schams is a region of the Canton Graubünden that was inhabited already by 1800 BCE. It lies southwest

of Chur, a *curia* of Roman times and later an episcopal see, where alpine routes from the European north converge and lead to several passes over the Alps to Italy. The Schams valley is marked in the north by the ravine of the Via Mala, the Bad Path, which leads to a plateau where "the traveler becomes aware both of the dangers he has overcome and of the deep liberating breath he now draws" (Murbach and Heman 1967:5). The region is famous for the church at Zillis built around 1130 CE; the ceiling has numerous paintings in the Romanesque style by an unknown artist of the twelfth century.

This song from the Schams, too, uses a series of rhetorical questions. Do you really want to sever the sacred bonds, the song asks the emigrants, that tie you to the mountains, the lakes, and valleys? "Do you, sons of Schams, really want to leave those meadows," the third stanza asks, "from where the sounds of cowbells melodiously fill the whole valley?" Are even the bonds with parents, brothers and sisters, and friends unable to keep you in the Schams? But in contrast to the previous song, the text relaxes its unbelief and acknowledges that the "far away land of gold" is calling in creating the hope of "building a better existence." The song then turns to a series of good wishes: May the emigrants succeed, may a lucky star shine upon the departing so that they may some day return enriched to the Schamsertal! May they leave then in God's name whose richest blessing may be upon them. Although this song, too, views "America" merely as a land where potential riches in the form of gold beckon, the emigrants themselves are viewed worthy of all blessings God can bestow and will, hopefully, return to the beloved Schams they are now leaving.

3. *The Disappointed as Emigrant.* In the third text of uncertain provenance (Röhrich 1985:72) the emigrant himself, not those staying behind, expresses his views. He, too, is attracted by the promise of gold:

> It pulls me to America
> into the goldland California,

he sings in the refrain. Yet there are other forces driving him: life at home had brought him bitter disappointment. Was it ill luck? Strife among family, friends, or neighbors? An unrequited love? He does not explain. But one thing seems certain: happiness was denied him in the old *Heimatland*, the land he cherished as his home. But then the song turns to an imagery dominant also in the previous texts and typically German-Swiss: he will miss the Alps with their mountains, forests, streams, and joyful herds. Yet there is a consolation: he knows that also over there he will remain "Helvetia's son," will build a new *Heimat* and, eventually, will find final rest in peace.

4. *A Tearful Adieu.* The emigrant, most likely a young woman on the day of leaving, also speaks in the fourth song (SVA 8327). She confesses of having shed many tears because she was about to leave her valley in the Canton Wallis, surrounded by mountains, forests, and streams. She would never leave of her own accord, yet the "dear father had decided thus!" How many bouquets of flowers had she tied, how often had she enjoyed the shade of mighty trees! Yet the day of departure had come: "Farewell, so I shout saddened into the valley from mountainous heights. Homeland, homeland, will I never see you again? Do I behold you for the last time?" But darkness sets in and the heart becomes heavy. As so often in migration, one person or another makes the decision, yet spouse, children, or the aged have no choice or face the dilemma of either losing their loved ones ready to depart or joining them, thereby losing all that is encompassed by *Heimat*, the land that means home.

5. *Ballad of a Migration.* The fifth song tells a story and contains in its earliest version some twenty-three stanzas. It is titled "The Obersimmentaler in America" or "Song of an Emigrant to America" and was apparently written in the United States. A printed copy in the Volkslied Archiv notes: "Composed by an immigrant from Obersimmental. One notices it from the language. He lives in Erie, in the State Bennzelvanien [Pennsylvania]. Copied by J. B. in Buffalo, on January 31, 1835." The song became quite popular and is reported in various versions.[6] A Gertrud Zürcher noted a version in the Baselland in 1929 (SVA 24071:3), and "in the [19]30s it was sung by a blind wayfaring little man among other places also in the Gurnigel region, [located about seven miles west of Thun], known also in the Simmental" (SVA 24071:3). Another version identifies the author as follows: "Written by Fritz von Känel, Simmental, more than 50 years ago. I heard it sung by my mother in M[erligen?] on the Lake of Thun. Is sung after the melody: 'A sad little tale, I will tell; girls, pay proper attention.' ['Es trurigs Stückli will i zelle, Meitleni gebt ordli Acht!']" A recent edition claims that "the pastor of Beatenberg had written down the song about the middle of the last century. A certain J. K. is supposed to have brought it back from Buffalo in 1835; in the [Bernese] Oberland it is sung at many places" (Hostettler 1979:122–123).

---

[6]See for instance Schweizer Volkslied Archiv (SVA) 27159 (1853); 17998 (1857); 24071 (1929); 202362 (1954); also Jenzer 1869:82–84; Tobler 1884:193–198). It was also printed in 1859 in the review *Die Schweiz* 2 (1859):60. For the most recent version in German and English, see in Silverman 1992:372–375.

The text was written about a year after the emigrants had left their homeland and explains that they had nearly perished from heartache at departure. When they reached the ocean, they viewed it with horror: it was "a terrifying puddle," incredibly deep and unbelievably large. Then came the endless rocking of the boat, the onset of seasickness, the terrifying storms, the boredom, and homesickness. Yet one day the experienced travelers announced to the others that land would soon be reached; and indeed, at first it looked merely "like a little cloud," but then hills came into view, houses: the ocean crossing would soon be over! How delightful to leave the boat, that miserable box, and to learn to say *wäriwell*. The emigrant soon realized that money ruled here too:

> Who has enough money, is on top.
> Who has none left, is here also out.

But where should one settle? Some wanted to go here, others there, but good land was expensive, until one finally settled on "a bit of bush" and built a log cabin. It was a strange way of doing things for those sturdy Bernese, and all kinds of creatures seemed to intrude on the living quarters, especially snakes. Farming, too, was a strange affair: the cattle roamed freely, clearing the land was arduous, and all work was done fast. The proverbial thoughtful slowness of the Bernese had no place over here. If only those back home could see across: some would love what they saw, while others would recoil in disbelief. Was it good, then, to emigrate? The emigrant could not say "Do come—or don't!" Certain was only that "life is but a shadow" until one enters eternal life where, hopefully, all will be reunited.

6. *Anatomy of a Homesickness*. The last song to be reviewed concerns an emigrant's *Heimweh*, homesickness. The text is one among many similar ones. J. J. Schäublin's songbook, for instance, which appeared first in 1855 and by 1911 had reached its 109th edition, contains four texts explicitly exploring the nature of homesickness (Schäublin 1911: Nos.157, 161, 162, 163); others allude to the phenomenon. Although probably a universal experience, it "has been observed above all among the Swiss," a treatise of 1735 claims; for others it rarely seemed to turn into that "strange and dangerous sickness which Swiss in foreign countries must endure" (Zedler 1735). It was first dealt with as a medical issue in a work of Johannes Hofer and published in Basel (Hofer 1688; see also Kreß 1985:778).

The experience of homesickness is intimately connected with *Heimat*, a concept pointing to a general primal human need, but developed differently by human communities.[7] For Swiss it means primarily *Landschaft*, the shape of the region in which one lives, with its unique contours of mountains, forests, and pastures; its changing face depending on the time of day, the weather, and the seasons. These are all experienced in the routines of daily work and in moves over paths leading along meadows, crossing forests, and ending on heights from which the lay of the land can be uniquely enjoyed. This creates an intense chthonic bondage to the region especially of one's youth, and no other *Landschaft* can replace that original experience that tends to remain normative and provides a unique rootedness. Leaving such a world creates in many an emotional crisis that may become serious, even life-threatening. A Swiss newspaper, for instance, reported dryly: "Father Heini of Lucerne, missionary in San Francisco, 25 years of age, died of Swiss homesickness, June 21, 1872" (Osenbrüggen 1874:203). It was not unusual to meet in forlorn Alpine heights people who had been to Australia or California, but eventually returned to the place they had known as home, as *Heimat* (ibid. 207).

The text for the song "Schweizerheimweh" was written by Johann Rudolf Wyss the Younger (1781–1830). He had studied theology in Tübingen, Göttingen, and Halle, then became Professor of Philosophy in Bern where he co-edited the almanac *Die Alpenrosen* and created a multivolume unpublished collection of Swiss folksongs.[8] The text was first printed in 1811, the melody composed by F. Meissner a year later (von Greyerz 1927:180). Perhaps Wyss described his very own experience when he asked: "Heart, my heart, why so sad? What's that pain all about?" And he stresses: "It is so beautiful in the alien land!" Yet something vital is missing.

No matter how nice it may be abroad, *Heimat* it could never become. Thus, everything pulled toward home, to father and mother, "to the mountain, rock, and forest." Therefore, one must go back to the place of one's youth because neither joy nor peace will return until one has reached one's village. In the last stanza Wyss exhorts his heart to accept the pain in God's name who will grant a speedy return home, if that is His will. These feelings are echoed in many other German-Swiss songs (von Greyerz 1927:180–181) and reflect a general human experience that seems to have been especially intense among the German-Swiss.

The six texts reviewed above contain in various mixtures the central elements of the German-Swiss mentality. The world of the mountains is celebrated as a world defended and consecrated by the blood of the forebears whose dedication and wis-

---

[7]See especially Greverus (1972) and Kreß (1985); also the nineteenth edition of the *Brockhaus-Enzyklopädie* that in vol. 9 treats as one of the two Schlüsselbegriffe the term *Heimat* (Bausinger 1989:617–619).

[8]Data on Wyss can be found in the *Historisch-Biographisches Lexikon der Schweiz* 7(1934), 608–609.

dom shaped a community proud of its communally understood freedom. The lure of the wider world in general and of "America" in particular lies in the "gold," in its concrete as well as symbolic meaning. The *Heimat* is only rarely rejected and America sought not as the land of freedom, but of hopefully only temporary opportunity to gain greater wealth and then to return. This does not mean a rejection of the country of destination either; it simply intimates that the local community of one's youth was *Heimat*. Its landscape dominated by mountains, forests, streams, and lakes, and dotted with compact villages dominated by the church steeple, remained unforgettable and for many the goal of an inexplicable yearning, if at all possible to be regained.

APPENDIX: SIX SONG TEXTS

Note: The translations of these song texts are literal and, as far as possible, follow the stanzas line by line and in the same order of words as in the German version, in order to make them accessible.

1. *Der Auswanderer*
Und willst du hier nicht länger weilen
im grünen Tal am blauen See?
Du willst der Heimat Los nicht teilen?
nicht deines Volkes Wohl und Weh?
So wandre nach Amerika!
Ich bleib im Land der Alpen da.

Refrain:
Fahr hin denn nach Amerika,
als freier Schweizer leb ich da!
Fahr hin denn nach Amerika,
als freier Schweizer sterb ich da!

Der Schweiz, die dich mit Mutterhänden
als Kind gepflegt so treu, so gut,
ihr kannst du kalt den Rücken wenden,
durchwallt dein Herz kein Schweizerblut?

Du willst den Bürgerbrief zerreißen
den dir das freie Hochland gab?
Du willst nicht länger Schweizerbürger heißen,
schwörst unserm Bund auf ewig ab.

Die Väter, die in Unglückstagen
nie feig aus ihrer Heimat flohn,
die Tell und Winkelriede klagen
um dich, um den verlornen Sohn.

So wühl ein Grab im goldnen Sande,
verschmacht am Sakramentostrom!
Im schönen Schweizerlande,
bei meinen Vätern will ich ruhn.
(Gaßmann 1961:91-92)

The Emigrant
And you don't want to stay here any longer
in the green valley at the blue lake?
You don't want to share your homeland's fate?
Not your people's good and bad days?
So migrate then to America!
I stay here in the land of the Alps.

Refrain:
So move then to America,
as a free Swiss I will live here!
So move then to America,
as a free Swiss I will die here!

Switzerland, which with mother hands
reared you as a child so well, so good,
to her can you coldly turn your back,
does no Swiss blood run through your heart?

You want to tear up your citizenship paper,
which the free highland gave you?
You don't want to be called a Swiss citizen any longer,
you foreswear our league forever.

The fathers, who in days of misfortune
never cowardly fled from their homeland,
the Tells and Winkelrieds lament
for you, for the prodigal son.

So dig a grave in the golden sand,
pine away at the Sacramento stream!
In beautiful Switzerland,
among my fathers I want to rest.

Soldatenlied
Willst du dein Dienstbüchlein zerreißen
das dir die teure Heimat gab?
Willst nicht länger Schweizerbürger heißen?
So reis ins Land Amerika! (zwei, drei!)

Soldiers' Song
You want to tear up your [military] service booklet
which the dear homeland gave you?
You don't want to be called a Swiss citizen any longer?
So travel to the land America!

Refrain:	
Ja, ja, das Land Amerika!	Yes, yes, the land America
ist weit vom Land Europia! (zwei, drei!)	Is far from the land Europia! (two, three!)
Ach wie bange (zwei!), ach wie bange (drei!)	Ah how anxiously (two!), ah how anxiously (three!)
klopft das, klopft das Herz mir in der Brust! (zwei, drei!)	beats the, beats the heart in my breast! (two, three!)
Dich locken Kaliforniens Felder,	California's fields are tempting you
wo man das Gold im Flusse wäscht.	where one washes the gold in the stream.
Was nützen dir die vielen Felder,	What good to you are the many fields,
wenn du die teure Heimat nicht mehr häscht?	if you don't have your dear homeland any more?
So leb denn wohl, ich wünsch dir gute Reise,	So fare then well, I wish you a good trip
vergiß das teure Hochland nicht,	don't forget the dear highland,
wo sich der Fremde Edelweiße	where the alien braids wreaths of
und Alpenrosenkränze flicht!	Edelweiss and alpine roses!
Es pfeift, die Ankerketten stöhnen!	It whistles, the anchor's chains groan!
am Sprachrohr steht der Kapitän,	at the bullhorn stands the captain,
bei solchen schauervollen Tönen	with such terrifying tones
hält's schwer, nach Amerika zu gehn.	it's hard to go to America.
Grab dir dein Grab im Wüstensande,	Dig your own grave in the desert's sand,
verdirb am Sakramentostrom!	perish at the Sacramento stream!
Ich bleib im lieben Schweizerlande,	I will stay in dear Switzerland,
bei meinen Vätern will ich ruhn.	among my forefathers I want to rest.
(Gaßmann 1961:93-94)	

---

2. *Lied der Auswanderer*	*Song of the Emigrants*
Wollt ihr scheiden Schamsersöhne	You want to part, sons of Schams
aus dem lieben Heimatland?	from the dear homeland?
Fesselt euch nicht mehr das schöne,	Doesn't chain you anymore the beautiful
freie, liebe Bündnerland?	free dear Grisonsland?
Wollt ihr fort von diesen Bergen,	You want to go away from those mountains
Die ihr schon von Kindheit an	which from childhood on you have
Treu geliebt in eurem Herzen?	faithfully loved in your heart?
Schaut sie nochmals innig an.	Look at them lovingly one more time.
Wollt ihr lassen von den Matten,	You want to leave those meadows
Wo der Herdenglockenklang	where the sounds of the herds' bells
So melodisch euch ertönet	so melodiously reaches you
Durch das ganze Tal entlang?	throughout the whole valley?
Wollt ihr scheiden von dem lieben	Do you want to part with the dear
Eltern- und Geschwisterkreis,	circle of parents and brothers and sisters
Wo von wahrem Liebesbande	where in a true bond of love
Jeder sich geliebet weiß?	each knows to be loved?

Alles dies ist nicht imstande
Euch zu fesseln an den Ort,
Wo in treuem Freundschaftsbande
Ihr gewechselt manches Wort.

Nach dem fernen Land des Goldes
Wandert ihr nun alle aus;
Bessre Existenz zu schaffen,
Meidet ihr das Vaterhaus.

Möge dies euch wohlgelingen.
Dieser Wunsch begleitet euch
Auf der Reise und auch da drüben,
Drüben in dem fernen Reich.

Mög' euch dort der Glücksstern scheinen
Günstiger als hier zu Land,
Um bereichert heimzukehren
In das liebe Schamsertal.

Nun, so zieht in Gottes Namen!
Gott im Himmel sei mit euch,
Bitte euch den reichsten Segen.
Dies wünscht euch manch' Herz so weich.
(Schweizer Volkslied Archiv: Nr. 24535)

All this is not able
to tie you to the place
where in a true bond of friendship
you exchanged many a word.

To the far away land of gold
all of you will now depart;
a better existence to create
you abandon the father's house.

May this go well for you.
This wish accompanies you
on the journey and, too, over there,
over there in the far away empire.

May there shine a lucky star on you
more favorably than over here,
in order to return enriched
to the dear valley of the Schams.

Now then leave in God's name!
God in heaven be with you,
beg for you the richest blessing
that wishes you many a tender heart.

---

3. *Der enttäuschte Auswanderer*
Ich habe hier kein Glück gefunden
In meinem alten Heimatland,
Des Bittern hab' ich viel empfunden,
Drum ziehts mich in ein neues Land:
Es zieht mich nach Amerika,
Ins Goldland California.

Und muss ich hier die Alpen missen,
Verlassen Berg und Wald und Strom,
ist doch ein Trost für mich zu wissen,
Ich bleib auch dort Helvetiens Sohn.
Mich zieht's fort nach Amerika,
Ins Goldland California.

So leb' denn wohl, du Schweizererde,
Ich will mir dort die Heimat bau'n.
Leb' wohl du Quell, du frohe Herde,
Auch dort lässt sich's im Frieden ruh'n.
Mich zieht's halt nach Amerika,
Drum lebet wohl ihr Alpen da.
(Röhrich 1985:72-73)

The Disappointed Emigrant
I have found here no happiness
in my old homeland.
Of the bitter things I have experienced much,
therefore I am drawn to a new land:
I am drawn to America,
into the goldland California.

And if I must give up the Alps here,
leave mountain and forest and stream,
it is yet comforting for me to know
that I remain there too Helvetia's son.
I am drawn away to America
into the goldland California.

So fare then well, you Switzersoil,
there I want to build me my home.
Farewell you spring, you happy herd,
there, too, one can find rest in peace.
I just am drawn to America,
therefore fare well you Alps.

4. *Tränenreicher Abschied*
Thränen hab' ich viele, viele vergossen
Dass ich scheiden muss von hier.
Doch mein lieber Vater hat es beschlossen,
Aus der Heimat wandern wir!
Heimat, heute wandern wir,
Heut' auf ewig von dir!
Drum ade so lebe wohl!
Drum ade, ade, ade,
Drum ade, ade, ade,
Drum ade, so lebe wohl!

Lebt wohl, ihr grünen, blumigen Felder,
Wo ich manches Sträusschen band!
Lebt wohl ihr Büsche, Lauben u. Wälder,
Wo ich kühlen Schatten fand!
Berg und Thäler, stille Au'n,
Werd euch nimmermehr schauen.
D'rum ade so lebet wohl!
D'rum ade, ade, ade!
D'rum ade, ade, ade!
D'rum ade, so lebet wohl!

Lebe wohl, so ruf ich traurig hernieder,
Ruf's vom Berg hinab ins Thal,
Heimat, Heimat! seh ich nimmer dich wieder?
Seh ich dich zum letzen Mal?
Dunkel wird es rings umher
Und mein Herz ist so schwer.
D'rum ade, so lebe wohl!
D'rum ade, ade, ade!
D'rum ade, ade, ade!
D'rum ade, so lebe wohl!
(Schweizer Volkslied Archiv: Nr. 8327)

Tearful Farewell
Tears so many, many I have shed
that I have to depart from here.
Yet my dear father has decided it,
from the homeland we will wander!
Homeland, today we will wander,
today forever from you!
Therefore goodbye, farewell!
Therefore goodbye, goodbye, goodbye,
therefore goodbye, goodbye, goodbye,
therefore goodbye, farewell!

Fare well, you green, flowery fields,
where I bound many a little bouquet!
Farewell you bushes, woods and forests,
where I found cool shade!
Mountain and valleys, quiet meadows,
I will behold you no more,
Therefore goodbye, so farewell!
Therefore goodbye, goodbye, goodbye!
Therefore goodbye, goodbye, goodbye!
Therefore goodbye, so farewell!

Fare well, I call down sadly,
I call from the mountain down into the valley,
Homeland, homeland! Will I never see you again?
Am I seeing you for the last time?
It is becoming dark all around
And my heart is heavy.
Therefore goodbye, farewell!
Therefore goodbye, goodbye, goodbye,
therefore goodbye, goodbye, goodbye,
therefore goodbye, farewell!

---

5. *Der Obersimmentaler in Amerika*
Gät acht, i will ech öppis zelle,
vom neue Land Amerika.
I ha das jetzt scho lang geng welle
u ha's de neue geng la gah.
Es ist jetzt de es Jahr gly scho,
dass mir von öch hi Abschied gno.

Wo mir vo ech ewäg sy 'gange,
do het's is weh tah nit e chly;
mer sy vor Härzweh fast vergange
bis mer es Mal sy von ech gsy;

The Obersimmentaler in America
Pay attention, I want to tell you something
of the new land America.
I wanted to do that for quite a while
yet I never quite got to it.
It is now soon already a year
that we have taken leave of you.

When we went away from you,
that did hurt us not a little;
we nearly perished from heartache
until we finally had been away from you;

danah sy mir bi Paris für
und über's Meer, dur ds Wasser dür.

after that we went through Paris
and over the ocean, through the water.

I muess ech z erst no öppis brichte
vom Meer und vo de Wälli druff,
u was das mängsmal cha verrichte
mit Lüt u Guet, da obe druff.
Es het mi mengist Wunner gno,
jetzt bin i usem Wunner cho.

I must first still tell you something
about the ocean and the waves on it,
and what that sometimes may do
to people and things, there above.
I had often wondered about it,
now I have come out of the wonder.

Es ist e grüselichi Glunte—
wer's nit gseh het, der gloubti's nit—
und tüüf ist's, dass me cha kei chlumpe
ganz z Bode lah am länge Siil.
Dir chöht e Jahr druff ummi gah,
dir gseht no numme Bitz derva.

It is a horrible puddle—
who hasn't seen it, won't believe it—
and it's deep that one can't make a clump
touch the ground on a long rope.
You can go on it for a year,
you see of it only a bit.

A Himmel uehi und y ds Wasser,
da cha me gugge, wenn es ist;
sust gseht me nit viel schöni Sache,
as hie u da e grosse Fisch.
U mengist sy da Wälli cho,
die ds Schiff hi ganz u d Syte gno.
Eh bhüetis Gott, wie het es gwalpet!
Gly wänes z uangerobe ghyt.
Da het me rächt gsit: "Gott es walti!"
u deicht, es müessi gstorbe sy.
E Tiil hi Aengste übercho,
u ds Lache het's is alle gno.

Up to the sky and into the water
one may look, if it is;
else one doesn't see many nice things
but now and then a big fish.
And sometimes waves did come,
which took the ship fully to the side.
May god protect us, how it rocked!
Soon as if it was turning upside down.
Then one truly said: "May God take care!"
and thought it had to have died.
One part did become anxious,
and laughter it did take from all of us.

Fast all, die uf em Meer wei ryte,
die wärde chrank die ersti Stund.
Das Waggle spürt me scho bi Zyte,
u chotze muess me wie ne Hun.
Mi sälber het es tüechtig gno;
i ha my Tiil fast übercho.

Nearly all who want to ride on the ocean,
they become sick the first hour.
The rocking one feels quite in time,
and one has to vomit like a dog.
I myself was thoroughly hit;
I nearly got my part.

Chei Wunner, dass me albi inist
öpp use gugget über d Wan,
u da su trurig stiht und gihnet
u deicht: o chämi numme Lan!
Langwylig ist es, das ist wahr,
u macht ihm ds Hihmweh sunnerbar.

No wonder that one once in a while
looked out over the wall,
and there stands sadly and yawns
and thinks: O if only land would come.
Boring it is, that is true,
and gives one strangely homesickness.

Oepp inist amme Morge gscheht es,
so säge die, wo's chenne, ihm:
"Jetz rückt es de, un ärstig giht es
mit üs zum neue Ufer hin!"

Then once one morning it does happen,
that those who know it tell it to one:
"Now it will move, and it will soon be
for us towards the new shore!"

Vor Freude wird's ihm da schier bang,
un eismal tönt es: "Lan, Lan, Lan!"
Me gseht's no numme im Blaue usse,
grad wie nes Wülchli näher cho.
Doch giht's nit lang, so cha me wüsse,
dass's Lan ist, mi gseht Hüble scho.
U gly druf hie u da nes Hus:
Gott Lob! jetzt hört de ds Walpen uf.

Me fährt gschwin yhi zu der Luke,
wo ds Meer da numme chlys meh ist.
Da bist am Lan, du chätzers Trucke!
Me packt si drus, was hest was gist.
Da steit me uf der neue Wäl
u seit scho englisch: wäriwell.

Me giht u gschuet afe d'Gägni
un öppe Städt u lost o d Lüt.
Da "helf ju self" so seit der Jenggi,
u "hilf dir selber," deicht der Dütsch.
Wer gnue Gäld het, ist obe druff.
Wer keis meh het, ist hie o uff.

Die Meiste wotte gäng bas yhi;
as gfallt ne neue niene rächt,
u wott ne si nit schicke z blybe.
's guet Lan ist z tüer u d Lüt sy z schlächt.
Z lötscht anhi chuft me denn e Bitz
des Gstrüpps und buut si druf e Sitz.

Das Buue ist es gspässigs Wäse
für dä im Busch, wo's chuum vermah;
me schleppt e Hufe Trömmle zamme,
öpp i der Längi so ugfahr.
Danah so bstellt me d Lüt e Tag,
und lüpft si uf und leit si grad.

De bruchts nüt meh as Dach u Bode,
zwi Pfester dry und öpp a Tür,
u de no Chleck mit Dräck z verschoppe,
susch blast ihm ganz der Luft dedür;
und hindenahi es Kamin;
das tuet's de fast und ghyt nit yn.

Verwiche han i afe Schlange,
de was der numme schö's wiit gseh,
in üser Stube inne gfange;
me schücht se nit—es soll o gscheh,
dass gwüssni Lüt ne no express

From joy one becomes nearly worried,
and then it sounds: "Land, land, land!"
One sees it only in the blue out there,
just like a little cloud come nearer.
But it doesn't take long, so one can know
that it is land, one sees hills already.
And soon after here and there a house
Thank God! soon the rocking will stop.

One quickly moves into the opening
where the sea is merely small anymore.
You are on land, you catish box!
One unloads it as quickly as one can.
There one stands on the New World
and says already in English: Very well.

One goes and strolls through the area
and about town and listens to people.
There "help yourself" so says the Yankee
and "hilf dir selber" thinks the German.
Who has enough money, is on top.
Who has none left, is here also out.

Most want to go right in there;
and like no place really,
and do not want to give in and stay.
Good land is too costly and people too bad.
Then in the end one buys a bit
of the thicket and builds on it a dwelling.

Building is a strange affair
for one in the bush who hardly has money;
one drags a lot of logs together,
in length about the same.
Then one hires people for a day,
and lifts them up and lays them straight.

Then one needs only roof and floor,
two windows in and perhaps a door,
and then the spaces with dirt to stuff,
otherwise the wind will blow through;
and in the back a chimney;
that's just about does it and doesn't fall in.

Til now I have driven out snakes,
then whatever nice ones you want to see,
I have caught in our living room;
one doesn't fear them—and it is said to happen
that certain people by design

in ihrne Stube hi es Näst.
Me het hie Vieh und milcht und metzget,
me gugget öppe und zieht si hi.
Me nimmt e Achs u giht u bäzget
im Holz a mängem grobe Buum.
Es git ech Arbit nit für Gspass,
hie zmitts im Wal, uf frischem Platz.

We ds Vieh furtluft, so muess me flueche—
das ist e tusigs Tüfels Gschicht!
Viel lieber wett i no ga sueche
bi öch uf d Allmit euers G'richt;
denn diesi Allmit giht ech no
vo Grenland bis nach Mexiko.

's ist nadisch nit, wie viel Lüt meine
hie alz so söfli fadegrads.
Wär's rächt grad will, ist bas dahinne
no öppe uf sym alte Platz.
Doch flinggi Lüt, die werhe meu,
die chömme numme, we si cheu.

Oepp ine söllti Glogge bringe
u no es Wüschli Gäld derzue;
hie Chüeh ha u ne Matte dinga,
der Schwyzerchäs, der gälti gnue.
Es wär nes lustigs Läbe da
für ine, dä rächt juchze ma!

Dir sölltit chönne dürhi gugge
u sälber gseh grad wie nes ist;
es würdi viellecht mänge gluste,
u mängi siiti: "Ni, ni gwüss—
wenn's sy muess, will i lieber no
hie um my lötschte Chrüzer cho!"

I chan ech wäger nit rächt rate
u säge: chömit—oder nit.
Denn üsers Läbe ist e Schatte,
bis dass mer gah y d Ewigkiit.
Dert finne mer enannere scho,
will's Gott, doch öppe frisch und froh.
(Hostettler 1979:122-23)

in their living room have a nest.
One here has cattle and milks and butchers,
and checks sometimes and drives it on.
One takes an ax and fells and cuts
in the woods on many a rough tree.
It means work that isn't a joke
here midst in the woods, on a new place.

If the cattle runs away, one must curse—
that is a thousand devils' story!
Much rather I would want to search
with you on the heights your cattle,
because these heights do stretch
from Greenland to Mexico.

By the way, it's not as many people think
that all is here in a straight line.
Who wants it straight is still back home
there on his old place.
But quick people who want to work
they shall only come, however they can.

Some should bring bells
and with it also a swash of money;
to have cows here and rent a farm,
the Swiss cheese, it is valued well enough.
It would be a fun life here
for one who feels like shouting of joy!

You should be able to peer across
and see for yourself just as it is;
perhaps it would entice many a one,
and many a one would say: "No, no surely—
if it has to be, I rather still lose here my last penny."

Thus I cannot advise you right
and say: do come—or don't.
For our life is a shadow
until we go into eternity.
There we surely will find each other,
may God will it, quite fresh and happy.

---

6. *Schweizerheimweh*
Herz, mys Herz, warum so trurig?
Und was soll das Ach und Weh?
's ist so schön i frömde Lande!

Swiss Homesickness
Heart, my heart, why so sad?
And what is that pain and woe?
It's so nice in alien lands!

Herz, mys Herz, was fehlt dir meh?
Herz, mys Herz, was fehlt dir meh?
Was mer fehlt? Es fehlt mer alles!
Bi so gar verlore hie!
Syg es schön i frömde Lande,
Doch es Heimet wird es nie.

Heart, my heart, what are you missing?
Heart, my heart, what are you missing?
What I miss? I miss everything!
Am so fully here!
Even if it's nice in foreign lands,
yet truly home it will never be.

Ach, is Heimet möcht i wieder,
Aber bald, du Liebe, bald,
Möcht zum Aetti, möcht' zum Müetti,
Möcht' zu Berg und Fels und Wald.

Ah, I want to be at home again,
but soon, you dearest, soon
want to father, want to mother,
want to mountain and rock and wood.

Uf und furt! Und führ mi wieder,
Wo's mer jung so wohl ist gsi;
Ha nit Lust und ha nit Friede,
Bis ig i mym Dörfli bi.

Up and off! And lead me again,
where in my youth I felt so well;
have no joy and have no peace,
until I am in my little village.

Herz, mys Herz! i Gottes Name,
's ist es Lyde, gib di dri!
Will's der Herr, so cha-ner helfe,
Dass mer bald im Heimet sy.

Heart, my heart! in God's name,
it is pain, but do give in!
If the Lord wants, he can help
that we will soon be back home.

(Schäublin 1911:216)

Bibliography

Baumann, Max Peter. *Bibliographie zur ethnomusikologischen Literatur der Schweiz. Mit einem Beitrag zu Geschichte, Gegenstand und Problemen der Volksliedforschung*, 7–79. Winterthur: Amadeus Verlag, 1981.

Bausinger, Hermann. "Heimat." *In Brockhaus-Enzyklopädie*. Vol. 9 (1989):617–619.

Bickel, Wilhelm. *Bevölkerungsgeschichte und Bevölkerungspolitik der Schweiz seit dem Ausgang des Mittlealters*. Zürich: Büchergilde Gutenberg, 1947.

Brady, Thomas A. Turning Swiss: *Cities and Empires, 1450–1550*. Cambridge: Cambridge University Press, 1985.

Breisach, Ernst. *Historiography: Ancient, Medieval and Modern*. Chicago: University of Chicago Press, 1983.

Foulquié, Paul. *Dictionnaire de la langue philosophique*. Paris: Presses Universitaires, 1969.

Furet, François. *In the Workshop of History*. Chicago: University of Chicago Press, 1984.

Gaßmann, Alfred Leonz. *Was unsere Väter sangen: Volkslieder und Volksmusik vom Vierwaldstättersee, aus der Urschweiz und dem Entlebuch*. Basel: G. Krebs Verlagbuchhandlung, 1961.

Gordon, Daniel. [Review Essay of M. Vovelle (1990)]. *History and Theory* 32 (1993):196–213.

Greverus, Ina-Maria. *Der territoriale Mensch: Ein literaturanthropologischer Versuch zum Heimatphänomen*. Frankfurt am Main: Athenäum Verlag, 1972.

Hofer, Johann. *Dissertatio medica de nostalgia oder Heimwehe*. Basel: Typis Jacobi Bertschii, 1688.

Hostettler, Urs. *Anderi Lieder: Von den geringen Leuten*. Gümligen: Zytglogge Verlag, 1979.

Jenzer, J. J. *Heimatkunde des Amtes Schwarzenberg*. Bern: Im Commissionsverlag der J. J. Dalp'schen Buchhandlung (A. Schmidt), 1869.

Kress, Hartmut. "Heimat." *In Theologische Realenzyklopädie* 15 (1985):778–81.

Kuhn, Gottlieb Jakob. *Sammlung von Schweizer Kühreihen und alten Volksliedern, nach ihren bekannten Melodien in Musik gesetzt*. 2nd, expanded edn. Bern: J. J. Burgdorfer, 1812.

La Capra, Dominic. "Is Everyone a *Mentalité* Case? Transference and the 'Culture' Concept." In *History and Criticism*. 71–94. Ithaca, NY: Cornell University Press, 1985.

Marchal, Guy P. "Die 'Alten Eidgenossen' im Wandel der Zeiten." In *Innerschweiz und frühe Eidgenossenschaft*, edited by Hansjakob Achermann, Josef Brülisauer, and Peter Hoppe, 309–403. Olten: Walter Verlag, 1990.

Morfaux, Louis-Marie. *Vocabulaire de la philosophie et des sciences humaines*. Paris: Armand Colin, 1980.

Murbach, Ernst, and Peter Heman. *The Painted Romanesque Ceiling of St. Martin in Zillis*. New York: Frederick A. Praeger, 1967.

Osenbrüggen, Eduard. *Die Schweizer. Daheim und in der Fremde*. Berlin: A. Hofmann & Co., 1874.

Röhrich, Lutz. "Auswandererschicksal im Lied." In *Der grosse Aufbruch: Neue Folge der Hessischen Blätter für Volkskunde* 17 (1985): 71–109.

Rüd, Luise. "Erinnerungen einer Arbeiterin aus dem Appenzellerland." *Schweizer Volkskunde. Korrespondenzblatt der schweizerischen Gesellschaft für Volkskunde* 58 (1968):31.

Schäublin, J. J. *Lieder für Jung und Alt*. Basel: Verlag Helbing & Lichtenhahn, 1911.

Schelbert, Leo. *Einführung in die schweizerische Auswanderungsgeschichte der Neuzeit*. Zurich: Leemann, 1976.

Schepping, Wilhelm. "Lied und Musikforschung." In *Grundriß der Volkskunde: Einführung in die Forschungsfelder der europäischen Ethnologie,* edited by Rolf W. Brednich, 399-422. Berlin: Dietrich Reimer Verlag, 1988.

Seeger, Anthony. "When Music Makes History." In *Ethnomusicology and Modern Music History*, edited by Stephen Blum, Philip V. Bohlman, and Daniel M. Neuman, 23–34. Urbana: University of Illinois Press, 1991.

Silverman, Jerry. *Mel Bay's Immigrant Song Book*. Pacific, MO: Mel Bay Publications, 1992.

Steinach, Adelrich. *Geschichte und Leben der Schweizer Kolonien in den Vereinigten Staaten von Nord-Amerika*. New York: Im Selbstverlage des

Verfassers, 1889. Reissue: *Swiss Colonists in Nineteenth-Century America.* New Introduction and Indexes by Dr. Urspeiler Schelbert. Camden, ME: Picton Press, 1995.

Tobler, Ludwig. *Schweizerische Volkslieder.* Frauenfeld: Verlag Huber, 2 vols., 1882–1884

U.S. Bereau of the Census. *Statistical Abstract (1920).* Washington, D.C., 1940.

von Greyerz, Otto. *Das Volkslied der deutschen Schweiz.* Frauenfeld: Verlag Huber, 1927.

Vovelle, Michel. *Ideologies and Mentalities.* Translated by Eamon O'Flaherty. Chicago: University of Chicago Press, 1990.

Weiss, Rudolf. *Volkskunde der Schweiz.* Zürich: Eugen Rentsch, 1978.

Zedler, Johann Heinrich. "Heimsuch, Heim-Weh." In *Grosses vollständiges Universal-Lexikon* 12 (1735): cols. 1190–1191.

4

COMMERCIAL ACCOUNTS OF EARLY MORAVIAN-AMERICAN MUSIC

Laurence Libin

Although their evangelical Protestant faith originated among followers of Jan Huss in fifteenth-century Bohemia and Moravia, the so-called Moravians (known officially as the *Unitas Fratrum*, or Unity of the Brethren) who emigrated to North America beginning in the 1730s were predominantly German in language, culture, and national identity, a result of their predecessors' having fled to Saxony to escape religious persecution. From headquarters at Herrnhut, established in 1722 on land provided by the sympathetic Lutheran count Nikolas Ludwig von Zinzendorf, the Moravians initially sent missionaries to Georgia; when that settlement failed, its survivors moved to Pennsylvania where in 1741 they began to build a new base in Northampton County on property purchased from the Methodist leader George Whitefield, a friend of Zinzendorf's. Here the Moravian immigrants created a successful sectarian community called Bethlehem, which soon bore offshoots in the surrounding area and in North Carolina around Salem.

Moravian life, as rejuvenated and organized largely by Zinzendorf—who rather than converting the Brethren to Lutheranism as he had intended, instead became a bishop and principal leader of their church—depended not on a systematized theology expressed in a formal creed but on customary rules of conduct drawn directly from the believers' understanding of the Bible as translated by Luther. Zinzendorf's doctrines centered on an emotional apprehension of God, accessible solely through love of Jesus. Sensual and nonintellectual, Moravian belief stressed the expression of personal religious feelings through shared social experience. To facilitate this sharing during every waking moment, all aspects of Moravian life were tightly regulated.

Communal music making served the Moravians as a powerful means for worship and for reinforcing social cohesion and attracting converts. Therefore, the

Moravians in America, as in Germany, cultivated music education and group performance, notably through congregational singing and ceremonial trombone ensemble playing as well as through domestic chamber music. In 1789, Bethlehem already had a chamber orchestra that included pairs of flutes, oboes, trumpets, and horns, in addition to the usual strings; a bassoon was added in 1800 and a contrabass in 1806 (Walters 1918:17). At this time Bethlehem's population did not much exceed thirteen hundred persons including four hundred children (Smaby 1988:86), but trombones, organs, spinets, pianos, guitars, and other instruments were routinely available, and concerts—thirty-six given in 1809 alone—presented American premieres of major recent works of Haydn (Walters 1918:17, 23).

As Bethlehem evolved from a village into a fully integrated urban industrial center (Gollin 1967), this vigorous musical tradition weathered the weakening of sectarian ties to Herrnhut and remained a local preoccupation. The Bethlehem Bach Festival, begun in 1900 under the direction of the distinguished Moravian musician and educator J. Frederick Wolle, underscores the city's German musical heritage; among other innovative programs, the nonsectarian Bethlehem Bach Choir presented, in the Moravian Church building, the first complete American performance of Bach's B-minor Mass, a work utterly foreign to the Moravian liturgy. Today, Moravian archives in Bethlehem and Winston-Salem, North Carolina, hold the most extensive collection of music written and performed in North America before about 1825. Since 1956 the Moravian Music Foundation has sponsored publication, public performance, and recording of this eclectic repertoire.

Despite its rich history, Moravian musical activity in America calls for more study to illuminate its personalities, economics, organization, and in particular its receptivity to outside influences. Fortunately, much evidence exists in carefully preserved commercial account books and related documents dating back to the 1740s. These accounts confirm that the early Moravian settlers were not culturally isolated but maintained close contact not only with Herrnhut, but also with Philadelphia, New York, and trade centers in Germany and England. Through these means, America's Moravians kept in touch with mainstream musical trends much as they followed political and other developments that affected their mission.

Starting in childhood, all congregants learned at least enough music to participate in sung services, but more was expected of those on whom God bestowed talent. Moravian schools, which attracted many non-Moravian pupils of German and British backgrounds, offered keyboard, violin, and singing lessons, and advanced students regularly performed for visitors. Trombone choirs and other bands generally involved more experienced performers. Respectable keyboard and compositional facility was required of schoolmasters, who commonly doubled as church musicians (Duncan 1989). However, individual virtuosity was not a goal, and ensemble playing predominated in keeping with music's participatory functions in the community. Keyboard solos were exceptional and served mainly didactic purposes.

This pious undertaking required large quantities of written music, instructional material, and suitable instruments either locally crafted or brought from distant sources. Once acquired, sheet music had to be copied and bound; instruments needed accessories such as strings and regular maintenance. The commercial accounts, which concern institutions and to a lesser extent individuals, record how often such items and services were obtained, from or for whom, and at what cost.

For example, the tinsmith Abraham Bömper (or Bemper) is cited in Bethlehem's diaconate Ledger B (1744–48) during 1747 in connection with violin strings perhaps bought in New York and destined for the Single Brethren's orchestra. On May 7 (f. 202r) he was credited 6*s*. 4*d*. in New York currency for violin strings and simultaneously debited the same amount (f. 203v), "[To] Abram Bömper [for] Violin Strings . . . Deduct 1/6 per £ to bring it into Pens:a Mony." On September 2 (f. 202r) Bömper was again credited, "[By] . . . 1 1/2 Doz. Fiddle Strings (13*s*. 6*d*.)." On average, therefore, these strings, very likely of double-length plain gut, cost 9*d*. each, a significant sum.

These purchases suggest that local musicians wore out strings at a rate that, if sustained, would have resulted in substantial expenditures. No wonder, then, that on September 17, 1759, the Gemein Conferenz Protocoll in Bethlehem noted, "Saiten vor Violinen werden verlangt. Sonderlich Quinten. Hellegas hat welche zu verkaufen. Es wird gewunscht man könnte welche hier machen." ("Violin strings are needed, especially E strings. Hellegas [Michael Hillegas, proprietor of America's first known music store, in Philadelphia] has some for sale. It is wished someone could make some here." Paul Larson of the Moravian College kindly provided this reference.)

Bömper's supplier may have been the New York merchant Henry van Vleck. Van Vleck, father of the Bethlehem musician Jacob van Vleck, received credit in diaconate Ledger C on December 8, 1752 (f. 192r), of 16*s*. 3*d*. for violin strings. On May 21, 1754, he received £2.5.5 1/2 for "3 doz white skins for organs" (reference from Paul Larson). On August 11, 1748, Ledger B simultaneously credited (f. 236r) and debited (f. 238r) van Vleck's account £8 in New York currency, equivalent to £7.8.– Pennsylvania money, for "a Crate of Viols."

This unexpectedly late reference to viols is not unique. In Ledger B, Samuel Powell received credit on July 28, 1747 (f. 196r), "[By] Society [for Furtherance of the Gospel], for an old Viol on 13th Inst. for Schomoco £1." (Schomoco was an Indian settlement.) Among other things, Powell was a bell founder; Ledger B records payment on August 4, 1747 (f. 204v), from the Society for the Furtherance of the

Gospel, "[To] Saml. Powell for Mettal and Coales to Make a Bell for Gnaden Hütten Wt 15 lb £1.11.–." (Gnadenhütten was another Indian mission.) More intriguingly, on September 3, 1747, Powell sold a violin to Justice of the Peace Henry Antes, possibly for the use of his seven-year-old son, John, who was to become the first known American-born composer of chamber music. Diaconate Ledger B debited the account of Henry Antes thus (f. 153v): "Samuel Powell for a Violin (by His order) for his Son £1.1.–," and simultaneously credited Powell's account (f. 196r), "[By] Hen: Antes for a Violin Which His Son had £1.1.–."

Other kinds of instruments and accessories also figure in early Bethlehem diaconate ledgers. For example, Ledger C shows that on January 13, 1749, Isaac and Thomas Noble split the cost of a flute purchased from Jasper Payne for a total of 18*s*. (ff. 45v, 46v). The Nobles must have been a musical family, for in Ledger B on January 15, 1747, the brothers Isaac and Thomas shared the 1*s*. 6*d*. cost of a half quire "good writing Paper . . . for a Musick Book," and Ledger D records on August 31, 1758 (f. 75r), a 3*s*. charge to James Noble for a "Spinnet Hammer" or tuning wrench.

On April 18, 1762, diaconate Ledger E (1762–1771) debited the nearby farm community of Christiansbrunn, where the Single Brethren had a band, 6*s*. on account of the "Brazier [Matthias Tommerup] for 2. Pipes to the Trumpets" (f. 51v). The same ledger debited Christiansbrunn's account on January 19, 1767 (f. 304v), "To Jonas Paulus Weiss for *R*15 12*g* paid for a Set of Sack Buts (:ein Chor Posaunen:) @ 5*R* pr. Span[ish] Pistole £4.3.8–3/4," and on May 16 (f. 304r), "To Freight of ye Sack Buts 5*s*. 2*d*." Weiss's supplier may have been Johann Gottfried Leydholdt or Leutholdt; the Moravian Historical Society in Nazareth preserves a tenor trombone inscribed "GEMACHT IOHANN. G. LEYDHOLDT IN DRESDEN ANNO 1761" (Mayes 1974: 98-99).

An inventory of supplies and equipment in the Bethabara, North Carolina, congregation house sheds further light on the Moravian instrumentarium. Preserved in the Winston-Salem archives (container G260, folder 1), this list dated August 14, 1766, begins (p. 1) by evaluating the following items under the heading *Zu Liturgischen Gebrauch*:

1 Orgel	15. –.–
1 Pass Geige	–.10.–
1 Violin	–. 5.–
2 Trompeten	–.10.–
2 Wald Hörner mit Krum Bogen und Aufsietze [?]	–.15.–
1 Mettallen Glocklein . . .	–. 5.–

The presence of crooks (*Krummbögen*) for tuning or transposing the horns is noteworthy but the following term is only half legible; Gombosi's reading, meaning "mouthpiece," is adopted here (Gombosi 1977:8).

Under the Bethabara inventory heading *Manuscripta* (pp. 7–8) the following items appear without valuation:

2 Volumina Musicalien vor Flute Travers
Riß und Erklärung vom Principal 8 Fuß
Zeichnung von einem Clavi Cordio

The technical drawings of an organ pipe rank and a clavichord indicate a practical interest in organ- and clavier-making on the part of a community resident who was perhaps inspired by the previously listed organ, which was brought from Bethlehem in 1762.

The American Revolution greatly disrupted Moravian life by imposing more contact with the outside world. The Bagge papers in the Winston-Salem archives include an urgent request dated February 15, 1779, from one Jo. Williams to the shopkeeper Traugott Bagge (container P602, folder 6, letter 65) asking, "If you have any brass headed nails such as wou'd Do for Drum-making pray let me have 500. & Charge them, let the price be as it will. you[r] mony shall be paid on sight." (Military drums were commonly decorated with geometric patterns of roughly twenty to one hundred brass nails.) During this period new instruments were difficult to obtain and old ones were moved from place to place as needed. On October 30, 1779, accounts of the boys' school at Nazareth Hall, preserved at Old Salem (inventory numbers 1042–42 and 1042–43), debit the Unitaets Administration £20 "für alte Orgel" (*Tage-Buch B*, 282) and also record "H. C. Schweiniz Dr. an . . . Meublen empfing von Ren[atu]s Lembke . . . für ein altes Clavier, in Gold £3.10.– *NB*. wurd am 19 Aug. 1780 bez[ahlt]" (279).

After the Revolution, Moravians resumed buying instruments, music, and related merchandise from Philadelphia and beyond. Buyers naturally preferred to deal through agents who spoke their language and in whom family and religious ties engendered trust. Prominent among Philadelphia's Moravian merchants was the firm of Boller & Jordan. John Jordan, who succeeded to Godfrey Haga's business on Third Street near Race Street in 1793, was an officer of Philadelphia's Moravian church, as were several men of the Boller family. Frederick, John, and Jacob Boller served the church successively as organists after 1785 (Sandwick 1985; Ritter 1857).

The Bethlehem general store's letter book (Bethlehem Moravian Archives) holds transcripts of purchase orders including one (8) dated February 28, 1797, from the storekeeper Johann Christian Reich to the important Moravian mercantile firm of Abraham Dürninger & Company in Herrnhut, covering freight and charges of 18 Reichthalers 16 groschen for a fortepiano shipped from Altona, near Hamburg; another entry refers to shipping a fortepiano together with two chests. Dürninger & Co. transacted considerable business with non-Moravians and probably obtained pianos from Saxon builders outside the Moravian orbit.

Salem's diaconate Ledger A for 1772–1790 also records occasional imports from Germany, and regular purchases from Bethlehem (Winston-Salem Moravian Archives). The musical instrument account (p. 140) shows a debit on April 30, 1785, "To Salem and Bethabara store, for Freight & Expences for a Chest to Altona & States Duty £5.17.–" and "To Administration paid to Geo. Weber in Herrnhuth £36.–.–". One year later the account was debited £11 for payment "in full" to Weber, and credited on March 12, "By Cash received from Salem & Bethabara £47.2.–" and "By Jacob van Vleck for his Share for Sundry Musical Instruments £11.14.10."

On August 26, 1786, the instrument account was debited "To Cash paid for Freight from Charleston &ca . . . £5.17.10." After a two-year hiatus, on April 30, 1789, the account was debited "To Administration, paid for Musicals [i.e., *Musicalien*] to J. B. Gebhard £17.10.6," followed by an additional £1.9.3 debit "for a Difference, caused by the Remittance of the Above." Two more debits followed exactly one year later: "To Journey Expences, paid for 24 G Fidle Strings 6*s*." and "To Administration for Fiddle Strings from Europe £5.8.9." Credits dated February 27 and April 30, 1790, balance the account, which totaled a healthy £83.11.4 over the preceding five years, most of it flowing out of Salem.

The music account in the Salem diaconate's Ledger B (1790–97) chiefly includes charges for music copying and instrument repairs, balanced by income from collections taken among Salem's residents. Charges (p. 59) include £2.10.– on July 14, 1790, for a music cupboard; 17*s*. on April 30, 1791, "for mending Instruments"; 5*s*. 4*d*. "paid to Fr. Peter, for Musicalien" on April 30, 1792, (the noteworthy composer Johann Friedrich Peter was Salem's former music master, now living in Bethlehem); and 10*s*. to Simon Peter in February 1793 "for writing Notes." "Sundry Musical Copies from Bethlehem" were purchased for £4.5.4 on April 30, 1794; Ann Green received £2.5.11 for the same purpose on July 9, 1794; and a further 5*s*. 10*d*. bought music from Bethlehem on January 31, 1795. On April 30, 1795, the account was debited 14*s*. "for repairing 2 Fiddle Sticks." On September 16, 1795, a bass was bought for £8, unspecified fiddle strings for £2.8.–, and "Notes &ca" for

£1.19.4. On February 18, 1796, 6*s*. went for writing paper and "Glueing 2 Bass's." Finally, on April 30, 1797, Gottlieb Schober received £1.17.4 "paid for Fiddle Strings," and £4.8.– was debited "To Administration, paid to Fr. Peter in Bethlm for 4 Choral Books for the Sackbuts."

Copying music was something of a Moravian cottage industry. An account book dated 1795 to 1806 from the Moravian general store in Nazareth (in the library of Old Salem, Inc., deposited at the Museum of Early Southern Decorative Arts, Winston-Salem) contains many entries for music copying and binding as well as for music purchases and lessons paid for through the store. This account records purchases of small and large music books—probably staff-lined copybooks, supplied by the bookbinder Joseph Oerter—and orders such as the following: February 13, 1798: "To cash, paid [David Moritz] Michael for [Joseph] Schweishaupt for copying Clavier Auszug vom Tod Abels" [by Johann Heinrich Rolle], at a price of 1*s*. 6*d*. per sheet not counting the cost of paper; March 31, 1798: "To Joseph Schweishaupt for writing Music," at 1*s*. 4*d*. per sheet; January 30, 1799: "To Jacob Van Vleck, for copying notes, the 146 Psalm"; July 2, 1803: "To Cash, paid Maria Weber, für copieren der Musik: Maria und Johannes" [by J. A. P. Schulz]; April 10, 1806: "To Cash, paid [J. F.] Peter for copying sundry pieces of Music"; and so on. Other entries refer either to copying or outright purchases of music including *sinfonien* of Graff, Gyrowetz, Haydn, H. [Johann Heinrich?] Miller, Mozart, Pleyel, Rosetti; overtures of Mozart; quartets of Haydn and Pleyel; sonatas of Nicolai and Pleyel; songs of C. R. Reichel and Schulz; Handel's *Messiah*; Haydn's *Stabat Mater*; November 11, 1796: "By Cash, received from [Nicholas] Höber for [Christian] Gregor's Choral-Buch £1"; October 25, 1797: "To Cash paid Catherine Levering for Grauns Tod Jesu £1.2.6 . . . 3 Violoncell Concertos von [Jean Balthasar] Trickler £–.15.– [and] 2 Quintettos von [Andreas] Lidel 11*s*. 3*d*."; May 8, 1801: "To D. M. Michael for . . . Befreyung Israel von Rolle, Lazarus [also by Rolle], Auferstehung und Himmelfahrt [C. P. E. Bach], Heilig [also C. P. E. Bach], 23. Psalm von [Justin Heinrich] Knecht" [altogether £6.19.–]; July 25, 1803: "To Joh. G. Cunow, for Music, sent by C. Fr. Reichel per Ordre on H. H. Zäslein £1.5.8"; April 1, 1804: "To Cash, paid [Johann Friedrich] Frueauff for Music viz Dawn of Glory 10*s*. 6*d*. [and] Dies Irae 7*s*. 6*d*." [both by Latrobe]; July 20, 1805: "To Boller & Jordan, pr Order of Geo. Willich to them for Musicalien [i.e., printed music] . . . £2.18.11"; September 14, 1805: "To Lewis West in Old England, for 3 Copies of Six easy Airs by [Christian Ignatius] Latrobe . . . £1.17.6" [probably Rev. Lewis West of Brockweir; see Grider 1873:11]; and so on. Payments recorded June 30, 1800, to Joseph Oerter for binding Johann Ernst Rembt's *Fugetten* and Johann Gottfried Vierling's *Orgel*

Stücke are especially interesting because of the paucity of Moravian references to solo organ music.

As a whole, this repertoire, mostly published around 1780 or later, shows the Moravians keeping pace with musical fashions abroad. Much of this music was doubtless destined for the boarding schools (including the new Girls' Seminary built in Bethlehem in 1790, mainly to educate outsiders' daughters), but as the congregation's economy deteriorated and parents, whose personal income was rising, assumed a larger role in rearing their own children, private homes accounted for a growing proportion of music and instrument purchases. Females, who increasingly outnumbered males in Bethlehem after 1764 (and by nearly two to one after 1784; Smaby 1988:55), may have become the main practitioners of domestic music in this period; many claviers were destined for their use.

Two purchases deserve special mention: on September 30, 1795, "To a Forte piano . . . made by Trute and Wiedberg in Philadelphia 110 doll[ars] £41.5.–"; and on November 28, 1799, "To Fr. Früauff, for a Clavecin royale £40.–." The short-lived partnership of Trute and Wiedberg, at 25 Filbert Street in Philadelphia, is remembered today chiefly for having made the only extant eighteenth-century Philadelphia harpsichord, a privately owned two-manual instrument dated 1794. Little is known about Wiedberg, but his partner Charles Trute had been making pianos and harpsichords in London since the 1760s. Trute emigrated about 1790 and not long after 1795 he moved with Wiedberg from Philadelphia to Wilmington, Delaware; there Wiedberg died and Trute ended his days as an innkeeper.

Früauff, a prominent minister, educator, and administrator, as well as organist and composer, might have brought the clavecin royale (a novel type of square piano or *Tafelclavier*) with him from Germany in 1788 and later decided to sell it. He was involved in another similar transaction: on May 1, 1804, the Nazareth store account records, "To Cash, paid J. F. Frueauff for a Forte Piano, in part £16.17.6" and "To Boller & Jordan as per order payable to J. F. Früauff for a ballance in full for the F. Piano £26.5.–."

The impressive diversity and frequency of music-related commerce in Nazareth, a community of only a few hundred inhabitants near Bethlehem, demonstrates the close integration of music and daily life. In addition to Johann Friedrich Peter (who brought a large collection of music manuscripts from Germany in 1770) and the organ builder David Tannenberg, other persons named in Nazareth's store accounts had important musical responsibilities in the community. Reverend Jacob van Vleck, a composer, performer, music teacher, and administrator, played the organ when George Washington visited Bethlehem on July 25, 1782. In 1788 van Vleck was involved in planning a new organ for Bethlehem's Moravian church. The organist, violinist, and watchmaker Johann Georg Weiss succeeded Johann Christian Till as music teacher at the Boys' School in Bethlehem and helped John Krauss tune an organ in 1801. Joseph Schweishaupt, organist and director of the Aufseher Collegium in Bethlehem, gave keyboard lessons at the Nazareth boys' school, while David Moritz Michael, a noteworthy composer, versatile instrumentalist, and also leader of the Bethlehem collegium, taught violin and singing at the boys' school. (Michael eventually returned to his native Germany and died in Neuwied; see Grider 1873:6, 8, 10; David 1942:33 ff.; McCorkle 1956:493.)

Among music-related entries, general store accounts mainly detail purchases of strings for bowed and keyboard instruments, which were heavily used under rugged circumstances. Strings figure in the Salem diaconate's account with Traugott Bagge for the Salem store (Winston-Salem Moravian archives, container S740, folder 4): for example, June 6, 1798, "1 Base fidlestring 1*s*."; July 5, 1798, "To 3 yds Catgut . . . 10*s*."; October 2, 1799, "fidle Strings 4*s*." Salem's deacons noted on January 12, 1802, "We are running short of violin strings, and Br. Schober was asked to order more from Br. Friedrich Peter in Bethlehem . . ." (Fries 1943: 2705–2706). Makers as well as players required strings: the 1804 inventory of David Tannenberg's estate at Lititz lists 33 pounds of brass and iron wire as well as rolls of harpsichord and clavichord strings (Brunner 1990:221), and the diary of the organ builder John Krauss records purchases of wire between 1796 and 1803, some of it bought in Philadelphia (Brunner 1990: 223–226).

To meet demand, Nazareth and Bethlehem general stores stocked wire and catgut strings in considerable variety. Interestingly, inventories and store accounts specify wire for spinets, clavichords, and harpsichords but not for pianos, although all these instruments used the same kinds of wire. The Nazareth store charged 7*s*. 6*d*. for two dozen spinet wires, or 3–3/4*d*. each (December 31, 1795), and 6*d*. for one roll of spinet wire (December 31, 1796). Annual inventories of the Bethlehem store list in increasing detail large quantities of gut strings and music wire including some of silver for machine-wound bass strings. Nominally, strings were stocked only for violins and cellos (then often called basses), but some of these same strings could also have been used on violas, double basses, harps, and certain other instruments.

The Bethlehem store inventory of May 31, 1761, lists (p. 4) only £3 worth of unspecified violin strings. The inventory of April 24, 1762, reports (p. 15):

2 Violin Basses	1/2	–.2.4
145 Do. Strings	/7	4.4.7

The March 31, 1766, inventory lists (p. 18):

88 Fidel Strings	. . .	1.10.–
3 Bass Do.		–.3 .–

and on p. 20, two dozen Jew's harps worth 7*s*. 3*d*. (on February 28, 1785, three dozen Jew's harps worth 6*s*. were on hand). Now, "bass" strings cost 1*s*. each, while single violin strings average a little over 4*d*., a significant drop since 1762.

The inventory of February 9–28, 1791, quantifies much brass and iron wire by weight, one stone equaling ten pounds. Brass clavichord strings, counted by the dozen, are gauged by a normal ascending German system, probably that of Nuremberg or Berlin. The presence of so many gauges of brass clavichord wire indicates that some instruments may have been entirely brass-strung, as occurred in Germany into the nineteenth century. At 7 1/2 *d*., 12*d*., and 15*d*. each, violin strings have risen in value:

8 doz. tin'd Jews Harps	1/6	–.12.– [p. 44]
5 stone Iron Wire No 1, 2 & 5	10/	2.10.–
3 do. 9, 10, 11	11/	1.13.9
10 do. 15, 16, 17, 18	12/6	6. 5.– [p. 48]
12–1/4 lb. thick brass Wire		
7–3/4 middling Do. }31-1/4 lb.	3/	5.17.2
11–1/4 fine sieve Do.		
. . .		
60 doz. brass Clavicord Strings fm No 0-7	@ 2/	6.–.–
20 doz. steel Do.	@ 2/	2.–.– [p. 50]
6–1/2 dz. 1st Violin Strings	7/6	2. 8.9
2–1/6 dz. 2nd & 3rd Do.	12/	1. 6.–
7 p[ieces] silver Bases	dz 15/	–. 8.9 [p. 53]

Instruments other than Jew's harps, which were regarded more or less as toys, and accessories such as cane for woodwind reeds do not appear in these inventories. Music books and scores, too, seem not to have been stocked by the general stores, but were specially ordered. Many receipts for music and instruments bought for institutional use survive in Moravian church archives, but private purchases were seldom officially recorded; therefore, commercial accounts like those discussed here offer possibly unique clues about the extent and nature of domestic musical activity.

The Moravians in America were not only consumers but also providers of music merchandise to buyers outside their fold. The pioneering contributions to American musical life of the organ builders John Clemm and David Tannenberg have been well documented (Brunner 1990) and the music of J. F. Peter and his contemporaries is becoming widely appreciated. The commercial accounts discussed here may shed further light on their influence, but seem to be most valuable in providing details of musical activity within the community. Transcription and analysis of these data will be a lengthy process, but from it should emerge a more comprehensive view of Moravian musical life.

This essay is a revision of the author's "Music-Related Commerce in Some Moravian Accounts," in *"Pleasing for Our Use": David Tannenberg and the Organs of the Moravians* (Bethlehem, PA: Lehigh University Press and Associated University Presses, 2000), pp. 79–115. The study was funded in part by a grant from the National Antique and Art Dealers Association of America and the Antique and Art Dealers League of America Travel Fund administered by The Metropolitan Museum of Art, and by a grant from the National Endowment for the Humanities.

Bibliography

Brunner, Raymond J. *"That Ingenious Business": Pennsylvania German Organ* Builders. Birdsboro, PA: Pennsylvania German Society, 1990.

David, Hans T. "Musical Life in the Pennsylvania Settlements of the *Unitas Fratrum.*" *Transactions of the Moravian Historical Society* 13, 1942. (Reprinted as *Moravian Music Foundation Publications* no. 6, 1959.)

Duncan, Timothy Paul. "The Role of the Organ in Moravian Sacred Music between 1740–1840." D.M.A. dissertation, University of North Carolina at Greensboro, 1989.

Fries, Adelaide L. *Records of the Moravians in North Carolina*. Raleigh: State Department of Archives and History, vol. VI, 1943.

Gollin, Gillian Lindt. *Moravians in Two Worlds: A Study of Changing Communities*. New York and London: Columbia University Press, 1967.

Gombosi, Marilyn. *A Day of Solemn Thanksgiving*. Chapel Hill: University of North Carolina Press, 1977.

Grider, Rufus A. *Historical Notes on Music in Bethlehem, Pennsylvania. From 1741 to 1871*. Philadelphia: John L. Pile for J. Hill Martin, 1873. (Reprinted as *Moravian Music Foundation Publications* no. 4, 1957.)

McCorkle, Donald M. "The *Collegium Musicum Salem*: Its Music, Musicians and Importance." *North Carolina Historical Review* xxxiii/4, 1956. (Reprinted as *Moravian Music Foundation Publications* no. 3, 1956.)

Mayes, Curtis S. "A Descriptive Catalogue of Historic Percussion, Wind, and Stringed Instruments in Three Pennsylvania Museums." M. M. thesis, Florida State University, 1974.

Ritter, Abraham. *History of the Moravian Church in Philadelphia from Its Foundation in 1742 to the Present Time.* Philadelphia: Hayes & Zell, 1857.

Sandwick, Charles M., Sr. *Jacobsburg: A Pennsylvania Community and Its People.* Jacobsburg, PA: Jacobsburg Historical Society, vol. 1., 1985.

Smaby, Beverly Prior. *The Transformation of Moravian Bethlehem from Communal Mission to Family Economy*. Philadelphia: University of Pennsylvania Press, 1988.

Walters, Raymond. *The Bethlehem Bach Choir: An Historical and Interpretive Sketch*. 1918. (Reprint. New York: AMS Press, 1971.)

II

Religion

5

LUTHERAN HYMNODY AND NETWORKS IN THE EIGHTEENTH CENTURY

A. Gregg Roeber

Historians of Lutheran hymnody in North America have noted for years the influence of Philadelphia and the Delaware River Valley upon the musical tastes of the first Swedish, Dutch, and German speakers in North America (Terry 1981). Until recently, however, few have realized that competitive networks of trade and communication, one dominated by clerics and teachers linked to German Pietism, the other by secular traders and entrepreneurs, both contributed to the curious mix of regional hymn traditions that made their way to North America. Furthermore, such networks built upon a preference among Lutherans in British North America for hymn texts and tunes that were not contemporaneous, but instead drew upon sixteenth- and seventeenth-century pieces. Although the major outlines for the sources of Lutheran hymnody are known to most readers, it seems best to review first what those sources were before turning to the issue of how hymnody and the communications networks intersected to create a peculiarly North American tradition for Lutherans by the 1790s.

Because the Marburg Hymnal (*Marburger Gesangbuch*)—first published in 1549 with its eighty hymns—was well-known throughout the Holy Roman Empire, one can understand why the greatly expanded version of 1747, with 615 hymns and paraphrases of the Psalms, became the hymnal of choice to be printed in 1757 by the very anti-Lutheran Dunkard printer, Christopher Saur, of Germantown, Pennsylvania. Heinrich Melchior Mühlenberg, the pastor called by three Pennsylvania congregations to serve them, arrived after his training in Halle and brief labor in Lausitz in 1742. He set to work compiling what emerged in 1748 as the order of worship, or *Agenda*, which explicitly names the Marburg hymnal as the source from which the pastor should select hymns "familiar to the whole congregation" (Schalk 1981; *Documentary History* 1898:14).

These seemingly innocuous words tell one a great deal about why the hymnal had achieved such broad popularity. Lutheran hymnody, both in musical style and in the texts the music conveyed, had, since the Reformation, come from the *Volkslied* tradition. Hymns were sung in unison by the congregation, unaccompanied, varying only slightly from simpler plainsong and the Latin responses, both of which still made up a considerable portion of the Lutheran liturgy well into the eighteenth century. The choir was left to do the more complex parts of both plainsong and the occasionally difficult vernacular chorales. During the Counter Reformation and the Thirty Years War, Lutheran hymnody tended to adopt themes reflecting these times of pestilence, warfare, and devastation. Many of the hymns dating from these times pursued lines of devotion to the sufferings of Christ. Even before the end of the seventeenth century, hymns from these earlier periods already tended toward the personal identification of the believer with the merits and sufferings of the Savior, although broader themes of Lutheran theology were never completely submerged. The tradition of hymn-singing extended beyond the congregation, especially cultivated by pastors' families, and in some regions, to actual singing schools for children of the parish (Söhninge 1984).

If the Marburg Hymnal reflected the compiled experiences of German speakers from throughout the Empire, the second type of major collections of hymnody brought to North America more accurately conveyed the regional flavor of Lutheran tastes in hymns. Of these collections, three in particular were of lasting significance: the so-called Halle Hymnal (Johann Anastasius Freylinghausen's *Geistreiches Gesangbuch*), the Wernigerode Hymnal (*Wernigerödisches Gesangbuch*), and the Württemberg collection (*Geistliche Erquickungs-Stunden*). Of these three, the first two reflected the theology of the clerics and teachers who came to North America, most of them from north and central Germany, and most educated at the Prussian pietist center at Halle. Most pastors sent to America were also ordained at the nearby pietist town of Wernigerode, technically a self-governing principality, but in actuality, after mediatization by Prussia in 1715, very much under Prussian political and religious influence. The last-named hymnal, by contrast, reflected the actual region from which most immigrants to British North America, that is, congregational members, came—the German southwest, where the Duchy of Württemberg stood as a bastion of Lutheranism surrounded by powerful Catholic and Reformed states and cities (Vann 1984).

The Prussian pietist center at Halle had been tied since 1701 to Dr. Thomas Bray's Society for Promoting Christian Knowledge (SPCK). August Hermann Francke had been elected to corresponding membership in the Society, and the Halle-educated lay preacher Wilhelm August Böhme functioned as Lutheran court chaplain to the prince consort, George of Denmark. Both the SPCK and Halle intended that New York, the destination of a first group of Württembergers and Kraichgau emigrants in 1711, should emerge as the center for a press, bookstore, and clearinghouse for a Lutheran-Anglican cooperative effort to further the growth of orthodox Protestantism in the colonies. Instead, Pennsylvania replaced New York, not in small part because the emigrants from the German southwest—the Palatinate, Ulm, Baden, and Alsace, in addition to those already named—prized above all else the absence of militia service, low or nonexistent taxes, and no official religious establishment, to say nothing of the proprietary colony's unusually pacific relations with Native Americans (Roeber 1991).

Despite contrary migration and demographic patterns, hopes for New York's future role among European and British authorities died hard. Failing to win German speakers' enthusiasm for the Book of Common Prayer in translation in the 1710s, British sponsorship for Johann Christian Jacobi's 1722 edition of the *Psalmodia Germanica* met with little success. Yet, of genuine significance, one notes the extraordinarily large number of hymns in this collection by composers from between one-half to a full century earlier. Indeed, Jacobi incorporated out of the sixty-two hymns and fifteen chorales eight by Paulus Gerhardt and eleven by Luther himself as opposed to a comparative few by the English dissenter Isaac Watts. As late as 1756 another version of this book was published by pastor Albert Weygand, pastor of Trinity Lutheran Church along with the trustees of King's College. Weygand also translated Luther's *Small Catechism* into English. But Trinity by the 1740s had been abandoned by late-arriving Lutherans who demanded German-language services, turning their backs on a Lutheran service in Dutch that had been in use since the days of New Netherland. The Württembergers insisted on building a brewery and a church next to it and procured their service—and hymns—in German. Weygand, born in Frankfurt am Main and educated at Halle, presided over a rump congregation that was in danger of collapse for lack of financial support. German speakers had signaled the lesson many a pastor has learned to his sorrow since: that it does not pay to ignore congregational tastes in hymns or language (Horn 1976; Terry 1981:86–87; Glatfelter 1981:162–163).

After the New York experience, the more likely network for the distribution of Lutheran hymnody might have evolved on the Savannah River in Georgia. For, in the 1730s, it was here that Halle planted its most famous experimental colony, Ebenezer, composed at first of exiled Salzburgers and Palatine servants. The former maidservants and unpropertied day workers from Salzburg who comprised the early congregation were guided by the Halle-trained pastors Johann Martin Boltzius and Israel Gotthilf Gronau. In keeping with the objectives Halle had in mind for the settlement, all aspects of the economic, spiritual, and social-geographical topography of the community remained securely in the pastors' hands. This quasi-monastic environment provided a laboratory in which pietist ideals of reconciling true belief with genuine social practice would be worked out, with a combination orphanage-old people's home-pharmacy at the center, modeled on the Francke Foundations' own nucleus of buildings and activities at Halle (Urlsperger 1972[1739]: VI; Jones 1984, 1992).

Lutheran hymnody was also intended to help transform these oppressed and uneducated former closet Lutherans into archetypal Lutheran pietists. Boltzius revealed in his journals the difficulties he had suppressing quasi-Catholic baptismal ceremonies and festivities, especially naming patterns and celebrations that went along with the baptisms. Since the Salzburgers had been forced to learn the catechism and hymns that they knew in secret, their store of hymn favorites was presumably small, explaining why Gronau recorded instructing his charges in singing without detailing which hymns were sung. Boltzius was particularly interested in music, having helped to found the *Collegium Musicum* at Halle, and not surprisingly, he used hymnody to inculcate his vision of piety among his charges. His journals, kept by Boltzius as by all of Halle's foreign workers by order of the Foundations as a record of activities, note hymns sung during each year. The hymn collections used were both the Wernigerode Hymnal and Johann Anastasius Freylinghausen's *Geistreiches Gesangbuch*, which with its supplements of 1704 and 1711 by 1741 contained 597 melodies and 1,581 hymns. Of some twenty-seven hymns sung in 1739 that Boltzius noted, the most—eight—were compositions by the ultra-orthodox confessional Lutheran, Paulus Gerhardt. Only four can be attributed to Freylinghausen or an eighteenth-century "pietist" author (Urlsperger 1972:VI, Appendix 1; VII, 9).

This same pattern repeated itself in Pennsylvania. By 1748, six years after Mühlenberg arrived, the Marburg Hymnal was chosen as the basis for hymnody in this mission field, although both the Halle and the Wernigerode hymnals were important sources as well. And, once again, from the lists of hymns that Mühlenberg made in his journals—for instance between 1764 and 1768—out of some sixty hymn titles, thirty date from before 1700 and most from before 1648. Again, Paulus Gerhardt leads the list as the favorite hymn composer, with Luther and other representatives of the period of Lutheran confessional orthodoxy. Whatever quarrels separated Halle from the orthodox Lutheran universities at Leipzig and Wittenberg, one should remember that Halle's instructions to its pastors in North America reiterated time and again that they were to remain unswervingly devoted to the *Unaltered Augsburg Confession*. The choice of Gerhardt, the man forced out of the prestigious pastorate at St. Nicholas's Church in Berlin in 1666 for his refusal to alter traditional Lutheran ceremonies at baptisms as ordered by the Elector, suggests how seriously this command was taken (Muhlenberg 1942–1958 [I]: 85, 193, 297; [II]: 243, 441–442).

Before turning to the issue of networks and the distribution of Lutheran hymnody, it would seem useful to explain exactly why Gerhardt was so popular among the pietists of north-central German states, and why, therefore, his influence among transplanted Lutherans in North America came to be so important. First, Gerhardt's popularity stemmed in the Empire itself from the quality of his poetry and the depth of his spirituality that was recognized by his own congregants in Berlin, and not because of his adoption by the politically or ecclesiastically powerful. Gerhardt continued the Reformation practice of composing powerful texts rooted in biblical themes that also drew upon observations of nature and daily life. His perennially popular composition, "Nun ruhen alle Wälder," managed to combine his own inclinations toward a mystical spirituality with a deep love of the natural world and simple, daily routines and observations. After Gerhardt's death in 1676, his work was collected and issued in three editions of 1707, 1717, and 1723. A biography followed in 1723, and a history of pietists, "the born-again" in Saxony in 1726, also noted Gerhardt's work and theology, which pietists claimed—erroneously, perhaps—matched their own (Fechner 1982; Reinitzer 1986).

Whatever else came to characterize Lutheran hymn-singing and liturgical piety in North America, one aspect would have struck the outside observer: whereas German Moravian hymnody heard in those congregations was dominated by contemporary eighteenth-century tunes and composers, Lutheran hymns of choice sung in congregational worship continued to reflect the theology and style of the sixteenth and seventeenth centuries (Ingram 1982; David 1959; Johanson 1980).

In no small part, Halle's own determination to preserve Lutheran identity in the midst of a riot of radical pietist options represented by Schwenkfelders, Dunkers, Dutch Labadists, and English dissenters seems best to explain this pattern. Perhaps, too, the Halle fathers, stung by the charges issuing from Leipzig that the pietist center had compromised on orthodox doctrine, evinced a determination to disprove critics in the city that hired, and then continually fought with, Johann Sebastian Bach over his orthodox, but emotionally gripping compositions (Petzoldt 1984).

Moreover, the choice of older, orthodox hymns stemmed from both pastoral preference and the Halle fathers' own awareness of congregational enthusiasm for familiar hymns, an awareness based on their own travels in the Empire. They rightly concluded that such choices could be used to encourage transcendence of many local and regional bounds. Halle's network of distribution and its representatives and factors had to compete, however, with more secular traders who shared few, if any, of the pietist "hopes for better times," times that would see a closer integration of belief and behavior. Instead, these traders were interested mainly in profits, and their connections depended heavily on the region from which they or their clients originated, usually the German southwest territories. The Francke Foundations had established a bookseller from Silesia, Daniel Weisiger, in Philadelphia as early as 1735 who distributed its pamphlets and books. But Halle enjoyed no monopoly on the trade in hymnals or the transfer of Lutheran hymnody. The earliest settlers who arrived between 1727—the date of the first substantial migration through Philadelphia—and 1776 came from the German southwest where inventories of estate reveal a Wernigerode. Private devotions in the German southwest centered not around the classic works of Johann Arndt, Philipp Jakob Spener, August Hermann Francke, or Gottfried Arnold, the great pietist writers of north and central German states. Rather, the prayer books of Johann Starck and Johannes Habermann, the sermons of the Eßlingen preacher Immanuel Gottlieb Brastberger, and the Württemberg hymnal provided spiritual solace not only for Württembergers but Kraichgauers and Palatine Lutherans as well. Even in the poorest homes, among those whose property never exceeded valuation at 100 gulden—worth perhaps four cows in current market value—at least four books could be found, the catechism, and invariably Starck, Habermann, and the hymnal. For weavers and day workers, the average was double this number; for propertied smallholders, even larger (Roeber 1993; Medick 1992). In Philadelphia proper, for instance, a late-arriving Württemberger established a household conventicle reminiscent of similar small pietist cells in the Empire. Theodorus Memminger was related through his wife to the great Württemberg chiliast pietist Johann Albrecht Bengel. And, it would appear that what these people sang in conventicle meetings and what they preferred to sing at funerals and other highly charged emotional events might have reflected a different theological and hymnodic tradition (Roeber 1993).

These emigrants to North America either brought copies of their own hymnals with them or relied on a number of traders and dealers in books and other goods who established themselves in centers like Philadelphia or Lancaster. Andreas Geyer, a bookbinder in Second Street, provided opportunity for purchase of hymnals, as did Christoph Lochner, formerly of Basel. Francis Hasenclever, a trader from Silesia, traveled often to London and the continent. Precisely how various Lutheran hymnal collections arrived in Philadelphia and more remote outposts remains somewhat of a mystery. One of the later arrivals at St. Michael's Lutheran Church in Philadelphia, the Badener Ernst Ludwig Baisch, may be representative of the process.

Baisch arrived in the colonies as a youth with his family in the 1750s. He became a well-known trader and traveler who for years plied the routes between Pennsylvania and the river valleys of the German southwest. His primary business seems to have been that of acting as designated attorney who acted to recover inheritances of emigrants now in the colonies. Centering his activities at Pforzheim, Baisch appeared in court cases in Württemberg, the Palatinate, the Kraichgau, and Ulm. In 1774, he undertook to provide a new edition of the Marburg Hymnal. No evidence suggests that Baisch himself had a hand in compiling a new edition. Rather, he must have arranged to obtain a printing in Germany and designated himself as sole distributor, largely from entrepreneurial motives (LCP; HSP; Wolf 1972; Häberlein 1991:120–126; Roeber 1993; Roeber 2000).

Most of these entrepreneurs naturally frequented the annual book fair at Frankfurt am Main as well as collecting hymnals from other regional centers like Basel, Stuttgart, or Heidelberg. By contrast, Halle relied on the annual fair at Leipzig, although the Francke Foundations hired a factor to represent its interest in Frankfurt and advertised in the imperial newspaper. The distribution of hymnals and pamphlets to North America, however, followed the route down the Elbe to Hamburg-Altona, and thence to Philadelphia, or in the case of Ebenezer, to Charleston or Savannah, where the packed chests were unloaded and taken overland or by smaller boats to the Salzburger settlement.

The competition for control of the type of hymnody that was to be sung, and the economic competition for control of its distribution could pit Halle's interests against those of other, regional suppliers. One of the most confrontational of the clergy in North America was the Halle-born and -educated pastor Johann Friedrich Handschuh. Arriving in America in 1748, Handschuh immediately got himself into difficulties in Lancaster where he discovered a large number of recently arrived Swabians who between 1748 and 1753 came to comprise perhaps the largest percentage of German immigrants to North America. At a funeral, these Württembergers requested that the hymn "Ich habe Lust zu scheiden" be sung. Handschuh refused, saying, "It cannot and shall not be done, for it is only a Swabian song." Other favorites, also mostly on the theme of death, such as "Ich hab einen guten Kampf gekämpft," reflected these Swabian pietist preferences. Removing to Germantown, Handschuh repeated his misguided attempt to dictate hymn tastes. When he was appointed to the shared pastorate of St. Michael's congregation in Philadelphia in 1757, his activities there almost destroyed the parish. Mühlenberg finally suggested to Halle that perhaps Handschuh ought to return to Germany. The obstreperous Hallenser attacked not only Württemberg pietists, but British Presbyterian evangelicals as well. To Gilbert Tennant, Handschuh remarked that "the whole English people lacked discretion and charity. . . . He believed that there was not a single truly pardoned and converted soul among them." Handschuh saved Mühlenberg further embarrassment by gracefully dying in October of 1764 (Muhlenberg 1942–1958 [I]: 437).

The records of German Lutheran congregational life in North America occasionally hint that the married women may have played an important role in forging the hymnodic traditions within Lutheranism in America. Certainly Swabian women who demanded their own traditional hymns and preferred that a pastor speak in a dialect similar to their own were among those who confronted pastors like Handschuh. This fact is reflected in the advertisement of Andreas Geyer, one of the bookbinders who advertised his wares in the Philadelphia newspapers. Geyer noted particularly his editions of the Württemberg prayer books by Habermann and Starck. But he also pointed out that he could provide a copy of Albertus Magnus's *Treatise on Wives and the Births of Children*. Mühlenberg noted in his journals that one of his congregants, a woman, requested that he announce from the pulpit her loss of the Württemberg hymnal, a request he complied with. These all-too-brief hints suggest, however, why the nature of hymnody changed once the Revolution destroyed the original networks of trade and communication between 1776 and 1783 and forced German Lutherans in North America to draw upon diverse backgrounds and tastes as they compiled the first American editions of hymnbooks.

Even before the Revolution disrupted networks, Halle's contributions to the mission fields in Pennsylvania and Georgia were in decline by the 1760s. The Revolution disrupted personal and family connections too, and the stream of immigrants ceased almost entirely until after the Peace of Paris, reviving between 1790 and 1817 to about a thousand persons per year arriving from German-speaking Europe (Grabbe 1988). Family connections that had brought hymns and prayer books also suffered accordingly. The publication of the first post-Revolutionary Lutheran hymnals in 1786 and 1795 in Philadelphia and New York genuinely reflected the dawn of a new era. Both in terms of liturgical style and in the choice of hymnody, the disruption of older networks caused by the Revolution portended important consequences for Lutheran theology and piety in the new republic.

In 1748 as Mühlenberg attempted to compile a liturgy for the German speakers from all over the Holy Roman Empire now in North America, he found himself faced with almost impossible differences in taste. As he complained, some of his choices of what was to be said or sung appeared Calvinist and "low church" to some; others were offended by "popish" rituals or chanting. The 1748 *Agenda*, modeled on the Savoy Chapel liturgy of London, was probably never experienced by most Lutherans outside of St. Michael's in Philadelphia. The use of chorales and hymns Mühlenberg had envisioned and which he had personally experienced in

Dresden and Leipzig could be used at St. Michael's because the parish school boasted over a hundred students and had a superb organ that was constructed at Heilbronn and shipped to Philadelphia. Its quality made the renowned David Tannenberg, the Moravian organ builder from Lititz, Pennsylvania, bemoan its deterioration in 1770 when he was asked to repair it. A well-thumbed copy of the *Agenda*—which was never printed but hand-copied and used by each clergyman of the Ministerium of Pennsylvania—survives at the Gettysburg Seminary Archives today. The document reveals that the liturgy was never used in its entirety. A truncated version of invocation, reading, sermon, and concluding prayers typified much worship. In such a context, one should also ask how rigorously the suggestions for hymns were followed that also appear in the original *Agenda*. The opening hymn to the Holy Spirit seems in fact to have been used. The English translations of that hymn appeared in the New York *Psalmodia Germanica* as well as the paraphrase of the "Gloria in excelsis" and the recommended hymn of the day, the beloved composition by Benjamin Schmolck, "Liebster Jesus wir sind hier" ("Holy Jesus, We Are Here"). Again, of some significance, Schmolck was a seventeenth-century representative of orthodoxy, and not a pietist, perhaps reflecting still the respect for older tradition that seems to have characterized Lutheran preferences for hymns in the North American setting (*Documentary History* 1898; Wolf 1977; Schalk 1981).

Halle's pietist preachers had struggled to keep the traditions of emotion, inwardness, emphasis on renewal, and "born-again" spirituality closely tied to the hearing of the Word and reception of the Sacrament. These efforts, however, may have been uprooted by the events of the Revolution. The first German-American hymnal, the *Erbauliche Liedersammlung* of 1786, contains pietist offerings from Freylinghausen's Halle Hymnal and fewer selections from the Marburg Hymnal. Mühlenberg commented on this negatively, underlining 534 pieces from the Halle hymnal and suggesting that the 216 hymns to be supplied ought to come from the Wernigerode, Halle, and Cöthen hymnbooks—the last-named his personal favorite. He especially seemed intent to eliminate hymn texts that indulged the eighteenth-century sentimental fondness for diminutives, a policy that eliminated not only Moravian hymns in large numbers, but struck out as well many pieces from the Württemberg collection (Folkening 1972; Muhlenberg 1942–1958 [III]: 524–525).

This 1786 collection of hymn texts, reissued repeatedly from St. Michael's and Zion parish in Philadelphia, appeared in enlarged form eight times before 1820 and went through another twelve reprints before 1850. The hymnal also included thirteen hymns composed by J. H. C. Helmuth, the last of the Halle-trained clergy to serve as chief pastor in Philadelphia (1745–1825). Zion, the larger of the two buildings in this combined parish, was known throughout the first part of the nineteenth century as a pietist church with little attention paid to liturgy. Partly, this fact was due to Zion's construction between 1766 and 1770 when parish indebtedness originally could not allow the new church to be outfitted with an organ. But by the 1780s, with the collaboration of schoolmaster David Ott, Helmuth labored to perpetuate the European tradition of choral singing, cantata performance, and liturgical composition he had learned at Halle. By 1790, Tannenberg completed the organ for Zion, which was dedicated both with a public ceremony and a private concert for President George Washington. Despite the outbreak of yellow fever in Philadelphia in 1793, the quality of both hymnody and liturgical music remained high at Zion, but suffered perhaps irremediably when the church burned on December 26, 1794. Not until 1811 was an organ reinstalled at Zion. Between 1809 and 1813 a tune book finally emerged to accompany the hymns collected in the 1786 *Erbauliche Liedersammlung*. As Edwin Wolf has pointed out, the choice of melodies for the 266 chorales breaks down to 127 dating before 1700, and 108 from the eighteenth century. Not only in terms of texts, but also in the emotive associations provoked by the music, a decided preference for older tradition marked Lutheran hymn inclusions, apparently regardless of regional background (Wolf 1977).

Outside these atypical environs at St. Michael's and Zion, however, the actual practice of choosing and singing of post-Revolutionary Lutheran hymns was quite different. What influences the growing evangelical revivals among Methodists and Baptists exercised on Lutheran households have never been investigated, nor the actual practice of hymn singing itself. If the few hints from the pre-Revolution period are any indication, household devotion may well have followed more local and regional patterns and reflected choices that connected many German speakers to the nonliturgical emotional revivalism of English-speaking evangelicalism. This probability would have been strongest where Halle's former networks had been weakest and congregations not challenged by the broader, cosmopolitan view of Lutheranism that Halle sought to inculcate among its adherents. This possibility, at least, would help to explain why even in Georgia, after the Ebenezer settlement was destroyed in the Revolution, a renowned Baptist preacher commented that former Lutherans made up some of his best converts (Jones 1984).

The disruption of networks of distribution, especially that dominated by Halle, but even those constructed by traders who connected families to their former homelands and villages in the German southwest, accounts for part of the complex story of German Lutheran hymnody in North America. So too, however, does the clear preference of Lutherans for both texts and tunes from a much earlier age. Presumably, such choices were ratified by congregations and were not merely the choice of pastors, since internal congregational peace could hardly be kept if a pastor contravened his flock's wishes in hymn singing. Handschuh's unfortunate confrontation with his Württemberg parishioners had proven that. In 1807 a Montgomery, Pennsylvania, manuscript "A Song of Summer" ([*Gesang*] *der Sommerzeit*) drew upon Paulus Gerhardt for its inspiration, suggesting how deeply the orthodox hymn composer's influence continued to be felt even in German-American folk art (Borneman 1937:31). The 1786 collection of hymns, drawing as it did on Marburg, Halle, Wernigerode, and Cöthen hymnals and supplemented by what was essentially a seventeenth- and eighteenth-century collection of tunes, perpetuated in North America a connection to the music of the Reformation era among Lutherans from diverse regional backgrounds one would not otherwise have predicted.

Yet, Mühlenberg himself hinted at this pattern when reporting on his suggestions for filling up the complement of hymns to be included in the projected 1786 collection. He especially pointed out that "the ancient and medieval hymns, which have been familiar to all Lutherans from childhood on, cannot well be left out; even though they sound somewhat harsh in construction, rhyme, etc., they are nevertheless orthodox" (Muhlenberg 1942–1958 [III]: 524).

How those selections and choices intersected with household piety and practices that evolved at least in part because of regional preferences in the German states we only dimly understand. At the least, however, the complexity of admixtures these remnants from the eighteenth century attest to should warn against easy reduction of hymn-singing and distribution to "popular" versus "elite" forms. Far more likely, the accidents of network distribution, availability of, and access to favored compilations of hymns, and the degree of support individual pastors—such as Helmuth—gave to music in general explain more about the relative popularity of hymns among German-speaking Lutherans in North America. The importance of the "orthodox" choices for hymns among Lutherans lay in the early determination of leading Halle-educated clerics not to become imprisoned by the regional or local origins of their mixed congregations, but to search for a broader base for instruction in the hymns of the more remote Reformation past. The creative tension between this "pan-Lutheran" hymnody among German speakers with the emotional associations created by local and regional preferences supplied the basis for a vibrant attention to hymn-singing that lasted at least until the beginning of the nineteenth century. As networks decayed and memory of the German origins of many Lutherans dimmed, a more provincial, North American context obscured what had been a lively debate over hymnody and identity only the pre-Revolutionary networks had made possible.

Bibliography

Borneman, Henry S. *Pennsylvania German Illuminated Manuscripts*. Norristown, PA: Pennsylvania German Society, 1937.

Beilage to the *Pennsylvanische Staatsbote:* Ab G 1760/8; Ab G 1773/20; Ab G 1773/23.

David, Hans T. *Musical Life in the Pennsylvania Settlements of the* Unitas Fratrum. Moravian Music Foundation Publications No. 6. Winston-Salem, NC: Moravian Music Foundation, 1959.

Documentary History of the Evangelical Lutheran Ministerium of Pennsylvania and Adjacent States. Proceedings of the Annual Conventions from 1748 to 1821. Philadelphia: Board of Publication of the General Council of the Evangelical Lutheran Church in North America, 1898.

Fechner, Jörg-Ulrich. "Paul Gerhardt." In *Orthodoxie und Pietismus*, edited by Martin Greschat. Stuttgart: M. Kohlhammer Verlag, 1982.

Folkening, John. "The First Lutheran Hymnbook in America: Mühlenberg's *Erbauliche Liedersammlung*, 1786." M. M. thesis, Concordia College, River Forest, IL, 1972.

Glatfelter, Charles H. *Pastors and People: German Lutheran and Reformed Churches in the Pennsylvania Field, 1717–1793*. Breinigsville, PA: The Pennsylvania German Society, 1981.

Grabbe, Hans-Jürgen. "Besonderheiten der europäischen Einwanderung in die USA während der frühen nationalen Periode 1783–1820." *Amerikastudien/ American Studies* 33 (1988): 271–290.

Häberlein, Mark. "Vom Oberrhein zum Susquehanna: Studien zur badischen Auswanderung nach Pennsylvania im 18. Jahrhundert." Ph.D. dissertation, Augsburg University, 1991.

Horn, Edward T. III. *A Colonial Liturgy in English*. Philadelphia: Fortress Press, 1976.

HSP = Pennsylvania Historical Society

Ingram, Jeannine S. "Music in American Moravian Communities: Transplanted Traditions in Indigenous Practices." *Communal Societies* 2 (1982): 39–51.

Johanson, John H. *Moravian Hymnody*. Moravian Music Foundation Publications No. 9. Winston-Salem, NC: Moravian Music Foundation, 1980.

Jones, George Fenwick. *The Salzburger Saga*. Athens: University of Georgia Press, 1984.

______. *The Georgia Dutch: From the Rhine and Danube to the Savannah, 1733–1783*. Athens: University of Georgia Press, 1992.

LCP = Library Company of Philadelphia, German Broadsides Collections.

Medick, Hans. "Buchkultur und lutherischer Pietismus: Buchbesitz, erbauliche Lektüre und religiöse Mentalität in einer ländlichen Gemeinde Württembergs am Ende der frühen Neuzeit: Laichingen 1748–1820." In *Frühe Neuzeit-Frühe Moderne? Forschungen zur Vielschichtigkeit von Übergangsprozessen*, edited by Rudolf Vierhaus, et al. 297–326. Göttingen: Vandenhoeck & Ruprecht, 1992.

Muhlenberg, Henry Melchior. *The Journals of Henry Melchior Muhlenberg*. Translated and edited by Theodore G. Tappert and John W. Doberstein. 3 vols. Philadelphia: The Evangelical Lutheran Ministrium of Pennsylvania / The Muhlenberg Press, 1942–1958.

Petzoldt, Martin. *Bach als Ausleger der Bibel: Theologische und musikwissenschaftliche Studien zum Werk Johann Sebastian Bachs*. Berlin: Evangelische Verlagsanstalt Berlin, 1984.

Reinitzer, Heino. *Paul Gerhardt: Ich bin ein Gast auf Erde*. Berlin: Hensel Verlag, 1986.

Roeber, A. G. "'The Origin of Whatever Is Not English among Us': The Dutch-speaking and the German-speaking Peoples of Colonial British America." In *Strangers within the Realm: Cultural Margins of the First British Empire*, edited by Bernard Bailyn and Philip Morgan, 220–283. Chapel Hill: University of North Carolina Press, 1991.

______. *Palatines, Liberty, and Property: German Lutherans and British North America*. Baltimore: Johns Hopkins University Press, 1993.

______. "German and Dutch Books and Printing." In *A History of the Book in America, Vol. I: The Colonial Book in the Atlantic World*, edited by Hugh Amorg and David D. Hall, 298–313. New York: Cambridge University Press, 2000.

Schalk, Carl F. "German Hymnody." In *Hymnal Companion to the Lutheran Book of Worship*, Marilyn Kay Stulken, 25–32. Philadelphia: Fortress Press, 1981.

Söhninge, Oskar. "Die Musik im evangelischen Pfarrhaus." In *Das evangelische Pfarrhaus: Eine Kultur- und Sozialgeschichte*, edited by Martin Greiffenhagen, 25-32. Stuttgart: Kreuz-Verlag, 1984.

Terry, R. Harold. "Lutheran Hymnody in North America." In Marilyn Kay Stulken, *Hymnal Companion to the Lutheran Book of Worship*. 85–95. Philadelphia: Fortress Press, 1981.

Urlsperger, Samuel. *Detailed Reports on the Salzburger Emigrants*. Edited and translated by George Fenwick Jones, et. al. vols. VI and VII. Athens: University of Georgia Press, 1968–1995.

Vann, James Allen. *The Making of a State:Württemberg 1593–1793*. Ithaca: Cornell University Press, 1984.

Wolf, Edward C. "Music in Old Zion, Philadelphia, 1750–1850," *The Music Quarterly* 58 (1972): 622–652.

______. "Lutheran Hymnody and Music Published in America 1700–1850: A Descriptive Bibliography." *Concordia Historical Institute Quarterly* 50 (1977): 165–75.

6

ETHNIC MUSICS/RELIGIOUS IDENTITIES: TOWARD A HISTORIOGRAPHY OF GERMAN-AMERICAN SACRED MUSIC

Philip V. Bohlman

In the beginning there were hymnbooks and hymnals. In the beginning, as they packed their trunks to emigrate, Germans saw to their spiritual well-being and the preservation of cultural identity by including their hymnals.[1] In the beginning the earliest colonial American printers, Benjamin Franklin and Christopher Saur, began to mass-produce German hymnals in the early decades of the eighteenth century (Bohlman 1992). In the beginning the devout and pietistic adherents of Amish, Mennonite, and Hutterite doctrines, having established their movements in martyrdom, turned to their songs and their hymnbooks to chronicle that history. In the beginning, as they founded new synods to reformulate the conservative values of German Lutheranism, mid-nineteenth-century Midwestern pioneers formed community bonds with new churches, parochial schools, and singing schools, their hymnals clasped in their hands and tucked in their pockets as if to solidify those bonds even more firmly.[2] In the beginning of their nineteenth-century immigration,

---

[1] J. G. Schnabel's early eighteenth-century novel *Insel Felsenburg* describes the preparation of supplies for the foundation of a German utopian community on Felsenburg Island as including twenty-nine songbooks "for the special grace of God," from a total of thirty-nine books the settlers brought with them, the other ten books being Bibles (1731:129). After the island community had thrived for several years, a further shipment of seven hundred books arrived, among which were four hundred sacred songbooks. Though fictional, Schnabel's story presages the printing activity of German religious-utopian communities in North America, which largely concentrated on the production of hymnbooks and Bibles. The Felsenburg Island utopia was not, in fact, religiously motivated in the novel, only its literary activities and production.

[2] For studies of the employment of German hymnals in singing schools, an inheritance from English-Protestant New England traditions, in the formation of new communities and denominational bodies,

the builders of German-Jewish Reform temples turned for leadership to their *hazzan*, their cantor, for spiritual and musical leadership so that they might later attract a rabbi (Slobin 1989:29–50). In the beginning the histories of German-American religious communities were inscribed in their songs, in their hymns and in their liturgies, and it is hardly surprising that music came to make the histories of these communities—indeed, to extend those histories—well beyond the beginning.

The hymnals and hymnbooks that we encounter in the foundational myths and historical moments I have here recounted differed from each other, often radically so, despite the rather small terminological pool used to identify them, that is, hymnals, hymnbooks, and songbooks in English, *Siddurim* in Hebrew, or *Gesang-* and *Liederbücher* in German, usually modified by *geistliche* or *kirchliche*.[3] The functions of their contents, too, differed dramatically, far more than suggested by the physical omnipresence implicit in the introductory paragraph. Some hymnals stayed in the pews; others accompanied their owners as an artifact of church life for further use in the home. Some were created as bastions against change; others literally ushered in change with innovations on their pages. Some included musical notation as a component of their contents; others included only the texts of songs, together with a reminder of tunes that were obviously well known in oral tradition.

In all cases, however, the hymnal was more than just a book, even a book of very special importance. The music that resulted from performing out of the hymnal was, in fact, a representation of the community, a representation animated through performance and animating because it brought the community into existence as they sang. The hymnal included hymns and sacred songs that praised God, but, more important, provided a musical means of establishing a specific relationship between God and individuals. The hymnal shaped the sacred boundaries of ethnicity and ascribed identity. The hymnal's music, moreover, perpetuated the community,

---

see Schalk 1965 for Missouri and Bohlman 1993 for Pennsylvania. The image of Lutheran farmers, clasping their hymnals as they gather to form a new parish in northern Wisconsin, appears in Alfred Ira's autobiographical novel (Ira 1923).

[3] The term *hymnbook* usually designates a collection of texts only; in contrast, a *hymnal* includes printed music, either a hymn's melody or a four-part harmonization (cf. Hinks 1986). The German terms *Gesang* and *Lied* both gloss as *song*, but *Gesang* is more frequently used for religious repertories or hymns. A hymn in the most general sense is a composed sacred song that is sung by the congregation; hymns often have flexible functions in the liturgy or paraliturgical functions altogether.

A *siddur* (pl. *siddurim*) is a prayerbook used for daily and weekly worship in the Jewish tradition. Literally, a *siddur* fixes the "order" of worship, and it provides the congregation with a means of joining in the performance of the order of worship. *Siddurim* most commonly include text only, though frequently in Hebrew with the vernacular translation (e.g., German) on a facing page, although *siddurim* in the Reform tradition also occasionally include printed music, usually in an appendix.

giving it a chance to resituate the past in the present, that is, to perform its history through a new sense of *communitas* immanent in the music of a religious body.

Sacred music, particularly that of the songbooks of the church and the synagogue, came to play a very special role in the making of history in German America, and it did so *despite* denominational and doctrinal differences, indeed, *despite* such profound differences as those between the institutions of Christianity and Judaism in America. It has been these "despites" that especially intrigued me and challenged me as I undertook the research for this essay, for rather than undermining the search for larger music historical processes by introducing a surfeit of exceptions, they have led me to ponder a more unified historiography for German-American religious music, in which differences emerge as the primary processes of unity. The sacred music and musical practices historically came to function in ways that were both German and American, and together these functions powerfully underpin German-American history and music history.

Historiography of German-American Religious Musics

In this essay I examine the larger problem of writing the music history of German-Americans. A muted consensus exists in many different areas of Americanist musical scholarship that the German-American contribution to American music was fundamental to a larger American music history. In filiopietistic scholarship, the mute has been stripped from that consensus, particularly when statistics about the German membership of American orchestras and in the history of American music education are trotted out.[4] This consensus about German elements or contributions notwithstanding, we have failed to formulate a music history—and a music historiography—of German-American music.[5] And so, we content ourselves again and again with trotting out the same statistics.

I also posit that it is and will remain impossible to construct a more sweeping narrative of German-American music history until we reassess the most basic his-

[4] The New York Philharmonic, for example, was ninety percent German-speaking in 1890. Orchestra founders, such as Theodore Thomas in Chicago, came overwhelmingly from Central Europe in the late nineteenth and early twentieth century, as did their successors as conductors during much of the remaining twentieth century.

[5] Richard Crawford, in a longer discussion of histories of American music (1993:3–37), identifies the attention to European origins as both a unifying factor and a stumbling block for American music historiography. "Our historians and works, however various, do hold certain things in common. All take Europe as a starting point. Indeed, no fact about the writing of American music is more characteristic than the looming presence of Europe" (1993:6). The historiographic "characteristic" notwithstanding, neither Crawford nor the historians he examines seems willing to transform it into a trope for ethnic music historiography or as evidence for the impact of European religious traditions on American music.

toriographic methods. The problematic of German-American music history, I argue further, bears a resemblance to the construction of other music histories in North America, music histories for other groups and communities whose musical practices specify and shape cultural identities. I refer, of course, to a broad range of unwritten—and "unconstructed"—music histories, those of women, people of color, gays and lesbians, the working class, migrant laborers, or the suburban middle class. While looking more closely at the music historical processes in German-American religious music, I am, therefore, not attempting to discern and reduce those processes that are unique, that would yield a music history unto itself. Instead, I deliberately seek the interrelations between German-American religious musics and those of other communities who have contributed their distinctive voices to a larger American music history.

The interrelatedness between different communities, regions, and subcultures often fails to appear in the historiographic models for American music. American music history forms either from a mosaic[6] or panorama[7] of different parts or from the tension of opposing binarisms (e.g., Hitchcock 1988, and Crawford 1993). H. Wiley Hitchcock therefore proposes that music history in the United States has formed from the tension between "elite" and "vernacular" musics, roughly the traditions emulating European art music or employing the conventions of written traditions and everything else. Searching for a somewhat more broadly applicable pair of historical processes, Richard Crawford proposes a pair he calls "cosmopolitan" and "provincial." Explicit, then, are the distinctions between musical practices that reach beyond the city, region, or subculture for which they were created and those that do not. The opposing binarisms of Hitchcock, Crawford, and others are useful historiographic methods for understanding that part of the pair—elite and cosmopolitan—in which history is implicitly present, but historiographically they falter when turned toward the "peoples without history," those whose musical practices are vernacular or provincial. It follows, then, that music history itself remains bound

---

[6] Gilbert Chase (1987), for example, begins at the beginning, which for him is the arrival of the Pilgrims in the early seventeenth century, and then allows historical diversity to accrue through the arrival of other immigrants or the development of new genres, so that the distinctiveness of the whole of American music history eventually results from its characteristically distinctive parts.

[7] The panorama that Daniel Kingman (1990) metaphorically uses is a vast painted canvas, whose scenes one views at different moments while nonetheless examining the entire sweep of a region or a series of historical events. The panorama, though not uniquely American, had a special significance in the ways in which the expanding West was represented in spectacles during the nineteenth century.

to literate, urban, and art traditions, whereas folk, ethnic, and religious traditions,[8] however generously treated, are largely ahistorical. It is hardly surprising that these traditions fall off the panorama or are at best tucked into the peripheries of the musical landscape of the United States as a whole.

Music history and historiography are subsets of general history, and musicians and music-making contribute to the making of general history. On one hand, we witness music embedded in the historical processes of constructing communities and identities because of music's essentially performative nature, in other words, in the reproduction of these communities and identities. On the other hand, we recognize that a general music history is itself constituted of subsets. Here, I investigate one such subset, namely the religious music history of German-Americans. This music history itself has a surfeit of subsets, each with distinctive musical practices and processes. It is a music history, moreover, that began in Colonial America and is still very much a part of contemporary American musical practices. It is a music history that continues to shape musical and religious identities. The connections between the past and the present are only rarely continuous. In a traditional music historical sense, this lack of continuity might even seem to be ahistorical. As the essays in the present book make abundantly clear, German-American musical identities have changed radically over time, sometimes proliferating and at other times consolidating. Any music history, accordingly, must take this into account.

I concern myself in this essay, then, with ways we might better begin to take the processes of proliferating and consolidating musical identities into account. To do this, I draw rather closely on historiographic methods forged by Michel Foucault, particularly on the concept of "archaeology," which he developed most extensively in *The Order of Things* (1970) and *The Archaeology of Knowledge* (1972).[9] My concern is archaeological insofar as I attempt to identify and locate an "episteme," namely a broad range of musical practices that constitute the ethnic-religious community's knowledge of itself. In a Foucauldian historiography, the recognition of the episteme in the community's self-knowledge, "apart from all criteria having reference to its rational value or to its objective forms," allows one to construct "a

---

[8] Here and throughout this essay, I recognize an important distinction between religious music created for sacred services or with fundamentally religious functions, and religious music composed for performance on the secular stage or with aspirations to primarily worldly functions, in other words, as art music with a religious text.

[9] In this sense I follow attempts to reformulate music histories, such as Gary Tomlinson's work on the Renaissance (especially Tomlinson 1993) and Georgina Born's ethnographic study of French musical modernism at IRCAM in Paris (Born 1995).

history which is not that of its growing perfection, but rather [a history] of its conditions of possibility" (1970: xxii).

History—or archaeology, as Foucault prefers to call it in such instances—is immanent in the "space of [musical] knowledge" and musical practices, in the use of music to embody community identity (1970: xxii). To music accrue the functions of creating the space in which musical practices take place, hence the context in which identity emerges and is perpetuated through music. Such functions depend on the institutions of power and the unfolding of power structures through history. I argue here that the hymnbook and the hymnal are just such structures of power because of the ways they connect German-Americans to their religious institutions, to the synagogue or church, and beyond to the movements and synods responsible for producing musical practices for a larger network of religious institutions. Music, therefore, contributes to the construction and reproduction of ethnic identity through its centrality in religious practice. Understanding the meanings embedded in German-American religious musical practices draws us closer to understanding German-American epistemology itself.

The archaeological notion of music history has a particular resonance for German-American music for several reasons. First, religious musical practices are frequently central to identity and to the knowledge of self. We recognize this in the vast range of styles and repertories, which is to say the vast range of German-American religious musical identities. Stated more precisely, in the United States there are more rather than fewer religious institutions conveying German identities than in Central Europe. Concomitantly, there are more rather than fewer German-American religious musical practices. Second, having created an epistemological field in which we are no longer describing histories of "growing perfection," in other words, a music that is specifically German-American, we can institute processes of comparison; that is to say, we can ask increasingly more complex questions about the relation of religious music to German-American identity.

It is because of this fundamentally epistemic quality of music and its interaction with religious institutions invested with power that I have constructed my comparison in this essay from two religious communities that probably offer an unlikely comparison at first glance. What is it about German-Lutheran and German-Jewish musical practices that makes them comparable? The object "music" differs, that is, it sounds different; the role of language in music and identity differs; should not such music histories be unique, channeled into separate-but-equal categories? If we only understand music as a symbol for identity, perhaps; but my purpose is to understand music as an episteme for the knowledge of self and the location of that knowledge in historical space. Before proceeding further, let me sketch some reasons that make comparison far more illuminating than one might have suspected at first glance.

The historical conditions that represent the major immigration of German-Lutherans and German-Jews in the nineteenth century were often quite similar. The largest immigration for both groups in the nineteenth century took place from about 1800 until 1880. During the first half of this period, immigrants, whether Lutheran or Jewish, were largely from the working class, or were disenfranchised and poor. Those who were not came in small sectarian (e.g., the "Old Lutherans" in Wisconsin in the late 1830s) or utopian (e.g., the "Harmonists" in Pennsylvania and Indiana), and they formed tightly knit communities in North America. After 1840 and particularly after the unsuccessful 1848 revolution, the immigrants in both groups were increasingly more elite and educated. In both forty-year periods, there were historical conditions that brought about an "American transformation" of community and religion, with the establishment of the major Lutheran synods and Reform Judaism by mid-century and their growing authority in German-American sectarian life thereafter, that is, with the establishment of institutions of centralized religious power in American urban centers, such as those promulgating Reform Judaism in Cincinnati.

Lutheranism in North America transformed and Americanized the institutional structures it brought from Central Europe. Whereas the centralized institution of power, the synod, was regionally based in Europe, especially in northern Germany, usually identified with a city that had a seminary or a university theological faculty, in the United States synods cut across regions. The Missouri Synod, for example, laid its roots in St. Louis, but it quickly spread throughout the United States, especially in the states of the Upper Midwest, which attracted the largest immigration of Germans in the late nineteenth century. Americanization meant, therefore, a decentralization, which is evident even today in the network of synodal seminaries and colleges (usually called "Concordia") throughout the United States. Other ethnic groups from Lutheran areas of Europe, especially Scandinavians, formed their own synods, meaning that religious institutions were isomorphically equivalent to ethnic institutions.

A second stage of Americanization has taken place in the twentieth century, as synods merged together, with the resulting consolidation of doctrinal, musical, and ethnic identities. That there has been resistance to these is evident in the struggles over which hymnal[10] a consolidated synod (e.g., the Lutheran Church in America or

[10] Or hymnals! It is not uncommon to find Lutheran churches that have several different hymnals in its pews, one that reflects the trend toward Americanization, and another that clearly embodies

the American Lutheran Church) would find acceptable. A similar process of consolidation has characterized American Judaism, and American Jewish songbooks and prayer books (e.g., the *Union Prayer Book*) reveal similar struggles over just how extensively hymnals can and should reflect ethnic identity.

Among the American transformations was the expanding musical hegemony associated with German Lutheranism and Reform Judaism. Both formed what we might describe as "musical mainstreams": standardized repertories and musical styles, and the means whereby to reproduce these. Moreover, these musical mainstreams were themselves distinctly American, for they resulted from sweeping musical changes that occurred in the first half of the century. Even sectarian and splinter groups came to be defined musically and theologically in relation to these two German-American mainstreams, for example, in the Wisconsin Synod of the Lutheran Church or the Conservative Movement in American Judaism.

Musical practices in the church and synagogue, too, intensified and perpetuated the presence of music in daily life and practice. German-Lutheranism and Reform Judaism relied extensively on literate musical traditions, though not just the publication of hymnals and prayer books, rather also their transformation into forms that could be transported to the home. Music became the product of not just the individual body, but of the body politic of the religious community, as the sanctuary underwent radical changes in North America, with new roles for women and instrumental music distinguishing traits of German-American Lutheranism and Judaism. Increasingly, then, musical practices came to embody the transformation of German into American religious practices.

Schriftlichkeit—Literacy

The music historical processes constructed by German-American religious communities are distinctive because of the central importance of literacy, that is, a core of musical traditions embedded in printed texts and the transmission through those texts because of their mass production. The importance of literacy is as true in German-American Judaism and Lutheranism as in Amish or Hutterite traditions. It is, in fact, this importance of literate and printed musical traditions that may have blinded many scholars of ethnicity and folklore from considering German-American musical traditions, both secular and sacred.[11] Far more interesting to most scholars

---

an ethnic epistemology, which might be appropriate for, say, holiday seasons or other moments in the year when ethnic and religious identities most tightly intersect.

[11] Singing "folksongs" from and mass-producing them with books is normative in many German-American communities. During fieldwork, when I invite my consultants to sing "folksongs" for me,

than the Amish *Ausbund* printed only a few years ago in Pennsylvania has been the wishful presumption that sixteenth-century German chorales have been preserved by the Amish through the oral transmission of melodies used to sing from the *Ausbund* (see, for example, Helen Martens's examination [1981] of Hutterite hymns as if they stemmed from a melody tradition that retained traditions from the *Meistersinger* of the sixteenth century).

Literacy has yet another importance, for German-American religious communities have used it to transform musical texts into historical texts. The hymns of the Amish or the Hutterites conflate devotion, faith, and knowledge of the self with a sweeping sense of communal history. The hymns themselves become embodied genealogies of the Amish (see Asad 1993:55–79). Such an embodied genealogy is evident in the first two and last two verses of the 140th hymn in the Amish *Ausbund*, the well-known "Haslibacher Lied." The following variant of the song comes from the first American version of the *Ausbund*, published by Christoph Saur of Germantown, Pennsylvania, in 1742 (cf. Bachmann-Geiser and Bachmann 1988:132–134).

Opening verses

Was wend wir aber heben an, Zu singen von ein'm alten Mann, Der war von Haßlibach, Haßlichbacher ward er genannt, Aus der Kilchöri Summiswald.	We turn now to pick up, And sing of an old man, Who was from Haslibach, He was called Haslibacher, From the Kilchöri in the Summis Woods.
Da das der lieb Gott zu thät lan, Daß er wurd hart geklaget an, Wohl um den Glauben sein, Da hat man ihn gefangen hart, Führt ihn gen Bern wohl in die Stadt.	Because he had given himself to God, So that he had been severely charged, To be strong in his faith, Therefore he was taken prisoner, And led to Berne into the city.

• • •

Closing verses

Der Henker der sprach mit Unmuth Heut hab ich gericht unschuldig Blut, Da sprach ein alter Herr,	The executioner spoke without courage, Today I have taken innocent blood, Then an old man spoke up,

---

they usually reach for a songbook and sing from it, with no sense that the repertory should conform to expectations that folksongs circulate in oral tradition.

Des Täuffers Mund hat gelacht im Hut,	The Baptist's mouth had laughed in the hat,[12]
Das bedeutet Gottes Straff und Ruth.	Which meant God's punishment and beating.
Der uns diß Liedlein hat gemacht.	He who created this little song for us,
Der war ums Leben in Gfangenschafft,	Was imprisoned for life,
Den Sündern thät ers zu lieb,	But he endeared himself to the sinners,
Ein Herr ihm Federn und Tinten bracht,	So a man brought him feather and ink,
Er schenckt uns das zu guter Nacht.	And he presented us with this gift for our salvation.

(Haslibacher Lied)

Literate hymn traditions further spawned historical processes because of their fetishization of language. On the one hand, this might mean the deliberate realization of the German past through the continued employment of Gothic style of type, a printing practice that German religious presses abandoned only in the mid-twentieth century, when, in fact, they ceased the production of German-language hymns altogether. Similarly, it meant that hymns preserved High German, which survives in song texts even when communities themselves speak in dialect or English (cf. Wulz in this volume). On the other hand, it was precisely this fetishization that allowed printers to juxtapose the German and the American, making each songbook a vehicle for stimulating different music historical processes. The *Pennsylvanische Sammlung von Kirchen-Musik* (1840), an example of which appears as Figure 1, did precisely this, creating a bricolage of diverse German and American traditions from which mid-nineteenth century immigrants could choose their own historical past and present (see Bohlman 1993). Standard German hymns, from different historical eras, are "translated" into shape-note hymns for the westward spread of American Protestantism, thereby preserving the archaic literary form of the German and introducing the distinctively innovative literary form of the American counterpart. Printing practices also essentialized Germanness, whether in the conservative Missouri Synod Lutheran or the liberal Reform Jewish hymnbooks, for they allowed the versions selected for these hymnbooks to epitomize the German chorale melody or the metricized German version of a Hebrew psalm, to evoke that special beauty that each hymnbook editor strove to find.

---

[12] Legend, as transmitted by the song, holds that Haslibacher's hat contained an image of the executed man's head after it fell from his head after beheading. When the image laughed, it signified a bad omen. The symbolic connection to John the Baptist is obvious, for the Amish were called "Täufer" or "Wiedertäufer," usually glossed as *Anabaptists* in English.

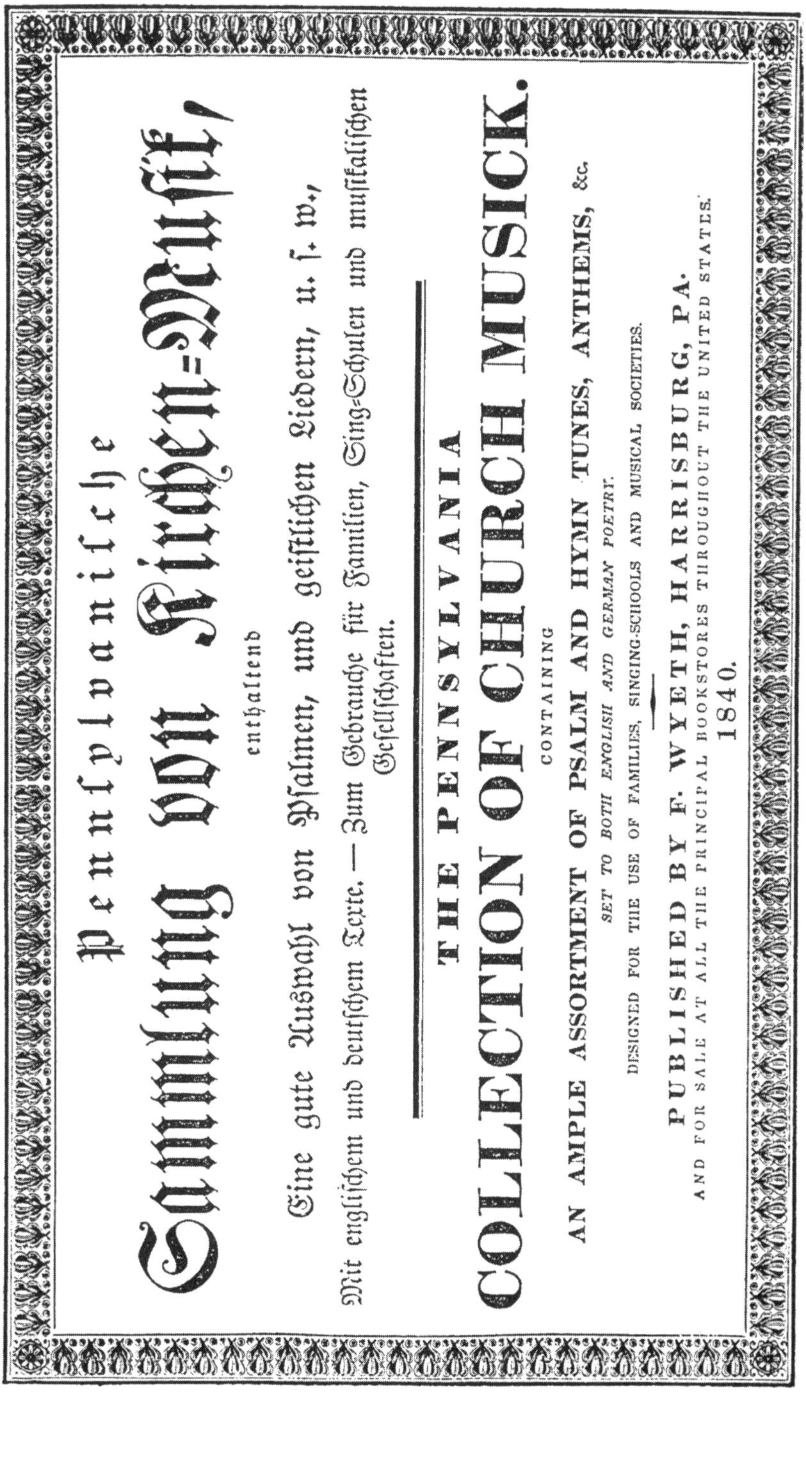

Pennsylvanische

Sammlung von Kirchen-Musik,

enthaltend

Eine gute Auswahl von Psalmen, und geistlichen Liedern, u. s. w.,

Mit englischem und deutschem Texte. — Zum Gebrauche für Familien, Sing-Schulen und musikalischen Gesellschaften.

THE PENNSYLVANIA

COLLECTION OF CHURCH MUSICK.

CONTAINING

AN AMPLE ASSORTMENT OF PSALM AND HYMN TUNES, ANTHEMS, &c.

SET TO BOTH ENGLISH AND GERMAN POETRY.

DESIGNED FOR THE USE OF FAMILIES, SINGING-SCHOOLS AND MUSICAL SOCIETIES.

PUBLISHED BY F. WYETH, HARRISBURG, PA.

AND FOR SALE AT ALL THE PRINCIPAL BOOKSTORES THROUGHOUT THE UNITED STATES.

1840.

Figure 1. *Pennsylvanische Sammlung von Kirchen-Musik* (1840).

Orality, Performance, and the Embodiment of Congregational Life

The literacy of German-American religious music, however central its functions, is not isolated. Instead, it exists in a sort of dialectical relation with orality, specifically an orality that depends on the performance practices of the congregation or community. Hymn- and prayer books that do not employ printed notation—the bulk of those examined in this essay—necessarily require that the congregation retain melodies through oral tradition. Oral tradition in these cases, however, is not a matter of individuals knowing a sufficient number of formulas to allow them to internalize large repertories with lengthy individual pieces. In contrast, oral tradition results from community practices, and it remains anchored to those moments when congregations, families, or singing societies sing together.

Certain religious-musical specialists, for example, may utilize knowledge of the written tradition in order to facilitate performance through oral tradition. The Jewish *hazzan*, or cantor, possesses not only specialized knowledge of biblical and prayer texts, but recites from a system of fairly rudimentary notation, which suggests no more than melodic direction and cadential patterns. The lead-singer in Amish and Hutterite hymnody, similarly, bridges oral and written tradition by employing the practice of lining-out (German, *ansagen*). Religious song, therefore, is frequently a site where the oral and written interact through complex performance practices.

At one extreme, oral tradition is virtually inseparable from written tradition, for example, in a congregational setting where an organist "remembers" the melodies for the community; here, I might note, is yet another reason that German-Jewish traditions lend themselves to comparison with German-Lutheran ones, for the organ had become virtually indispensable in synagogues by the mid-nineteenth century, that is, at a moment coeval with the rise of the Jewish hymnal and prayer book in the United States.[13] At an opposite extreme, oral tradition depends on the ways in which the portability of hymn- and prayer books allows them to be used in a constellation of community settings: in schools, in social gatherings, in the home. Nevertheless, it is again the group that "remembers" the melodies, that reconstitutes the music through performance. We might think of oral tradition, then, as a fluid process transported with the songbooks themselves, therefore part of the literacy of the tradition yet brought to life only through performance as a group or community.

---

[13] Throughout the nineteenth century the so-called *Orgelstreit* (quarrel over the organ) raged in Central European synagogues, with Reform synagogues embracing the musical possibilities opened by the organ and Conservative or Orthodox synagogues rejecting the presence of instrumental music altogether. See Frühauf 2000.

Performance, then, empowers the group or community to have knowledge of itself. It provides a moment of epistemological knowledge for the community. Even more important for the genealogy of the religious-ethnic community, the public performance at the core of hymnody means that it provides the community with a possibility of reproducing its epistemological knowledge musically, within and without community ritual. We recognize in community performance, therefore, what Foucault would call subjectification, "the way a human body turns him- or herself into a subject" (cf. Rabinow 1984:10–11 and Foucault 1984). Historically, self-knowledge of this type results from an extensive genealogy, the musical tradition itself, constantly reproduced with hymn- and prayer books. Necessary for the perpetuation of the tradition, moreover, is the investment of both the music with some sense of authority, as well as external authority figures in the religious-musical life of the community.

As we examine the genealogies of German-American hymn traditions, a remarkable genealogy of authority figures also turns up. The eighteenth-century Christopher Saur, for example, literally left his imprint on musical traditions for several religious communities, the Moravians, the Brethren, and the Amish among them. The founding figure of Missouri Synod Lutheranism, C. F. W. Walther, was not only the spiritual leader of the synod, but a well-known organist, hymn composer, and musical didactician. David Einhorn, to whose Reform Jewish hymns I turn below, was so beloved as to be "incarnate" in the hymns on the pages of the prayer book that bore his name in the title; as his translator put it: "We know that there will always be a few congregations that will continue to love *their* Einhorn; for many decades they have by this book been led to the fount of true edification" (Einhorn 1896:v; emphasis in the original).[14]

Power accrued to these authority figures as they did to the hymn traditions themselves and the performance space in which history was made and remade, in the sanctuary of the church and the synagogue. Increasingly, then, music was the link among these various components in the genealogy and history of the religious community. Increasingly, music embodied those processes that made the history of the community itself.

Music Making History

Fundamental to the processes of modern music history is a tension that resolves itself over time in unexpected, even contradictory ways. This tension might arise

[14] In other hymn traditions as well figures of authority play significant—even iconic—roles. The journal of the Hymn Society of America, *The Hymn*, usually includes a picture of a well-known hymn composer on its cover.

from the encounter of one musical tradition with another, say, through cultural contact, colonialism, or class conflict. It may stem from the seemingly contradictory trajectories of oral and written traditions, the first pulling in one direction, the second tugging in another. The tension may intensify because of the skewing of power relations or the political economy of musical tradition. Obviously, these conditions of tension are commonplace in the modern world, and they very well may have been normative in the music histories of other times and places.

If music history unfolds as a result of these tensions, it necessarily acquires the ability to follow a number of trajectories, some of them resolving the tensions, others circumventing them, still others intensifying or multiplying them. Musics and musical practices, it follows, accrue to these histories in vastly different ways. A situation of culture conflict may mean that one community appropriates the music of the other, a sort of lock-stock-and-barrel swipe of musical style and repertory; Anthony Seeger (1991) has convincingly argued that musical thievery is, in fact, normative to the music history of the Suyá people of Amazonian Brazil, and that these music historical practices seem to be frequent among other North and South American native peoples.

Musical appropriation cuts across the religious-musical practices of German-American communities. Conservative, isolationist sects, such as the Hutterites, borrow hymns and other sacred songs not only from other German-speaking sects, notably the Mennonites, but also from folk- and popular-music repertories in surrounding English-speaking communities. Music history grows from these acts of borrowing in quite different ways, with change and stasis interacting in a complex dialectic. Composers of Reform and even Conservative Jewish liturgy also borrow from Christian religious repertories, especially from the Protestant traditions of North Germany.[15]

These religious communities make history as situations of tension afford them ample opportunities to hear other musics and cobble together new musics of their own. Considered only as repertories of pieces, the musics of modern music history begin to seem all mixed-up, but we might perceive instead that their being all mixed-up is also a measure of their responsiveness to the complex experiences of their history. Hence, we observe in essays in the present volume that German-Americans have musics that contain Czech polkas and English rock music; American country and western music and, even, German ballads.

---

[15] The cantor-composer who created the "Vienna Rite," Salomon Sulzer, commissioned many non-Jewish composers for the repertory that became the foundation for the rite *Schir Zion*. Franz Schubert, for example, is represented by a setting of the 92nd Psalm. When building the Vienna *Stadttempel* (city temple), the Viennese Jewish community commissioned a work by Beethoven, which he failed to complete, however, before his death.

The German-American experience offers a prime example of the conditions of tension I have just described, and religious communities encounter these conditions as if in a flood. Tensions, religious or otherwise, spur individuals, families, and groups to abandon one continent for another. New cultural tensions face the immigrant in a new environment, both those from within the community through power struggles, and from without, in other words, as a result of the usual pressures to acculturate.

Both of the larger religious groups examined here responded to these tensions in distinctive ways. German Lutherans often accepted the tensions of cultural confrontation and empowered their history to resist them. German Jews recognized the various possibilities of acculturation, the opportunity for which they were denied in Europe, and they saw to it that their history benefited from these when appropriate. The musics of German-American religious communities, moreover, became means of confronting these tensions and giving voice to their responses. Their musics, too, borrowed from Methodist hymnody or a Southern shape-note sound; their musics, too, insisted that women's voices and the organ belonged in the synagogue; their musics, too, responded to the conditions of American history in unexpected and creative ways.

German Lutheranism

Opening the *Lieder-Perlen*, by far the most common home songbook among German-Americans in the Midwest, one reads of its origins in the "Vorwort," prepared by *Das Committee* in St. Louis, in February 1894:

> The songs in this book were anthologized and arranged by a committee of the St. Louis teachers' conference, together with Mr. F. Färber, for the book commission and the directorship of the Concordia Publishing House. The title, "Lieder-Perlen" ["Pearls of Song"], is certainly just the right one, for, from the huge number of possible songs, we have unquestionably chosen only the most beautiful and most appropriate. Moreover, the original songs in the volume come from the pens of competent men, such as Brauer, Breuer, Burhenn, Färber, Feiertag, Grote, Ungemach, and others. We should like to express our warmest thanks to these, especially to Prof. A. Gräbner, who particularly contributed to the book by editing the text. God grant that these "Lieder-Perlen" might sing praises to him and serve the edification and joy of young and old, and that they might everywhere find a joyous reception (*Lieder-Perlen* 1894:Vorwort).

For rural German-Americans in northern Wisconsin, the *Lieder-Perlen* is *the* embodiment of their musical identity (see Figure 2). Part hymnbook, part collection of folk songs, part sampling of hymns and patriotic songs in English, part popular songster, the *Lieder-Perlen* had an enormous range of functions, all of them, however, transmitting and underscoring the authority of the Missouri Synod of the Lutheran Church, and by extension shoring up the centrality of conservative bulwarks of German Lutheranism in the rural areas throughout the Midwest that had attracted the major waves of north and northeastern German immigration between the Civil War and World War I.

The *Lieder-Perlen* is a remarkable musical document because it became a means of negotiating so many different German-American identities, while at the same time its publisher, the Concordia Publishing House of the Missouri Synod, had in fact only a single goal, that of employing music as fences to contain the flocks of German immigrants settling in rural and urban American communities, particularly in the Midwest. The Missouri Synod was a relative newcomer in the history of German-American immigration, and it is surely significant that the first decade of its history, the 1840s, witnessed the initial opening of the states of the western and northern Midwest to agricultural settlement. It was an immigrant institution waiting to welcome the major waves of immigration to these regions in the second half of the nineteenth century.

The doctrines of the Missouri Synod were a complicated mixture of rejections. On one hand, there was a rejection of the State Church of Saxony, which had effected a union of Reformed and Lutheran churches.[16] On the other hand, there was a rejection of other Lutheran synods that had undergone contamination by various forms of American rationalism, both religious and secular (Luebke 1990:5–6). The dilemma posed by these two forms of rejection forced the Missouri Synod to turn inward, that is, to establish a religious-cultural path independent from the past, yet channeled by a unique sense of Germanness and Americanness. To achieve this complex, far-reaching synthesis, the Missouri Synod turned to music, even as to the privileged cultural domain from which it could construct its own German-Americanness.

Music served the historical mission of the Missouri Synod with remarkable effectiveness, and precisely because it became the most sweeping tool of community building. Already in the 1840s, the founders of the Missouri Synod experimented with a number of pre-existing hymnals and sources for religious music, and

---

[16] Both Reformed and Lutheran churches are Protestant, with Reformed traditions anchored in the doctrines of John Calvin, Lutheran traditions in the doctrines of Martin Luther.

Figure 2. *Lieder-Perlen*, cover illustration.

from those sources the church founders anthologized new books, that is new repertories, that were mass-produced by the synod's Concordia Publishing House. Underlying the mass production and commodification of these brand-new German-American musical traditions was what might be called a "democratic spirit," a belief that any and all German-American Lutherans could and should take part in them. The publishers recognized that it was not so much the repertory itself that would attract everyone in the community, but rather the formats and functions of the books. Ready access to the musical traditions would bring about their perpetuation. If the songbooks of this invented German-Americanness were everywhere to be found, so too would the German-American be enveloped by the sounds and symbols of her culture. And the church founders were indeed quite correct.

The Concordia Publishing House produced its songbooks and other religious musical publications in a variety of formats, albeit in formats that targeted very specific functions in community life. At one level, there were publications that belonged to the church, hymnals that remained in the pews and chorale books that familiarized the liturgy of the church. At another level, there were songbooks intended for use in the schools, and these grew in importance as the massive parochial-school system of the synod spread across the Midwest. The title page of the *Lieder-Perlen* announces one of its primary functions as use in "our schools." At still another level, music should penetrate the home, and for this various personal hymnals were used (see Figure 3), and music also appeared on the pages of the myriad almanacs and family magazines that the Missouri Synod sent through the mails. Finally, there were the spaces in-between: publication design facilitated portability. If one wanted to do so, one could stick a portable hymnal or the *Lieder-Perlen* in one's pocket, taking it to the rehearsal of a local *Gesangverein*. These songbooks filled the entire space of the community. They were, in a very real sense, ubiquitous; and with them so was music ubiquitous, filling the entire space of the community.

Even its own chroniclers refer to the Missouri Synod as the most conservative form of Lutheranism in the United States, and with this in mind, I should like to caution that the reader not confuse my brief sketch of the literate underpinnings of music produced by Missouri Synod institutions with a larger music history of German Lutheranism in this country. We have glimpsed but one part of that larger music history. Still, it is a significant part, for it so strikingly results from the conscious appropriation of music to construct German-Americanness. The more closely we examine the musical texts representing the history of this German-Americanness, the more we witness that the malleability of musical traditions and the flexibility of even so-called conservative patterns of cultural identity can be rallied to the same ends.

Kirchen=Gesangbuch

für

Evangelisch-Lutherische Gemeinden

ungeänderter

Augsburgischer Confession,

darin des sel. Dr. Martin Luthers und anderer geistreichen
Lehrer gebräuchlichste Kirchen=Lieder enthalten sind.

St. Louis, Mo.
CONCORDIA PUBLISHING HOUSE.
1905.

Figure 3. Title page of *Kirchen-Gesangbuch.*

In a songbook like the *Lieder-Perlen* we hear this in the juxtaposition of German folk songs and hymns composed by C. F. W. Walther (1894:53), the spiritual founder of the Missouri Synod in America. We witness it when we open the *Lieder-Perlen* to be regaled with fantastic icons of America, the secular English and sacred German world facing each other on opposite pages (Walther 1894: Anhang, 60–61), or "The Star-Spangled Banner" printed in Bar-form (see Figure 4), as if it were a hymn created by Martin Luther (Walther 1894: 169–171). By inscribing "The Star-Spangled Banner" in the most traditional formal style of German hymnody, the anthem of Americanness becomes also an icon of German Lutheranness (cf. Schalk 1995).

The German-Jewish Reform Tradition

The Reform tradition of Judaism began as an early nineteenth-century German response to a theology, polity, and liturgy formed by Talmudic law and deemed resistant to the potential for emancipation and modernization unleashed by the Enlightenment (cf. Elbogen 1993:297–307). German in origin, Reform Judaism flourished in the United States, and its mainstream presence was a primary force shaping the Jewish community well into the twentieth century (Elbogen 1993:319–333). German-speaking immigrants allied themselves with Reform Judaism almost entirely until the final decades of the nineteenth century, and the mainstream presence of the Reform tradition remained so pervasive until the 1920s that we find observers, such as the following, equating it with the most basic symbols of Americanization: "The free spirit of American institutions is impatient of the restraints of rabbinical legislation as embodied in the *Shulchan Aruch*. The descendants of the immigrants, even in the first generation, are so affected by the free school, the free state, and the free atmosphere in which they live and move and have their being that they can impossibly entertain the religious views of their Orthodox forebearers" (quoted in Idelsohn 1929:333).

There are various historical explanations for this centripetalizing presence of Reform Judaism (see especially Meyer 1988). Because Jewish immigration until 1880 was almost entirely German—particularly so since 1800—and because these immigrants, in accordance with the German-American predilection for an intensive *Vereinswesen* had thoroughly institutionalized American-Jewish religious life, one explanation holds that Reform Judaism had what amounted to a hegemonic presence. Reform Judaism embodied a remarkably American form of religious identity, a syncretic blend of theology and American pragmatism. It created this blend, nonetheless, out of German elements. In many ways, the music of the Reform tradition became *the* voice for this blend, which is to say that it became a way of performing

183. The Star-spangled Banner.

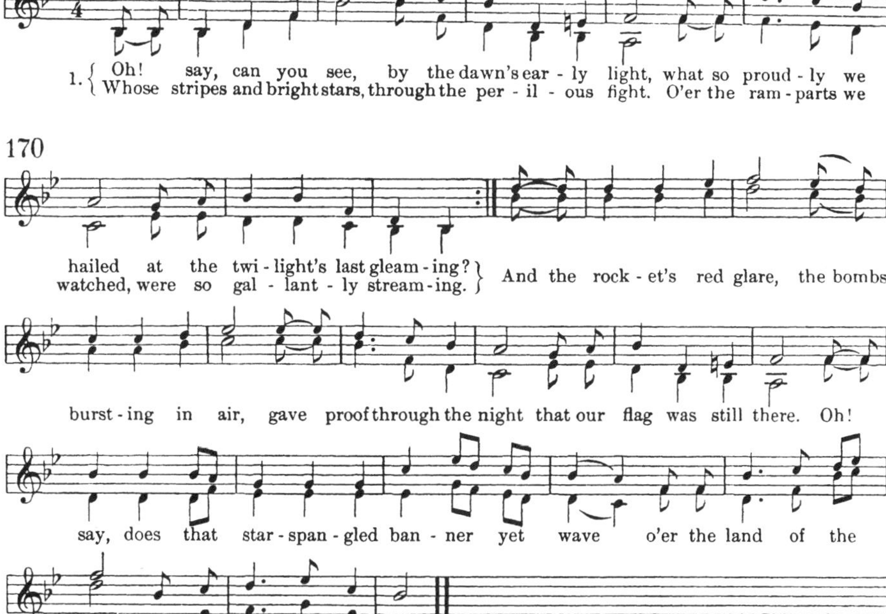
1. { Oh! say, can you see, by the dawn's ear - ly light, what so proud - ly we
Whose stripes and bright stars, through the per - il - ous fight. O'er the ram - parts we
170
hailed at the twi - light's last gleam - ing?
watched, were so gal - lant - ly stream - ing. }
And the rock - et's red glare, the bombs
burst - ing in air, gave proof through the night that our flag was still there. Oh!
say, does that star - span - gled ban - ner yet wave o'er the land of the
free and the home of the brave?

2. On the shore, dimly seen through the mist
of the deep,
Where the foes haughty host in dread silence re-
poses,
What is that which the breeze, o'er the towering
steep,
As it fitfully blows, half conceals, half discloses?
Now it catches the gleam of the morning's first
beam,
In full glory reflected, now shines on the stream;
'Tis the starspangled banner, oh! long may it wave
O'er the land of the free and the home of the brave.

171

3. And where is that band, who so vauntingly
swore,
Mid the havoc of war and the battles confusion,
A home and a country they'd leave us no more?
Their blood has washed out their foul foot-steps
pollution;
No refuge could save the hireling and slave
From the terror of flight or the gloom of the
grave,
And the star-spangled banner in triumph shall
wave
O'er the land of the free and the home of the
brave.

4. Oh! thus be it ever when freemen shall stand
Between their loved home and the war's desola-
tion,
Blest with victory and peace, may the heaven res-
cued land
Praise the Power that hath made and preserved us
a nation.
Then conquer we must, when our cause it is just,
And this be our motto: "In God is our trust."
And the star-spangled banner in triumph shall
wave
While the land of the free is the home of the
brave.

Figure 4. "The Star-Spangled Banner," #183 in the *Lieder-Perlen*.

the American acculturative experience into being. Abraham Zvi Idelsohn, himself a new immigrant from Germany (though Latvian in upbringing) in the late 1920s, wrote of the Americanization immanent in synagogue song in 1929.

> True to the principle that the song is the tonal expression of ideas and sentiments, of modes of life and the combats of life, the Synagogue song had to undergo changes in order to become once more a genuine expression of that group of Jews which was being remolded under new conditions. . . . More than in any other cultural sphere [the] psychological change [in the second immigrant generation] manifested itself in the Synagogue song, song being a genuine expression of emotions and sentiments. Fundamental changes could be expected here. . . . Scattered in small groups throughout the vast country of predominant Anglo-Saxon *milieu*, imbued by its culture, educated in its schools, carried along by its train of thought, the heart of the young generation from its infancy on vibrated to the sound of Anglo-Saxon song. The Germanized Synagogue song, which the Ashkenazic immigrants had brought with them to this country, was thus more and more Occidentalized, and the Oriental-Jewish elements gradually deteriorated to a meaningless exotic chant (Idelsohn 1929 318–319).

The music of the American Reform tradition consisted therefore of three historical levels: the traditional Ashkenazic,[17] with its modal system and largely oral transmission; the German, influenced by congregational Protestant traditions; and what Idelsohn calls the Anglo-Saxon, whereby he refers to the American tradition of hymnody.

We should not presume, however, that these three historical levels just settled out in a musical style history. Quite the contrary, the attempt to create a Reform hymnody for American congregations was aggressive, and it reflected the processes that undergirded the formation of immigrant Christian hymn traditions. Briefly stated: the American hymnbook was a vessel into which all sorts of songs were dumped, often regardless of denomination and not unusually with an aesthetic of convenience. Today, it strikes us as strange to find Christian hymns and obviously Protestant forms in the Jewish liturgy and hymnals of the nineteenth century. Moreover,

---

[17] The Hebrew word *ashkenaz* means simply "German." Ashkenazic Jewish communities are those from Central and Eastern Europe. Speaking German or Yiddish as vernaculars, Ashkenazic Jewish communities have folk-music repertories that reflect the centuries of residence in Germanic-speaking areas. Ashkenazic liturgies have distinctive melodic styles and modal repertories (cf. Werner 1976).

these often predominated in hymnals that had only a handful—and I mean literally four or five—of songs in Hebrew, with the rest in English and German.

Such hymnals, prayer books, and *siddurim* are strange only if we try to place them in a historical model that presumes a pre-immigrant prototype for German-Jewish musical practices and then a gradual transition to an American form of worship that perpetuated a single tradition. Again, a more archaeological perspective and methodology would better serve us as we seek explanations for the contradictory ways in which music represented the Reform tradition in America. I should like to trace the path of Americanization in a single prayer book, David Einhorn's *Gebetbuch für Israelitische Reform-Gemeinden*, which first appeared in Baltimore in 1858, and then was published in a "new translation after the German original" in 1896 by Emil Hirsch of Chicago (see Figure 5). Assuring the prayer book's user that the book could not be tampered with because David Einhorn's "very soul . . . found incarnation in the pages of the book" (Hirsch in Einhorn 1896:iii), Hirsch takes us on an extended journey, in which every possible form of German-Americanization is explored or at least tried out for its potential efficacy.

This translation pretends to be nothing more than what the word implies. Inspection will show the departures from the original to have been few. The changes introduced were suggested by the desire to adapt the book more readily to its practical uses. For this reason, in Part II, the full text of the hymns has been added. The hymns are partly original by the translator; partly they are adaptations and translations from the German, made by him; a few have been taken from the translator's scrapbook and are from the pen of anonymous contributors to periodical literature. It will also be noticed that many of the Hebrew poems, which in the German edition are rendered in rhymed prose, are here presented in a metrical form. For this, the translator, too, is responsible. He trusts that his attempts in this direction will not be found too much below the high plane of their surroundings. It may have been a hazardous venture on his part to add a few prayers not found in the original. This was done in order to meet the demand expressed by some of the colleagues of varying occasionally the text of the prayers read. These additional prayers will be found to be recasts, largely, of thoughts expressed by Einhorn, and to follow his own method of utilizing biblical passages. The Week-Day Service, as given here, is also an enlargement of the formula contained in the German edition. In some of the congregations using Einhorn's ritual, the Week-Day (Sunday) Service has become a permanent institution, and it was with a view of meeting this circumstance that the translator made bold to introduce what changes he has. The order of "Taking out the Scroll" differs also from that in the German. The reasons that prompted this revision are plain. To make the choral features a more prominent part seemed desir-

עלת תמיד.

Gebetbuch

für

Israelitische Reform-Gemeinden.

עלת תמיד העשיה בהר סיני לריח ניחח אשה ליהוה.

Ein beständiges Ganzopfer, dargebracht am
Har-Sinai zum lieblichen Geruche,
ein Feueropfer dem Ewigen.
(4. B. M. 28, 6.)

Baltimore.
Gedruckt bei C. W. Schneidereith No. 61 Sharp-Straße.
1858.

Figure 5. David Einhorn, *Gebetbuch für Israelitische Reform-Gemeinden* (1896).

able. The responses assigned to the choir, have been, as far as possible, rendered in the rhythm of the German original so that the music written for the German text can be used also for the English (Hirsch in Einhorn 1896:iv–v; parentheses in the original).

To perform the hymns in Hirsch's edition of Einhorn's prayer book is to perform one's Jewishness, Germanness, and Americanness. The feeling of the German language is not lost in the English settings; nor is a growing American confidence to be lost upon the Jewish worshiper using the book, whose contents have grown and multiplied in the new edition.

Hymnals and synagogue song in America have continued to grow and expand to the present, with some standard German-Jewish Reform books still forming the mainstream, notably the *Union Prayer Book* and the *Union Hymnal*, but numerous other influences, such as Reconstructionism, have also entered, not least as American Judaism assumes a new position vis-à-vis the international Judaism made possible by the establishment of Israel in 1948. As American-Jewish history was being made, however, the music of American Jews, raised in song and embodied in congregational life, was present in the making (see Summit 2000).

The Many Voices of German-American Music History

> The hymnal is a unique tool for worship. It is a treasury of theology, poetry, music, history, liturgy, and praise. . . . [I]t is truly "the people's book." (Wisconsin Evangelical Lutheran Synod 1993:9)

> The flowering of popular hymnody is the greatest of the artistic contributions of the Lutheran churches. . . . The hymnal was conceived as a collection for Lutherans who had become Americans in speech and culture. (*Lutheran Book of Worship* 1978:6, 7)

If we found that, in the beginning, there were hymnals and hymnbooks, we have also discovered them to exert a persistent presence in the music histories spawned at these beginnings. Change, debate, disagreement, innovation, composition, and multicultural juxtapositions—the nature of religious music histories in North American have changed not at all since the beginning; if anything, change and the power invested in hymnals have increased. As the epigraphs opening this section make clear, moreover, there is little doubt about the actors and agents, the musicians and the music-makers in the music history that I examine here: the hymnal truly is "the people's book," and it has been generations of immigrants and the transformation of ethnic communities that have made a people's music history.

Surely, the hymnal has proved to demonstrate an unexpected presence in the archaeology of knowledge whose complex levels I have examined here, although I might dispel any notions that this presence should be unexpected by turning momentarily to recent history. First of all, I should observe that my own fascination with the effect of these archaeological objects on the performers of tradition resulted from my ethnographic pursuits, in other words, my own fieldwork in several German-American religious communities—Lutherans in the Upper Midwest, Jews in Pittsburgh. Not only did I encounter the hymnals in the church, synagogue, or home, but I found that their owners sang from them, that is, that these hymnals continued to function in the performance of community and self-knowledge. We might pause, then, and ask ourselves: Why was this possible? And what does it signify?

The hymnal has also not ceased making history for the Missouri Synod or in any of the other historically German-American synods. During a period of conciliation and liberalization in the 1950s and 1960s, the Missouri Synod moved to broaden its dialogue with other Lutheran synods, particularly the larger multi-ethnic synods undergoing consolidation themselves. Consolidation assumed specifically theological, musical, and ethnic forms. At an institutional level, this meant the formation of commissions to reform worship among Lutherans. At an epistemological level, this meant the attempts to create a common hymnody, beginning first in 1945, with a second period of reform beginning again in 1965. Resistance to this reform movement broke out in the late 1960s and intensified in the 1970s, the result of which was a reaffirmation of conservatism in the Wisconsin Evangelical Lutheran Synod and the Missouri Synod, the dominant German-American Lutheran traditions (Luebke 1990: 11–12). The battle within the Missouri Synod was fought on theological grounds and won because of a realignment of the authority structure. The Wisconsin Synod, in fact, chose not to do battle at all, embarking on a path of reform that would lead to the publication—again, after some 150 years of church history—of its own hymnal in 1993.[18]

---

[18] The Wisconsin Synod, nonetheless, interpreted its reform of the hymnal as both conservative and innovative. "The phrase 'new/revised' in the synodical resolutions was interpreted to mean a hymnal which *preserved* the Christian and Lutheran heritage of liturgy and hymns from *The Lutheran Hymnal* and at the same time *improved* and *expanded* it" (Wisconsin Evangelical Lutheran Synod 1993:8, emphases in the original). To achieve the seemingly contradictory goal, the compilers retained the core repertory of four hundred hymns and then just added to it hymns that would serve as the markers of Americanization at the end of the twentieth century. "The last three decades have seen a strong resurgence of creativity and interest in the writing of hymns. Therefore, congregations will enjoy a greater variety of hymns than formerly. In addition to Lutheran chorales and traditional English hymnody, a wide selection of plainsong hymns, spirituals, folk hymns from Appalachia, Wales, Ire-

The battle among the different German-American Lutheran synods primarily employed musical weapons: ultimately, it was a struggle over hymnal reform.[19] In brief, the contested turf was the matter of retaining the Germanic basis of Missouri Synod hymnody and the liturgical order that the hymnal had embodied, intentionally so, as a pure representation of the piety of the early centuries of the German Reformation. Few congregations still used the German language, but it was not language that was at issue, rather the ability of the hymnal itself to reflect a changing congregational body. In the end, after a bitter struggle, attempts at compromise were dropped, and the Missouri Synod implemented a new version of its traditional hymnal, but it also participated in the commission to reform a common hymnal, *The Lutheran Book of Worship* (1978). Individual congregations implicitly retained the right to choose between the two, or combine aspects of the two, and in so doing, they were able to assert numerous aspects of their ethnic and religious identities. With a response to hymn reform, the Missouri Synod made a powerful statement about its own German and American histories.

The music histories of the Missouri Synod and Reform Judaism are only several of the thousands that have characterized the lives of German-American religious communities. Some of these histories have been long, and they have changed only gradually; there were certainly many music histories that were so brief, so fleeting that we may not yet have learned of their existence. The Amish confront the martyrdom of their founders each time they crack open the *Ausbund* (1742), but there are other groups that may have lost track of who their founders were. Some of the competing Jewish Reform hymnals and prayer books of the early twentieth century may have had a decidedly Protestant influence on their contents, but others reformed the reform, returning to the traditional melodies and repertories, perhaps guided by the authority of highly schooled cantors, yet another product of an American music culture (cf. Slobin 1989).

When we put all these traditions together, juxtaposing them as I have deliberately done in this essay, we shape the religious musical traditions into a whole that has many parts, many of which stick out and seem not to want to fit. We create, in

---

land, and elsewhere, gospel hymns, and contemporary hymns in different styles are included" (Wisconsin Evangelical Lutheran Synod 1993:9).

[19] As if to recall the struggle itself, every major Lutheran hymnal produced during and after the period of reform includes a description of its relation to the issues of reform in an "Introduction." Even by beginning at the beginning of the hymnal, so to speak, the user—the worshiper or singer—immediately realizes where she or he enters the history symbolized by the hymnal in use by a particular congregation.

fact, a postmodern historical whole, and within this new patterns and new musical connections take shape. I have already used the term *bricolage* to describe the coexistence of these histories, their insistence on being different, and yet their coherence within a larger German-American religious music history. Contradictory yet representative of many of the same immigrant and ethnic experiences, religious musics have responded to German-American history with many voices. Giving voice to that history, animating the reflexivity implicit in the hyphen between German and American, religious musics embody a constant redefinition of the many identities German-Americans have constructed in their knowledge of themselves.

Bibliography

Asad, Talal. *Genealogies of Religion: Discipline and Reasons of Power in Christianity and Islam*. Baltimore: The Johns Hopkins University Press, 1993.

Ausbund. Ausbund, Das ist: Etliche schöne Christliche Lieder, Wie sie in dem Gefängnis zu Passau in dem Schloß von den Schweitzer-Brüdern, und von anderen rechtgläubigen Christen hin und her gedichtet worden. Germantown: Christoph Saur, 1742. (Reprinted as *Mennonite Songbooks, American Series I*. Edited by Irvin B. Horst. Amsterdam: Frits Knuf, n.d.)

Bachmann-Geiser, Brigitte, and Eugen Bachmann. *Amische: Die Lebensweise der Amischen in Berne, Indiana*. Bern: Benteli, 1988.

Blackwell, Carolyn S. "German Jewish Identity and German Jewish Emigration to the Midwest in the 19th Century." In *Emigration and Settlement Patterns of German Communities in North America*, edited by Eberhard Reichmann, LaVern J. Rippley, and Jörg Nagler, 310–321. Indianapolis: Max Kade German-American Center, Indiana University-Purdue University at Indianapolis, 1995.

Blum, Stephen, Philip V. Bohlman, and Daniel M. Neuman, eds. *Ethnomusicology and Modern Music History*. Urbana: University of Illinois Press, 1991.

Bohlman, Philip V. "Music in the Culture of German-Americans in North-Central Wisconsin." Master's thesis, University of Illinois at Urbana-Champaign, 1980.

________. "Deutsch-amerikanische Musik in Wisconsin–Überleben im Melting Pot." *Jahrbuch für Volksliedforschung* 30 (1985): 99-116.

________. "Religious Music/Secular Music: The Press of the German-American Church and Aesthetic Mediation." In Geitz, ed., 69–90, 1992.

________. "Die 'Pennsylvanische Sammlung von Kirchen-Musik': Ein Lehrbuch zu Deutsch-Amerikanisierung." *Jahrbuch für Volksliedforschung* 38 (1993): 90–109.

________. "'Still, They Were All Germans in Town' – Music in the Multi-Religious German-American Community." In *Emigration and Settlement Patterns of German Communities in North America*, edited by Eberhard Reichmann, LaVern J. Rippley, and Jörg Nagler, 275–293. Indianapolis: Max

Kade German-American Center, Indiana University–Purdue University at Indianapolis, 1995.

Born, Georgina. *Rationalizing Culture: IRCAM, Boulez, and the Institutionalization of the Musical Avant-Garde*. Berkeley: University of California Press, 1995.

Chase, Gilbert. *America's Music: From the Pilgrims to the Present*. Rev., 3rd edn. Urbana: University of Illinois Press, 1987.

Conzen, Kathleen Neils. "Germans." In *Harvard Encyclopedia of Ethnic Groups*, edited by Stephan Thernstrom, Ann Orlov, and Oscar Handlin, 405–425. Cambridge, MA: Harvard University Press, 1980.

Crawford, Richard. *The American Musical Landscape*. Berkeley: University of California Press, 1993.

Dobkrowski, Michael N. "'The Fourth Reich'—German-Jewish Religious Life in America Today." *Judaism* 27(n.d.): 80–95.

Elbogen, Ismar. *Jewish Liturgy: A Comprehensive History*. Translated by Raymond P. Scheindlin. Philadelphia and New York: The Jewish Publication Society and The Jewish Theological Seminary of America, 1993.

Einhorn, David. *Book of Prayers for Jewish Congregations*. Trans. by Emil G. Hirsch. Chicago: S. Ettlinger, 1896.

Foucault, Michel. *The Order of Things: An Archaeology of the Human Sciences*. New York: Random House, 1970.

________. *The Archaeology of Knowledge and The Discourse on Language*. Translated by A. M. Sheridan Smith. New York: Pantheon, 1972.

________. "Space, Knowledge, and Power." In *A Foucault Reader*, edited by Paul Rabinow, 239-56. New York: Pantheon, 1984.

Frühauf, Tina. "Orgeln und Orgelmusik jüdischer Gemeinden im deutschsprachigen Raum." Doctoral dissertation, Folkwang-Hochschule Essen, 2000.

Geitz, Henry, ed. *The German-American Press*. Madison: Max Kade Institute for German-American Studies, University of Wisconsin–Madison, 1992.

Glazer, Nathan. *American Judaism*. 2nd edn., revised. Chicago: University of Chicago Press, 1989.

Hinks, Donald R. *Brethren Hymn Books and Hymnals, 1720–1884*. Gettysburg, PA: Brethren Heritage Press, 1986.

Hitchcock, H. Wiley. 1988. *Music in the United States: An Historical Introduction*. 3rd edn. Englewood Cliffs, NJ: Prentice Hall, 1988.

Holzapfel, Otto. *Religiöse Identität und Gesangbuch: Zur Ideologiegeschichte deutschsprachiger Einwanderer in den USA und die Auseinandersetzung um das 'richtige' Gesangbuch*. Berne: Peter Lang, 1998.

Idelsohn, A. Z. *Jewish Music in Its Historical Development*. New York: Holt, Rinehart, and Winston, 1929.

________. *Jewish Liturgy and Its Development*. New York: Henry Holt, 1932.

Kingman, Daniel. *American Music: A Panorama*. 2nd ed. New York: Schirmer Books, 1990.

Levine, Joseph A. *Synagogue Song in America*. Crown Point, IN: White Cliffs Media Co., 1989.

Lieder-Perlen. St. Louis: Concordia Publishing House, 1894.

Luebke, Frederick C. *Germans in the New World: Essays in the History of Immigration*. Urbana: University of Illinois Press, 1990.

Lutheran Book of Worship. Lutheran Book of Worship. Minneapolis and Philadelphia: Augsburg Publishing House and Board of Publication, Lutheran Church of America, 1978.

Martens, Helen. "Die Lieder der Hutterer und ihre Verbindung zum Meistergesang im 16. Jahrhundert." *Jahrbuch für Volksliedforschung* 26 (1981): 31–43.

Meyer, Michael A. "German-Jewish Identity in Nineteenth-Century America." In *Toward Modernity: The European Jewish Model*, edited by Jacob Katz, 247–267. New Brunswick, NJ: Transaction Books, 1987.

________. *Response to Modernity: A History of the Reform Movement in Judaism*. New York: Oxford University Press, 1988.

Peck, Abraham J., ed. *The German-Jewish Legacy in America, 1938–1988: From Bildung to the Bill of Rights*. Detroit: Wayne State University Press, 1989.

Pennsylvanische Sammlung. Pennsylvanische Sammlung von Kirchen-Musik. Harrisburg, PA: F. Wyeth, 1840.

Peterson, Brent. "Masthead Iconography as *Rezeptionsvorgabe*: Producing *Die Abendschule*'s Family of Readers." In Geitz, ed., 91–117, 1992.

Rabinow, Paul. "Introduction." In idem, ed., *A Foucault Reader*, 3–29. New York: Pantheon, 1984.

Schalk, Carl. *The Roots of Hymnody in the Lutheran Church—Missouri Synod*. St. Louis: Concordia Publishing House, 1965.

________. *God's Song in a New Land: Lutheran Hymnals in America*. St. Louis: Concordia Publishing House, 1995.

Schnabel, J. G. *Insel Felsenburg*. Volker Meid and Ingeborg Springer-Strand, eds. Stuttgart: Reclam, 1979 [1731].

Seeger, Anthony. "When Music Makes History." In *Ethnomusicology and Modern Music History*, edited by Stephen Blum, Philip V. Bohlman, and Daniel M. Neuman, 23–24. Urbana: University of Illinois Press, 1991.

Slobin, Mark. *Chosen Voices: The Story of the American Cantorate*. Urbana: University of Illinois Press, 1989.

Strauss, Herbert A. "The Immigration and Acculturation of the German Jew in the United States of America." *Yearbook—Leo Baeck Institute* (1970): 63–94.

Summit, Jeffrey A. *The Lord's Song in a Strange Land: Music and Identity in Contemporary Jewish Worship*. New York: Oxford University Press (American Musicspheres), 2000.

Tomlinson, Gary. *Music in Renaissance Magic: Toward a Historiography of Others*. Chicago: University of Chicago Press, 1993.

Werner, Eric. *A Voice Still Heard: The Sacred Songs of the Ashkenazic Jews*. University Park, PA: Pennsylvania State University Press, 1976.

Wisconsin Evangelical Lutheran Synod, ed. *Christian Worship: A Lutheran Hymnal*. Milwaukee: Northwestern Publishing House, 1993.

7

MUSICAL LIFE AMONG THE CANADIAN HUTTERITES

Helmut Wulz

Jetzt ist die Zeit und Stunde da, Daß wir ziehn nach Amerika. Die Pferde sind schon angespannt, Wir ziehen in ein fremdes Land:	The hour of decision is now upon us, For us to go to America. The horses are already hitched up, We are traveling to a foreign land.
Seid alle männlich und seid stark, Macht uns den Abschied nicht zu hart. Wir ziehen ja nicht aus der Welt, Auch da ist Gott, der uns erhält.	Act like grown men and be strong, Do not make departure all too hard. We are not leaving the world altogether, There is also God, who receives us.
Und wenn das Schiff zur See einschwimmt, Dann werden Liedl angestimmt. Wir fürchten keinen Wasserfall, Der liebe Gott ist überall. (Hutterite *Gesangbuch*)	And when the ship is out to sea, Then we raise our voice in song. We're afraid of no waterfall, Because dear God is everywhere.

The history of the Hutterites lives in their songs. Indeed, the identity of the Hutterites—their sense of who they are in relation to the world around them—is transmitted through their songs, not only those contained in the 3,404 pages of the Hutterites' three volumes of *Chronicles* (Figure 1) and their *Gesangbuch* (Songbook), but also in the everyday songs they draw from a mixture of oral and written traditions. The "everyday," however, does not exist separated from the ongoing history of the Hutterites, but rather the everyday provides the opportunity to reenact and remember the history of what it is that has fixed the identity of the Hutterites so firmly. There is no more important means of reenacting and remembering that identity than the songs the Hutterites sing.

This is because Hutterite identity in North America resides on the surface of Hutterite culture: the simple clothing the Hutterites wear, the strange sounds of the language they speak with each other, the overt "skin of pastness" that covers an even deeper layer of strangeness. For Europeans—in my case, for an Austrian from the southern state of Carinthia—Hutterite identity may also be manifest on the surface, but we are drawn immediately beneath the surface: by highly symbolic dress, by the language that is more familiar than strange, and by songs that narrate a history that derives from our own. The Hutterites, however, live in North America, where they live out their past in the midst of a modern world. Although there are Hutterites in Europe, they are few in number, and their communities are small and dispersed; the residents in most of these communities, moreover, came originally from North America.

The journey to the Hutterites and to the history that intersects with our own European and rural Austrian sense of identity means, therefore, traveling to North America. It is a journey that begins with modern transportation, but ultimately it is a journey that enters the narrative space of Hutterite songs. The journey begins with the strangeness of the surface but continues with the familiarity underneath, the familiarity of song and the past that Hutterite song embodies and uses to confront and challenge modernity.

This chapter is the account of one such journey to the Canadian Hutterites. At the beginning, it was my intent to discover something common about a shared Austrian identity, more specifically, a shared Carinthian identity. When I initially undertook my research, I believed that I was in search of "old songs" about the past. At the end, I realized that the songs I heard and recorded were also about the present and about the maintenance of identity in modern North America. The Hutterite journey of history is itself old, having begun in the sixteenth century, but it is ongoing and palpable today. The songs that narrate the Hutterite journey of history are therefore not just surviving traces of its earlier stages: those songs connect us through the past to the present and to a German-American musical culture that, in all its strangeness, becomes strangely modern when we listen to the music of the Hutterites in North America.

Familiar Language—Foreign Sound: Following the Trail of the Hutterites

For many in North America the term *Hutterites* is not a foreign word, devoid of associations, but rather a reference to an ethnic group, whose members have chosen to live an existence isolated by the language, religion, and socioeconomic structure of their community. If North Americans also sometimes confuse Hutterites with other German-speaking religious sects—the Amish and Mennonites, for example—they nonetheless have a sense of the cultural components that give Hutterite ethnicity its distinctiveness: intense practices of Christianity, language maintenance over many

Geschichtbuech
vnnd kürtzer durchgang von anfang
der welt / wie Gott sein werck inn seinem
volck auff erden angericht / gehandlet /
vnnd triben hat.

Demnach:

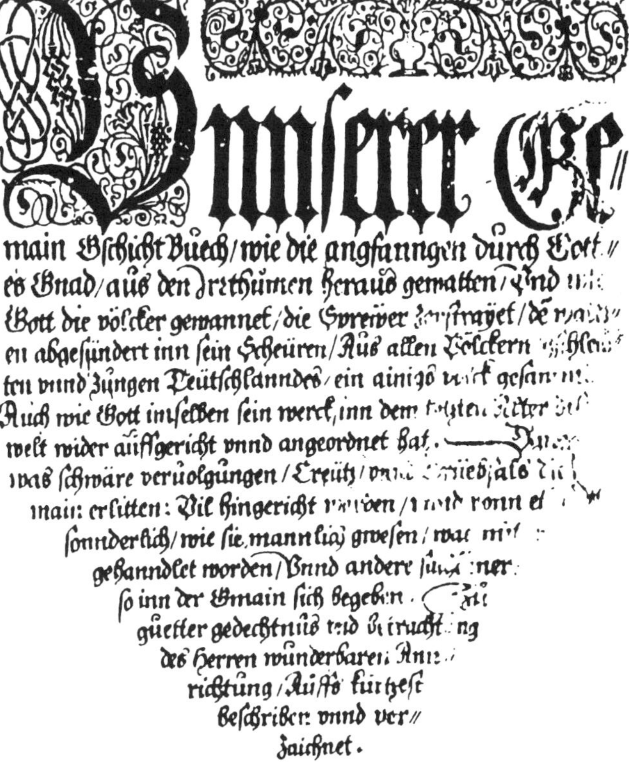
Vnserer Ge=
main Gschicht Buech / wie die angfanngen durch Gott=
es Gnad / aus den Irrthümen heraus gewatten / Vnd wie
Gott die völcker gewannet / die Spreiuer zerstrayet / de [illegible]
en abgesündert inn sein Scheüren / Aus allen Völckern [illegible]
ten vnnd Zungen Teütschlanndes / ein ainig volck gesam[illegible]
Auch wie Gott inselben sein werck, inn dem letzten Alter der
welt wider auffgericht vnnd angeordnet hat. —— Vnd
was schwäre veruolgungen / Creütz / vnnd [illegible] als die
main erlitten: Vil hingericht worden / [illegible]
sonnderlich / wie sie mannlich gwesen / was mit [illegible]
gehanndlet worden / Vnnd andere [illegible]ner
so inn der Gmain sich begeben. [illegible]
güetter gedechtnus vnd betrachtung
des Herren wunderbaren An=
richtung / Auffs kürtzest
beschriben vnnd ver=
zaichnet.

Figure 1. Title page of the *Hutterer-Chronik* or *Geschichtsbuch der hutterischen Brüder* centuries, characteristic and highly symbolic dress, and song. Most Americans and Canadians who have centuries of experience with diverse languages and cultures in North America are also aware of the fact that the prairies of the American and Canadian West provide the optimal conditions for the cultivation of such distinct and isolated ways of life, for they permit relative self-sufficiency. The ethnic identity and history of the Hutterites, while uniquely their own, have taken shape in North American cultural contexts. Like other North American ethnic groups, the Hutterites found in North America a place in which they could cultivate their sense of self.

In Austria, however, knowledge of the history of the Wiedertäufer (literally, "those baptized again") movement and the specific historical stream of the Hutterite brotherhoods is not widespread but rather remains the purview of scholarly investigations. Indeed, those interested in the Hutterites have largely been linguists studying the phenomenon of isolated language communities, the so-called *Sprachinseln* or "speech islands," that contain the traces of Central European expansion since the Middle Ages (cf. Weber-Kellermann 1978, Weber-Kellermann 1975, and Schaaf 1975).

European interest in the Hutterite communities of North America, which bear the self ascription of "sacred arches in an ocean of sin" (Mumelter 1986), increased when Michael Holzach (1982) and Bernd G. Längin (1986) published their journals and observations of contemporary life among the Hutterites. Recent television and radio accounts further contributed to European awareness of the Hutterites. Though written from different perspectives, these accounts shared a common fascination with the survival of European cultural elements, particularly language. As European awareness of the Hutterites in North America grew, so too did the tendency to portray them as cases of marginal survival or speech islands that had never succumbed to the melting pot.

This was particularly true in the Austrian province of Carinthia, whose Lutheran emigrants (Buchinger 1980), in German called *Transmigranten* (transmigrants), joined with the Hutterite brotherhoods in the middle of the eighteenth century, rather than diminishing in size and eventually disappearing altogether. Today, these former Carinthian Pietists constitute the main part of the so-called "Schmiedeleute." Accordingly, it is not by accident that the Hutterite community with the largest number of members remains under the spiritual guidance of Jakob Kleinsasser, who does not refer to himself as a bishop, but as a "respected elder," retaining the Lutheran tradition.

My first personal contacts with Hutterites date back to 1958, when, as a member of a touring Viennese choral group (Wiener Akademie Kammerchor), I encountered a group of women and men in Winnipeg wearing clothing that distinguished them from everyone else: women with full-length skirts and bodices in muted colors, wearing black scarves with white polka dots; fully bearded men with black suits, plaid shirts, wearing suspenders and black hats.

Although I was a student at the University of Vienna at this time, working extensively in dialect research, I failed to use this opportunity to learn more about the dialect spoken by the Hutterites. There was, indeed, no awareness at this time of the connections between the language spoken by the Hutterites and the dialects studied by Austrian linguists. It would be fifteen years later that my interest in the dialect of the Hutterites became stimulated, when I came across a letter written in that dialect in Hermann Prasch's cultural history of Upper Carinthia (Prasch 1990). The letter had been included in Prasch's volume in response to an inquiry from the Mennonite Research Center Weierhof, asking for surviving evidence about Hutterites (with the names Hofer, Glanzer, Waldner, Wurz, and Kleinsasser) whose homesteads were believed to have been near Spittal an der Drau, the town chronicled in the book.

The popularity of genealogy in the 1970s stimulated an interest among North American Hutterites in the "homeland" of their ancestors. As early as 1974, Jakob Kleinsasser and some of his brethren visited the Kleinsasserhof (literally, the Kleinsasser farm) in Oberamlach near Spittal, which had become an alpine tourist resort. Following Kleinsasser's visit, I proposed that Austrian Television (ORF) make a film documenting life on a Canadian Hutterite farm, but it was ten years before this could be realized, and then only as a brief cultural spot accompanying the news, in which linguistic and folkloristic aspects of the Hutterites received only marginal attention. At about the same time, regional television in Tyrol produced a documentary on the Hutterites, and this film heightened public awareness in Austria of an economically developed rural community in North America whose daily lives adhered closely to the teachings of the Bible and whose roots were Austrian.

During the past twenty years, the interest in Hutterite identity has grown both in Canada and Austria, and one might argue that it has stimulated a process of exchange and searching for a mutual selfness. Hutterite teachers from Canada, endeavoring to strengthen language instruction in their communities, have been attending language courses in Rothenburg ob der Tauber in Germany. While attending the language institutes, these Brethren also make excursions to the memorials of Brethren and Hutterite martyrs in Southern Tyrol (the German-speaking northeastern part of Italy), Austria, Slovakia, and the Czech Republic.

In the summer of 1990, Gertrud Gasser, current owner of the resort where the Kleinsasserhof used to be, asked me if I might bring the Hutterite teachers traveling

Figure 2: "Der Herr ist mein getreuer Hirt" (The Lord Is My Shepherd—Psalm 23)

in Austria to the radio and television station in Klagenfurt, the capital of Carinthia. Aware of the Hutterite reservations about contact with electronic media, I decided that the appropriate way to respond to Gasser's request was simply to give the Hutterites a tour of the station and respond to their questions about the responsibility of regional television to the maintenance of local culture. Such questions of local culture and identity—What goes into maintaining Carinthian identity through radio and television?—were of great interest to the Hutterites, and they responded in kind, granting me an interview in which they provided a detailed account of life on a Hutterite farm and described their initial impressions of Europe on this trip.

We had entered into a dialogue of exchange, with each side learning more about the other, but by extension learning more about themselves. At a certain point, the Hutterite teachers, who had come from different communities in Canada, burst spontaneously into song, as if to bring us to yet another common language. This was, in fact, my first encounter with Hutterite song, and it would be a critical moment in the European encounter with the importance of song in the crucial Hutterite maintenance of their own identity. From this first, critical moment, two aspects of Hutterite song were immediately evident. First, Hutterite song provided a means of representing certain aspects of Hutterite identity that words or conversation alone could not convey. Second, these men sang out of natural enjoyment. For the Hutterites, the most profound and the most joyful aspects of their own identity overlap, indeed, find their origins, in song.

Just as striking as the singing was the Hutterite language employed in song and in everyday conversation. I was familiar with it as a dialect from Upper Carinthia that was still used on isolated farms in the western part of the province where I had conducted fieldwork. My initial impression was that this dialect had remained relatively intact for 250 years. It was the recognition of these connections between

Carinthia and Canada that brought about the field research upon which I base much of this article, namely a trip to the Hutterite colony of James Valley in Manitoba. David Hofer, one of the teachers in the community, offered me his assistance and hospitality. The community also took it upon itself to provide me spiritual preparation, and Hofer sent me two important books on the Hutterites, the new editions of the *Großes Geschichtbuch der hutterischen Brüder* (The Large History of the Hutterite Brethren) (Wolkan 1923) and *Die Lieder der hutterischen Brüder* (The Songs of the Hutterite Brethren) (Hutterische Brüder in Kanada 1982/1983).[1]

It was significant that my introduction to current Hutterite identity comprised books on history and collected songs. The narratives of songs and historical accounts often intersect in Hutterite teachings, with many songs being explicitly historical and many historical texts employing songs as the most effective means of telling their stories. I should like, therefore, to turn to the historical background of the Hutterites in order to describe the conditions that determine the functions and characteristics of their song tradition.

Disciples of Christ: A History of Centuries of Persecution, or a Short Chronicle of the Hutterites

Der Henker tat ihn nehmen.	The executioner took him.
Führen auf den Platz der Stadt	Led him to the main square of the city
Und ihm die Zunge abschneiden	And cut out his tongue
Nach dem tyrannischen Rat.	As ordered by the tyrannical council.
Dem nach auf den Wagen schmieden.	After that, he was drawn and quartered.
Waren mit dem noch zufrieden.	But still they were not pleased.
Ihm mit feurig glühenden Zangen	Fiery, glowing pincers
Zweimal sein Leib angangen. . . .	Were twice driven into his body. . . .
Noch konntens nit satt werden	Still, they could not get enough
An allem wie gehört.	Of everything they felt was owed them.
Er wird von dieser Erden	He was entirely murdered, till death,
Ja ganz zum Tod ermördt.	And from this earth he departed.
Zum Aschen und Pulver verbrennt.	He was burned to ash and powder.
Also gings mit ihm zum End.	And thus he came to his end.
Welches ist doch zum Erbarmen,	Because of this we pity him,

[1] Combining these two monumental primary sources with some of the secondary case studies by German and Canadian folklorists and folksong scholars (especially Brednich 1981a, 1981b, 1981c, and 1982/1983; and Martens 1981) allows one to establish the relation between song and singing practices to the maintenance of early Hutterite communities through a rural, agricultural economy.

Daß die Gottlosen so tyrannisch sind. That the godless were so tyrannical.
"Aus meines Herzens Grunde" (From the Depths of My Heart)[2]

The Hutterites claim their origins in the Anabaptist movement ("Täuferbewegung") of the early sixteenth century. This movement, like those of other early Protestants, came into being as a protest against the interpretation of communion and against the power struggle within church politics. The Hutterites believed in adult baptism and following Christ literally according to the Bible, and they strongly objected to any form of oath-taking, bearing arms (except for a designated group called "Schwertler," or sword-bearers), and the holding of public office. In the sixteenth century, both the Reformed Protestant and the Roman Catholic church hierarchies responded to the Wiedertäufer by persecuting, deporting, and killing them. Moravia was the first land to offer refuge and freedom of religion to the persecuted Wiedertäufer from southern Germany, Switzerland, and Austria. The first religious community was founded in the Moravian city of Nikolsburg (today Mikulov) in 1526, but it disintegrated soon thereafter because of disagreement over military service. The so-called "Stäbler," who opposed any form of military service, left Nikolsburg and established a community in Austerlitz and then later in Auspitz, where they determined to share all community property equally. By so doing, the Stäbler believed they were following biblical injunctions against owning personal property.[3]

In 1533 Jakob Huter, a hat maker[4] born in Moos in the Puster Valley of Tyrol and baptized in Carinthia, joined the brethren in Auspitz. Recognized by all as a "faithful servant to the Holy Scripture," Huter became the community's spiritual leader. Huter was a strict leader, nonetheless, and under his leadership the rules of the Hutterite brotherhood took canonic shape.

Persecution against the Wiedertäufer grew during the course of the sixteenth century, and religious wars, initiated by Dutch Anabaptists, broke out in Münster in western Germany and spread quickly to Moravia, eventually forcing some of the brotherhoods to dissolve. Huter was able to escape the religious conflicts in Moravia and to return with his wife and a companion to Tyrol, where he lived undercover until he was discovered in the town of Klausen in November 1535 and then impris-

---

[2] This song narrates the torture and murder of Michael Sattler, one of the earliest Hutterite martyrs, executed according to the song on May 21, 1527, in Rottenburg am Neckar (Holzach 1982:16).

[3] The communal ownership of property may also have been a reaction to early capitalism in the sixteenth century, when the increased tax pressure placed on farmers throughout the alpine regions created an uproar of protest and brought about increasing support for the Anabaptist movement.

[4] Huter means "hat maker."

oned. After repeated interrogation and torture, Huter was burned at the stake on February 25, 1536, in front in the public square of Innsbruck. In this historical way, the specific origins of the Hutterites begin in Austria, with the life and martyrdom of Huter.

In Moravia and Slovakia the landowners soon recognized the value of reassembling the Hutterite communities, for the Hutterites had excelled as craftsmen. In particular, the Hutterites contributed to the development of the local pottery tradition —Habanerkeramik—that came to represent the regional tradition of Moravia and contributed to the material well being of the Hutterite communities (see Kalesny 1985). During the Thirty Years' War (1618–1648) the Hutterites, as pacifists, were trapped in the middle and subjected to persecution from both sides. As many as twelve thousand fled to Slovakia, which was then part of the Hungarian Empire. These were forcibly dispersed, for example, when two hundred were deported eastward to Transylvania, where they founded the community of Winz/Vintus.

As the Counter-Reformation and attempts to restore Catholicism in the Austrian countries diminished in the eighteenth century, Transylvania (in modern Romania) assumed a new role as a center for Hutterite growth. Protestants migrated eastward from Austria to Transylvania, among them Lutherans from Carinthia who settled near Winz. Their charismatic leader, Josef Kühr, encouraged some forty Carinthians to join the Hutterite community, and new practices of communal ownership quickly led to economic success and the founding of new communities, for example Deutsch Kreuz and Stein. When new Jesuit moves against Carinthian Protestants intensified in the mid-eighteenth century, another group of seventy-eight Hutterite Brethren opted for emigration in 1767 and attempted to settle in the eastern Carpathians. Here, they were greeted by soldiers from the Russian-Turkish War, who plundered their communities and forced them farther to the east. A community of sixty-six survivors eventually escaped into Ukraine, settling near Kiev in 1770.

At the beginning of the nineteenth century and then again in 1819, the Hutterite communities in Ukraine foundered, making it necessary to abandon the practice of communal property ownership. It was to the great fortune of the Hutterites that Mennonites, another German-speaking Anabaptist sect, had settled in Ukraine and southern Russia, offered economic and material assistance, helping the Hutterites to establish several new communities near the Black Sea called Huttertal, Neu-Hutterdorf, and Johannisruck. Pressure increased upon both the Hutterites and the Mennonites to pay taxes and do military service, which threatened their religious belief systems and economic survival. With the centuries of persecution in Europe motivating their migrations away from Central Europe, the Hutterites decided to immigrate to the United States.

The organization of the Hutterite communal life that persists even today in North America took shape in southern Russia. It is important to recognize that these patterns are not an insignificant factor in the ways in which European and North American components of Hutterite culture have mixed together over the past century and a half. The blacksmith (German, *Schmied*) Michael Waldner formed a group of Hutterites known as "Schmeideleut."[5] The preacher Darius Walter became the spiritual leader of the "Dariusleut." The last group of Hutterites to leave Russia was the so-called "Lehrerleut," under the leadership of their teacher (*Lehrer*) and preacher, Jakob Wipf. The Dariusleut and the Lehrerleut strictly adhered to the principles of the brotherhood, whereas the Schmiedeleut generally were less orthodox in their adherence to these principles. All three groups have lived in mutual understanding of each other, although intermarriage is relatively rare.

After establishing the first Hutterite community in Bon Homme, South Dakota, the Hutterites practiced their religion and developed their economic system without external interference. World War I changed all this because the Hutterites refused to take part in military service. Because of their German and Austrian origins and the fact that they still spoke German, the Hutterites' pacifism was interpreted as lack of loyalty, and many Hutterite families suffered acts of violence and prejudice. The maltreatment of the Hutterites in the United States was so extreme that many moved to Canada, where they bought large tracts of farmland in Manitoba, Saskatchewan, and Alberta. The Prairie Provinces provided the opportunity to lead a life of isolation, modesty, and devotion to "work in the name of God." Despite growing pressures to modernize, most Hutterites remained content at this time to observe the strict rules governing their belief system and their way of life. It was this impression that greeted me in 1990, when I conducted fieldwork in the James Valley Colony and its neighboring Hutterite communities.

The Importance of Music for Hutterite Belief and Community Life

Eine Stadt will ich Euch nennen,	I shall describe a city for you,
Die liegt in Hessenland,	Which is found in Hesse,
Hamburg heißt sie mit Namen,	Its name is Hamburg,
Ist manchem wohlbekannt.	And for many it is famous.
Da wohnt ein Bürger fromm und gut,	There lived a citizen, devout and good,
Sein Handwerk ein Radgießer,	Who was by trade a wheelwright,
Ward reich und wohlgemut.	And he was rich and happy.

[5] The German *Leute* means "people." In Austrian German, the final *e* is deleted in vernacular usage. The resulting *Leut* often carries the more intimate meaning of a group of people joined in common purpose.

Sein Name heißt Jerg Schneider,	His name was Jerg Schneider,
Ward er allda genannt,	This was how he was known,
Hat im Ehestand gelebt	He lived in marriage,
Bis vierunddreißig Jahr,	Until he was thirty-four,
Thät fromm und gottesfürchtig sein	He feared God and was faithful
Und hat mit seinem Weibe	And together with his wife
Ein einzig Töchterlein. . . .	Had a single daughter. . . .
Darauf die Tochter verschwunden	[Into the abyss] the daughter disappeared
Samt den feurigen Gasbock.	Together with the fiery ram.
Vor Schrecken man nichts sahe,	Out of fear one saw nothing,
Denn nur das selbe Loch,	Only that same abyss,
Darin die Tochter versunken war,	Into which the daughter had sunken,
Kläglich höret man schreien	One heard her voice crying
Ihre Stimme etlichs Mal.	In pain several more times.

(Song accounting episode in the Hutterite "creation myth," oral tradition)[6]

When I first entered the James Valley Colony, I had the great fortune not to be regarded as a total stranger. David Hofer, whom I had met when he visited the ORF studio in Klagenfurt, met me with his wife at the Winnipeg airport. Whether because of this initial familiarity or because of the purpose of my visit, which was to learn more about Hutterite song, Hofer immediately turned to music as a means of intensifying our communication. Leaving Winnipeg at dusk, he surprised me by asking, "Derf ma a Abendliadle singan?" (May I sing an evening song?) Before I could even tell him how much I would appreciate it, he began singing with a strong and nasal voice; his wife, Mary Hofer, joined in at the octave. As soon as I grasped the melody, I joined in at the third stanza, reading the singers' lips, standard practice when one is accustomed to learning new songs. The fact that I could sing with them not only broke but melted the ice. By sharing their dialect and music—two of their most important forms of identity—I had also crossed the border into the two most important domains of Hutterite communication, language and song.

My assumption that the Hutterites had a song for every situation in their daily lives and in their religious practice was confirmed during the next few days. Initially, I had hoped to find songs that might have survived from the period of emigration from Carinthia, which would have proved the existence of typical Carinthian

[6] This song was sung to Michael Holzach by the elders of a Hutterite community in Alberta to clarify the ways in which sixteenth-century Germans responded to the temptations of sin. The song, performed by the community's preacher, was the only form in which this narrative existed (see Holzach 1982:44–45).

melody and harmony.[7] I soon abandoned this hope. Despite certain distinguishing traits, Hutterite singing is not choral, but rather it is based on a repertory of lyrics that have been inscribed in songbooks and on a tradition of melodies transmitted orally. These melodies are specific to special situations and functions in the community, hence the North American contexts. I had partly realized this prior to the field research when I had studied the *Großes Gesangsbuch* (Large Songbook), a massive collection of Hutterite songs, with 347 song texts and 32 melodies printed as early as 1914.[8] Most of these songs are narrative histories of the martyrs and other witnesses to the faith of the Hutterites, appearing in rhymed verse (see the epigraphs in this article). Other songs serve as prayers, and still others paraphrase biblical passages. Together with the two books devoted to the history of the Hutterites, the songs constitute the main body of Hutterite faith and identity. The preface of the *Großes Gesangbuch*, moreover, quotes the biblical principles on singing, which Peter Riedmann summarized in his volume, *Rechenschaft* (Accountability), in 1556 (Riedemann 1556):

> Paul said: "Sing and present psalms to the Lord in your hearts with psalms and songs of praise and sacred songs" (Ephesians 5:13). We say, therefore, that it is good to sing sacred songs and, moreover, to be pleasing before God according to what is correct, which means that it correctly expresses the fear of the Lord and the inspiration from the spirit of Christ. These should be sung. They were called sacred songs (II Peter 1) because they were composed and created through the spirit of God and through his inspiration, and so that they can move and inspire men toward the spirit of God. . . . Where this does not happen and men sing from the pleasures of the flesh or because of the beauty of sound, or because he seeks something from singing, they transform music into flesh and the worldly, and they fail to sing the sacred, but rather literal songs. . . .
>
> The same goes for those who simply want to hear songs; they hear literally and not spiritually, and therefore have no fear of the Lord. Because inappropriate melodies are used, sung, and heard, he sins severely against God, he, who does such things (Psalm 50), because he has transformed his

---

[7] The choral tradition of Carinthia is one of the most distinctive traits in Austria. Families and communities, as well as other social institutions, support smaller and larger choral ensembles that have extensive repertories of harmonically complex folksongs.

[8] The tunes are identified by name only, usually at the beginning of the texts.

> word that should be devoted to healing and inspiration of faith into the passion of the flesh and used it for sin. . . .
>
> He, who, however, sings with faith, seeks for the words that bring the greatest service, where and as far as it is appropriate, and (II Timothy 3) how it brings about his improvement.
>
> One either sings well, or it is futile. We do not allow, moreover, that songs other than the sacred songs can be sung among us.

The songs from the *Großes Gesangsbuch* constitute part of the hymns used during Hutterite religious services, where unison singing only is permitted. There are also songs intended for the school and home, published in the *Gesangbüchlein* (Little Songbook) in 1919 (see Hutterische Brüder in Kanada 1982), and these had less strictly defined performance parameters. The popular didactic song, "Loblied auf die Rute" (Song Praising the Rod), appears in a secular version, "Song on the Wicked Daughter." Uniting the two versions is the emphasis on the values of strict education and upbringing. Rolf Wilhelm Brednich has identified Hutterite hymns that still retain the original functions intended for them when they first appeared as religious broadside ballads or newspaper songs centuries ago (Brednich 1982/1983).

The two Hutterite songbooks differ from each according to the reliability of song transmission. Whereas the number of songs in the *Großes Gesangbuch* has remained unchanged since it was first published, the *Gesangsbüchlein* has been enlarged several times. The first edition (1919) included only 135 songs, but the eleventh edition (1982) includes 195 different texts. We can surmise from this growing repertory that song practices are expanding and that Hutterites have officially (i.e., through the use of official community publications) perceived the need for allowing new songs to enter the communities.

There are other songbooks that are popular among the Hutterites, which, though they come from outside the communities, are sanctioned in them. By and large, these songbooks are in use in other German-speaking Pietist or Anabaptist sects, especially the Mennonites and the Amish. Perhaps the most important of these borrowed songbooks is the Russian Mennonite *Gesangbuch* (Songbook; see *Gesangbuch* 1989), which was first published in 1859, when Mennonite and Hutterite communities were in close contact prior to emigration from Russia; Canadian Mennonites and Hutterites remain in close contact until the present (cf. Klassen 1989).

The Hutterites also draw upon songbooks of the Amish, not only the standard hymnbook, *Ausbund* (1564), but also the *Unpartheyisches Gesang-Buch* (Impartial Songbook) (1841), which has most recently appeared in a reprint from 1988. Although this collection is "modern" in its use of printed music, it retains its traces of older styles, for example, the setting of several tunes in alto clef. Newer Hutterite songs also come from a German-language social songbook called *Reichs-Lieder für Evangelisation und Gemeinschaftsleben* (Imperial Songs for Evangelization and Social Life) (1909), which had sold more than one million copies by the time of its 1909 printing, the one current among Canadian communities. The most recent songs, too, owe their origins to a Mennonite songbook, the *Gesangbuch der Mennoniten* (Songbook of the Mennonites) (1949), whose first American imprint from 1942 contains songs that are especially popular among the Hutterites.

Apart from the recent additions to the Hutterite repertory, their songs often survive in archaic forms due to the fact that they have been isolated for centuries from traditions in Central Europe and have not experienced the concomitant linguistic change that would have resulted from contact with that tradition. The contents of their songbooks, for example, were reproduced literally, without making changes. This process of "stereotypic reproduction" also characterizes other expressive practices, such as sermons, prayers, and historical writing, all of which uses a form of German usually referred to as "Predigthutterisch" (sermon Hutterite), which is formally related to High German.

The everyday language of the Hutterites is a characteristic alpine German dialect, far more flexible than the fixed forms of High German in Predigthutterisch. The everyday language, nonetheless, has preserved typical elements of the Upper Carinthian dialect of southern Austria, such as the extreme lengthening of vowels and the insertion of marker or separation syllables such as *lei*. Even though this Carinthian dialect is the most extensively used form of discourse among the Hutterites, its influences are almost not found at all in the song tradition.

The primary influences on Hutterite song come from the written rather than from the oral or vernacular side of their lives. Helen Martens (1981) has examined the origin of Hutterite tunes and has suggested the following hierarchy of sources: songs sung in European courts, "Meistergesang" (master song), Gregorian and Lutheran chants, hymns of the Reformed Protestant church, hymns of free churches, and folksongs. When the Hutterites absorb tunes "from the outside," these tunes enter the tradition only to become fixed, as in the use of the high language itself. I found this to be true even when songs from American popular music or country and western entered Hutterite sacred repertories in Canada. The process of acquiring immediate stability, which in turn symbolizes the stability of faith and the strictness of Hutterite life, clearly characterizes the Hutterite transformation of song so that it can ascribe Hutterite identity.

Because singing has always been regarded as an expression of religious belief, it follows that there are many reasons for singing in the daily lives of the Hutterites.

A family begins the day with a morning song, and it ends the day with an evening song. The main task of kindergarten (*Klana Schuel*) instruction is the memorization of songs and prayers. Learning songs is also the primary activity of the *Deutsch Schuel* (German school), which is held daily from October to May, before or after the obligatory instruction in English for the older children.[9] The *Sonntags Schuel* (Sunday school) provides religious teaching for those not yet baptized, in other words, all Hutterite youths. Hymns, furthermore, constitute an important practice in the community's evening prayer (*Gebet*) and Sunday service (*Lehr*). Songs accompany the Hutterites as they work communally, and they are an essential component of the family's life together each evening. Religious holidays and festivals have extensive singing practices, and it can be said that all rites of passage during a Hutterite's life have special musical practices associated with them.

A special feature of vocal performance practice is *Ansagen*, that is, lining-out, or the reading of single verses by the preacher, teacher, or the eldest family member and then the repetition by the others. In this way, songs with many verses can be sung without great difficulty. It is a common practice to sing the so-called "Väterlieder" (songs of the forefathers), which have over one hundred stanzas. Hymns addressing the passion of Christ have as many as fifty-four verses, and traditionally these will be sung in broken groups over several days or even weeks. Oral tradition, therefore, benefits from the role of the lead singer in the *Ansagen*.

Hutterites sing with considerable volume, and they consciously use a nasal vocal quality that is emphasized through the slurring of intervals. To justify this style, Hutterites frequently quote the biblical enjoinment, "Let us cry so that the throat breaks." They interpret this to mean that singing as loudly as possible increases the passion for the subject about which they are singing. Hymn tunes themselves often employ the free meter of the late Middle Ages, as well as the modal structures of pre-tonal hymn traditions. Intonation problems often arise because of the extensive modality of the melodies, which contrasts with the tonal framework of other traditions. The younger generation, especially, tries to introduce harmony into the performance practice. During my fieldwork, for example, I was asked to help in the preparation of songs for a wedding, especially by making suggestions for harmonizations of the songs. My response was to reject the invitation and to emphasize the special importance of singing in unison. Just how long the commu-

[9] Hutterites are required by Canadian law to provide schools with English-language instruction to their children. In most communities, a teacher from a nearby town comes to the community school to provide such instruction. The "German school" supplements the English-language instruction, and it contrasts with the education from the external world by emphasizing rote learning of sacred and musical traditions.

nities can avoid the influences of singing with harmony remains an open question. Part-singing has made considerable inroads into communities such as Crystal Springs, and it seems likely that other communities may make this concession to "music from the outside" in the future.

Similarly, it is not clear how much longer the strict prohibition of instrumental music can remain in force. Whereas Riedemann's *Rechenschaft* (1556) gives unequivocal guidelines, which are respected by the older generation, community youths have turned to instrumental music, even if this takes place in secret.[10] The *Geigele* (literally, "little fiddle," but in fact a mouth organ) is the one instrument that is more or less acceptable.

Elderly Hutterites can sing at least one hundred different songs. The foundation for this repertory is laid in school. From October to May, pupils must learn the words and tunes of two hymns per week. The order in which young Hutterites acquire their repertory is relatively fixed: six morning and six evening songs first, then funeral hymns, then Christmas songs, and finally New Year's songs. At this point, children first begin to learn traditional hymns from the *Großes Gesangbuch*, which then leads to learning of songs with a more general character. The next stage of memorization includes hymns for Easter, Ascension, and Pentecost. A child's repertory is therefore quite extensive even at an early age, and children should ideally be able to sing from that repertory on appropriate occasions. There is even a system of examination, for children must stand up before the family or community on Saturdays and, one by one, sing the two songs they have learned during the previous week. Performed in this way, the songs first function as different parts, but gradually they fit together, forming the whole of their communities. As they grow older, therefore, children are acculturated into the life of the community by joining its singing as a communal whole. Quite literally, they sing themselves into Hutterite adulthood.

Diversity within Unity

Die Gmeinschaft ward zerstört	The community was destroyed
Nach der Apostelzeit,	After the age of the apostles,
Unterdrückt und verkehrt	Repressed and turned around
Durch Teufels List und Neid.	Through the devil's cunning and envy.

[10] Instruments such as the harmonica may be used in special gatherings of young people that are designed to bring about socializing, but more specifically to allow marriageable couples to form pairs (Holzach 1982: 138–140). Holzach and others who have lived with the Hutterites report incidences of transistor radios, smuggled into the beds of young Hutterites, that therefore provide sources of country and western music.

Doch hat jetzt Gott der Herr	Therefore, God the Father has now
Aus seinem Gnadenreich	From his kingdom of grace
Sein Gmein erwecket mehre,	Awakened his people,
Die Apostellehre	To see that the teachings of the apostles
Im Wort und Werk ist gleich.	Are equal in word and deed.
Die Gmein, die christlich Mutter,	The people, the Christian Mother,
Die hat viel Söhn verlorn,	Have lost many sons,
Bis auf den Jakob Hutter,	Even unto Jakob Hutter,
Den hat Gott auserkorn.	Whom God had chosen.
Ein frommer Mann er ware,	He was a devout man,
Feind allem Eigennutz,	An enemy of all selfishness,
Mit ihm ein kleine Schare,	A small group [followed] him,
Doch so war Gott ihr Schutz.	And thus was God their protection.

"Gemeinschaftsliedl" (Community Song)[11]

The following musical examples illustrate the varieties of sound and style that characterized the Hutterite singing traditions that I experienced during my fieldwork in the James Valley Colony of Manitoba. When the Hutterite teachers from different Canadian communities came to Klagenfurt, the first song they agreed to sing together was "Welt ade, ich bin dein müde" (Farewell to the world, I am weary with you; see Figure 3). In Europe this is a well-known song, but the version that is best known utilizes five-voice polyphony set by J. Rosenmüller. The first verse of the song is inscribed on many Hutterite tombstones, and the song is a part of a larger repertory shared by all Hutterites. The text, however, appears in neither of the two Hutterite songbooks, but it does appear in the Mennonite and Amish songbooks used by the Hutterites (*Gesangbuch* 1989, and *Unpartheyisches Gesang-Buch* 1988).[12]

The melody type used by the Hutterites can also be found in the *Gesangbuch der Mennoniten* (Allgemeine Konferenz der Mennonitengemeinschaft Nordamerikas 1949), though there are metric shifts, such as from the triple meter of the early eighteenth-century "Halleluja! Schöner Morgen" (Hallelujah! Beautiful Morning) to duple meter (see Figure 4).

Typically, Hutterite performance practice utilizes lining-out, which I experienced for the first time in the *Deutsch Schuel* (German school) when the pupils

---

[11] Sung by school children in the Wilson Colony of Alberta (Holzach 1982:23).

[12] In the Amish *Unpartheyisches Gesang-Buch* (1988), the milder "ade" in the title is replaced with *hinweg*, a stronger sense of "away with you!"

practiced the song in Figure 5, "Erwacht vom süßen Schlummer" (Awakened from Sweet Sleep). In the standard collection of German folksongs, the *Deutscher Liederhort* (Erk and Böhme 1893), the text of the song (1772) is attributed to Johann Kaspar Lavater and the melody (1812) to F. K. Ludwig Scholinus.

When Hutterites memorize song texts and prayers, they do so using a reciting tone, in which cadential points are indicated. The impression one has of such memorizing sessions is of a mechanical rattling off of syllables and words, for at this point the meaning of the texts is of only secondary importance. While memorizing the texts, the children are under considerable stress, for Hutterites use corporal punishment to discipline those with poor memories; this practice, however, follows the biblical passage, "He who loves his son shall beat him." Usually, the reciting of texts is so fast that little can be understood.

Songs accompany the daily lives of all Hutterites. The "Dirnen" (girls between fourteen and twenty-one)[13] are particularly eager to sing, and they have an extensive repertory of recent songs. These songs do not possess the sobriety of the ancestor songs or the martyr melodies, but rather more often employ the melodies of folksongs. The new songs, instead, often employ two- or three-voice settings, with the added voices harmonizing in thirds. There is, moreover, an added harmonic sense in the third voice, which often acquires dominant-tonic functions. The text of "Gott ist die Liebe" (God Is Love; see Figure 6) is in the Mennonite *Gesangbuch* (1989), as well as in the *Reichs-Lieder* (1909). August Rische (1819–1906) wrote the text, and the melody is taken from a popular folksong in Thuringia in eastern Germany.

This song still possesses its functional context as an accompaniment to work, whereas Figure 7, a choral piece, is typical of the style used for stage performance. As I have already mentioned, the Schmiedeleut and, especially, the Crystal Springs Colony are more open to influences from the outside and are more willing to respond to Hutterite dogmas with flexibility. These communities have, in recent years, attracted new members who often do not understand German, making it necessary to deliver some parts of the sermon in English. Other members offer considerable resistance to this practice, feeling that their cultural identity is being undermined. It is perhaps no accident that these colonies have a highly industrialized production of the agricultural goods they raise, necessitating a more open attitude toward the world. Accordingly, the song repertory and the related choral practices reflect this openness, permitting even mixed choruses.

---

[13] The Austrian *Dirndl* is based on this word, designating, in other words, a dress worn by a young woman.

Figure 3. "Welt ade, ich bin dein müde"

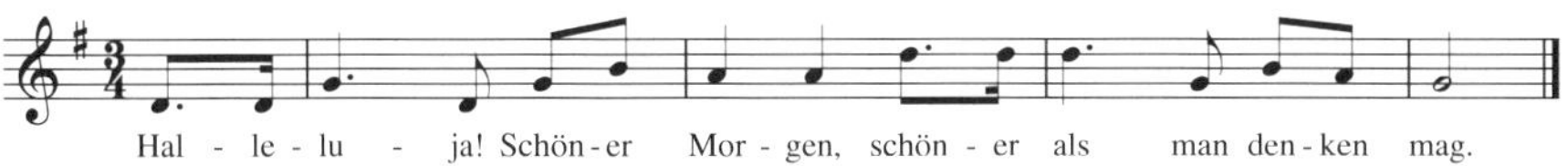

Figure 4. "Halleluja! Schöner Morgen"

Figure 5. "Erwacht vom süßen Schlummer"

Figure 6. "Gott ist die Liebe"

I arrived at the James Valley Colony with a religious hit song by Peter Strauch that the group Die Wasserträger (The Water Bearers) had popularized throughout German-speaking Central Europe. The Hutterites took the melody from written tradition and then adapted it for their own interpretive ends. It goes without saying that this type of singing has strayed from the principles set down by Peter Riedemann in 1556. Rather, it symbolizes a sense of expansion, of reaching out to the world, which is perhaps also evident in the biblical source for the text, Psalm 31:

Figure 7. "Meine Zeit steht in Deinen Händen" ("My Time Is in Your Hands")

There are interesting parallels with Carinthia in the passion song, "Ihr Sünder, kommt gegangen" (You, Sinners, Continue to Come), which the James Valley Colony maintains in its current tradition (see Figure 8). Only the Hutterite *Gesang-Büchlein* (Hutterische Brüder in Kanada 1982) contains a written source for the four-verse text. I am unable to locate the melody in any other written source. There is, nonetheless, a striking similarity to a song from Carinthia with the same title. The conjunct melody and a meter that shifts between duple, triple, and compound duple meters show a structural similarity to the "Lied style" of the sixteenth century, though I believe it is too inconclusive to claim direct connections. The ornamentation in the Carinthian version (line b in Figure 8) reveals that this version is more recent because of its parallels to the Baroque song tradition of the alpine countries. Although the Hutterites do not themselves recognize a specific similarity between the two songs, they exhibited a certain surprise when asked to consider the possibility.

It is well-known that the communal life in Hutterite communities limits space for personal interests. The single private place in a Hutterite's life is the small trunk, in which a Hutterite might keep officially forbidden objects, such as pictures, books, cosmetics, and even pocket calculators, cameras, or cassette players. In this way, young Hutterites gain access to dance music and other forms of popular entertainment.

Figure 8: "Ihr Sünder, kommt gegangen"— a) Hutterite version; b) Carinthian version.

Only a few hours before my departure from the James Valley Colony, my hostess, Mary Hofer, asked me to record—as discreetly as possible—a "song" that her son Dave and his cousin wanted to sing for me. She explained to me that I should need to go to a remote mobile home, where the two "sinning" singers were actually waiting for me. The songs I heard there were, according to Hutterite values, "from Hell." Riedemann would have observed that the songs were not sung in the "spirit" but rather in the "flesh." I found the performance of the two cousins quite remarkable; especially because their harmonization followed principles they themselves had developed through a filtered contact with the tonal basis of popular music. When later researching the song "Am blauen See im grünen Tal" (By the Blue Lake in the Green Valley), I identified its writers to be K. Götz and K. Hertha, and that the song had been made famous by the Jacobs Sisters, who had enjoyed popularity in Germany for over thirty years.

Figure 9: "Am blauen See im grünen Tal."

The Hutterites' predisposition toward "literal" (*buchstablich* in dialect) singing —in other words, monophonic singing—excludes the possibility of instrumental accompaniment, or at least makes it difficult to reckon with the possibility of musical instruments. When I suggested that in the Psalms[14] one could find quite an ex-

[14] For example, the following are relevant verses:

Psalm 33, verses 2 and 3:
2. Praise the Lord with the lyre,
make melody to him with the harp of ten strings!
3. Sing to him a new song,
play skillfully on the strings with loud shouts.

Psalm 81, verses 3 and 4:
3. Blow the trumpet at the new moon,
at the full moon, on our feast day.
4. For it is a statute for Israel,
an ordinance of the God of Jacob.

Psalm 68, verses 24 and 25:
24. Thy solemn processions are seen, O God,
the processions of my God, my King,
into the sanctuary—
25. the singers in front, the minstrels last,
between them maidens playing timbrels:

Psalm 150, verses 3-6:
3. Praise him with trumpet sound;
praise him with lute and harp!

tensive instrumentarium for the praising of God, the eldest member of the community, Jacob Hofer, responded that King David had very little understanding for the Hutterites and their faith.[15] The fact remains, nonetheless, that the banning of instrumental music is increasingly disregarded by young Hutterites in the community. Older members are suspicious of the "innovations" of the young, but they avoid direct confrontation of the issue. Whatever the official position, they were proud to "fiddle" for me, observing that I was an outsider. This practice is striking for me because the word *fiddling* (aufgeigen) is used in the same way in Carinthia. The Hutterites, however, have replaced the violin with the mouth organ, allowing them to hide the small instrument among their personal possessions. The repertory they fiddled for me consisted of choral works, simple dance tunes, and country and western music. There are also pieces that the older community members find acceptable, for example, Figure 10, "Tirol, du bist mein Heimatland" (Tyrol, You Are My Homeland):

Figure 10. "Tirol, du bist mein Heimatland."

I should like to include as my final example a song that I recorded almost by accident during my fieldwork in the James Valley Colony, in fact on my final day during the automobile ride to the Winnipeg airport. Just as he had greeted me with song, my host, David Hofer, sang the song in Figure 11 as a means of bidding

---

4. Praise him with timbrel and dance;
   praise him with strings and pipe!
5. Praise him with sounding cymbals;
   praise him with loud clashing cymbals!
6. Let everything that breathes praise the Lord!
   Praise the Lord!

Further Psalms with direct references to instrumental music include Psalms 71, 92, 98, 105, 108, and 149.

[15] The Hutterites are well aware of Psalm texts that stand in direct opposition to their belief system, such as the opening of Psalm 144, which strongly contradicts the Hutterites' pacifism: "Praise be the Lord, my rock, who teaches my hands to struggle, and my fists to wage war."

Figure 11: "O Jesus, süßes Licht"

farewell: "O Jesu, süßes Licht" (O Jesus, Sweet Light). The text and melody harken back to an older generation of songs, although neither of the two standard Hutterite songbooks includes it. "O Jesus, süßes Licht" does appear, however, in the *Unpartheyisches Gesang-Buch* (1988), without authorial attribution, but recommending the melody of "Nun danket alle Gott" (Now, All Give Thanks to God). There are similarities to other early hymns, such as Joachim Lange's (1670–1744) version of "Nun danket alle Gott" in the *Gesangbuch für die evangelische Kirche in Württemberg* (1893; first edition 1791). With shifts in meter and modal ambiguity (e.g., the move to Lydian in the second part), this song signifies an older, if not archaic style. Hofer was closing my fieldwork with an unequivocal symbol of the pastness of the Hutterites, a pastness that marked the identity of the Hutterites today.

Conclusion

Der dies Lied neu hat g'sungen	He who sang this song
Geörg Prukmair ward er g'nannt,	Was named Geörg Prukmair,
Hat für die Wahrheit gerungen	And he had struggled for the truth
Zu Riedt im Baierland.	At Riedt in Bavaria.
Durchs Schwert den Tod erlitten,	Having suffered death by a sword,
Um Christi Glauben gut,	In good faith toward Christ,
Hat ritterlich gestritten,	He struggled in knightly fashion,
Bezeugt mit seinem Blut.	As testified by his blood.
Dies Lied schenkt er den Frommen,	He presents this song to the faithful,
Zur Anzeig' Dankbarkeit,	As evidence of thankfulness,
Er hat's vom Sirach g'nommen,	He took it from Sirach,
Der auch zu seiner Zeit	Who was also much praised by the faithful
Viel der Frommen tut loben,	During his own time,

Also ein anderer mehr, Dies G'sang kurz weiter zogen Und g'sungen bis hieher.	Thus yet another, Brought this song a little farther And sang until it reached the present.
Nun sei Gott Lob und Danke, Der den Seinen gibt Kraft, Daß sie von ihm nicht wanken, Sondern bleiben sieghaft In Christo, unserm Herren, Der steht uns allen bei, Daß wir zu seinen Ehren Bis ans End' bleiben treu. Amen. "Vater Lied" (Father Song)[16]	Now, give praise and thanks to God, Who gives strength to his own, So that they do not turn away from him, But rather remain victorious, In Christ, our Lord, Who stands by each one of us, That we shall remain true to his honor Until the end. Amen.

Paradox and incongruity characterize the lives of the Canadian Hutterites. It is a life that seems isolated and dependent on isolation, and yet the means for creating and reinforcing isolation come from within the community. Their distinctive identity with the past and with their own history of martyrdom notwithstanding, the Hutterites enjoy a remarkable and enviable degree of economic success. In many parts of the Plains Provinces of Canada, the Hutterites own the largest farms and the most modern farming equipment. Whereas the personal lifestyle of community members may appear ascetic, Hutterites drive cars and exercise no ban on certain kinds of modern conveniences such as electricity. Although the guidelines about moral behavior are strict and instilled in children from an early age, there are moments in a young Hutterite's life when a degree of social experimentation is permitted, which is to say, is conveniently not observed by the community. Hutterite identity comes from within, and it is not primarily a reaction to the "other world" without.

The presence of music as a component in Hutterite identity is not just explicit: music is essential to defining and reproducing Hutterite identity. At the risk of sounding banal, one must say that the Hutterites are a singing people. Songs accompany all religious and secular events in the course of a year and of a lifetime. At home and at work, at school and during communal worship, there are frequent moments for singing, and these constitute a ritualization of Hutterite communal life. Children learn to sing early, and throughout their formal education, song provides a

[16] This historical song, composed by Jörg Pruckmair in the sixteenth century, consists of 105 verses, the final three of which appear here (Holzach 1982:267-277).

primary means of learning to be Hutterite, which is fundamental to the nature and function of formal education in Hutterite communities.

The omnipresence of song, moreover, transcends aesthetic significance. The nature of musical sound, its aesthetics, is highly theorized, using treatises such as Riedemann's *Rechenschaft* (1556) that prove remarkably effective in their applicability to musical phenomenon in a way that Riedemann could not have imagined in the early years of Hutterite history. The core of the Hutterite repertory is sung in unison and without dynamic shading. Volume is extreme, and it is clear that singing in unison as loudly as possible provides a symbolic coalescing for the community, a chance for the community to perform its own identity. Hutterite performance practices, such as lining-out, enforce unity. When outside influences successfully find their way into that performance practice, it is because the Hutterites perceive these influences as contributing to the unity and identity of the community. Even instrumental music, when it contributes to the socialization and cohesiveness of young Hutterites, may be tolerated, if indeed still not fully embraced. Significant only is that all music supports Hutterite identity from within rather than disrupting it from without.

The Hutterite identity that one finds in Hutterite music exhibits paradox only on its surface. The elements of folk and popular music are there to be found; dialect connects the language to Carinthian roots, but also to centuries of interaction with other German-speaking religious sects and to the host cultures encountered by the Hutterites on their spiritual journey. If we interpret the paradoxical mixture of internal archaisms and external encroachments as evidence that the Hutterite journey is reaching its end, we err. Hutterite song continues to narrate the paths of that journey—past, present, and future. Like Hutterite singing itself, the sense of community identified through the sacred journey is all the more meaningful because it is conveyed loudly and in unison.

Bibliography

Allgemeine Konferenz der Mennonitengemeinschaft Nordamerikas, ed. *Gesangbuch der Mennoniten*. Rosthern, SK: Allgemeine Konferenz der Mennonitengemeinschaft Nordamerikas, 1949.

Ausbund: Etliche schöne Christliche Geseng. Facsimile of the original edition: Vol. 1, Mennonite Songbooks, German series. Nieukoop: De Graaf, 1564.

Brednich, Rolf Wilhelm. "Beharrung und Wandel im Liedgut der Hutterischen Brüder in Amerika: Ein Beitrag zur empirischen Hymnologie." *Jahrbuch für Volksliedforschung* 26 (1981):44–60.

________. "Erziehung durch Gesang: Zur Funktion von Zeitungsliedern bei den Hutterern." *Jahrbuch für Volksliedforschung* 27/28 (1982/83): 109–133.

________. "Die Funktion von religiösen Erzählliedern bei den hutterischen Wiedertäufern in Kanada." 12. *Arbeitstagung über europäische Balladenprobleme der SIEF-Kommission für Volksdichtung Jannina 1980*. Jannina: 1981.

________. "Ein Stück alpenländische Kultur in der Neuen Welt: Die Hutterer." *Österreichische Zeitschrift für Volkskunde*, New series, 35 (1981):111–153.

Buchinger, Erich. *Die "Landler" in Siebenbürgen: Vorgeschichte, Durchführung und Ergebnis einer Zwangsumsiedlung im 18. Jhdt*. Munich: (Buchreihe der Südostdeutschen Historischen Kommission, 31) 1980.

________. "Der lutherische Zuzug zu den Hutterischen Brüdern im 18. Jahrhundert." In *Die Hutterischen Täufer, Geschichtlicher Hintergrund und handwerkliche Leistung*, edited by Bayrisches Nationalmuseum. Weierhof: Mennonitische Forschungsstelle, 1985.

Erk, Ludwig, and Franz Böhme. *Deutscher Liederhort: Auswahl der vorzüglicheren Deutschen Volkslieder nach Wort und Weise aus der Vorzeit und Gegenwart*. Leipzig: Breitkopf und Härtel, 1893.

Gesangbuch: Eine Sammlung geistlicher Lieder zur allgemeinen Erbauung und zum Lobe Gottes. Scottdale, PA, and Waterloo, ON: Mennonitisches Verlagshaus, 1989.

Gesangbuch für die evangelische Kirche. Gesangbuch für die evangelische Kirche in Württemberg. Stuttgart: 1893.

Holzach, Michael. *Das vergessene Volk: Ein Jahr bei den deutschen Hutterern in Kanada*. Munich: Hoffmann und Campe, 1982.

Hutterische Brüder in Kanada, eds. *Gesang-Büchlein: Lieder für Schule und häuslichen Gebrauch*. 11th edn. Elie, MB: James Valley Colony, 1982.

________. *Die Lieder der Hutterischen Brüder*. 5th edn. Cayley, Alberta.

Kalesny, Frantisek. "Die Wiedertäufer in der Slowakei." In *Die Hutterischen Täufer, Geschichtlicher Hintergrund und handwerkliche Leistung*, edited by Bayrisches Nationalmuseum, Weierhof: Mennonitische Forschungsstelle, 1985.

Klassen, Doreen Helen. *Singing Mennonite: Low German Songs among the Mennonites*. Winnipeg: University of Manitoba Press, 1989.

Längin, Bernd G. *Die Hutterer: Gefangene der Vergangenheit, Pilger der Gegenwart, Propheten der Zukunft*. Hamburg and Zurich: 1986.

Martens, Helen. "Die Lieder der Hutterer und ihre Verbindung zum Meistergesang im 16. Jahrhundert." *Jahrbuch für Volksliedforschung* 26 (1981): 31–43.

Mumelter, Gerhard, et. al. *Die Hutterer*. Innsbruck: Hayman-Verlag, 1986.

Prasch, Helmut. *1000 Jahre Grafschaft Lurn-Ortenburg, 800 Jahre Spittal an der Drau*. Spittal/Drau: 1990.

Reichs-Lieder: Deutsches Gemeinschaftsliederbuch. Neumünster in Holstein: Vereinsbuchhandlung G. Ihloff, 1909.

Riedemann, Peter. *Rechenschaft unserer Religion, Lehre und Glaubens: Von den Brüdern, die man die Hutterischen nennt*. 1556. (Reprint. Cayley, AB: 1962.)

Schaaf, Karlheinz. "Das Volkslied der Donauschwaben." *In Handbuch des Volksliedes. Vol. 2: Historisches und Systematisches—Interethnische Beziehungen—Musikethnologie*, edited by Rolf Wilhelm Brednich, Lutz Röhrich, and Wolfgang Suppan, 199–219. Munich: Wilhelm Fink, 1975.

Unpartheyisches Gesang-Buch. Unpartheyisches Gesang-Buch, enthaltend geistreiche Lieder und Psalmen, zum allgemeinen Gebrauch des wahren Gottesdienstes. 1841. (Reprint. Lancaster County, PA: Verlag von den Amischen Gemeinden, 1988.)

Weber-Kellermann, Ingeborg. "Probleme interethnischer Forschungen und Südosteuropa." In *Handbuch des Volksliedes*. Vol. 2: *Historisches und Systematisches—Interethnische Beziehungen—Musikethnologie*, edited by Rolf Wilhelm Brednich, Lutz Röhrich, and Wolfgang Suppan, 185–198. Munich: Wilhelm Fink, 1975.

________, ed. *Zur Interethnik: Donauschwaben, Siebenbürger Sachsen und ihre Nachbarn*. Frankfurt am Main: Suhrkamp, 1978.

Wolkan, Rudolf. 1923. *Geschicht-Buch der Hutterischen Brüder*. Macleod, AB: Standoff Colony, 1923. (Reprint. Cayley, AB: MacMillan Colony, 1982.)

III

Modern Identities

8

THE GERMAN CONCERTINA IN THE UPPER MIDWEST

James P. Leary

The American Century of the German Concertina

For six months in 1893 the Midwestern metropolis Chicago offered the Columbian Exposition, a sprawling mile-long celebration of "the World's Science, Art, and Industry," to vast, varied, and enthusiastic crowds (Bancroft 1893). Like prior "world's fairs" or "international expositions" in London (1851), New York (1853), Paris (1867), and elsewhere, the Chicago event juxtaposed the "industrial achievement," fine arts, and imperial triumphs of Western nations with exotic "raw materials" and "exhibits of primitive 'others'" gathered "from peripheral territories or colonies" (Hinsley 1991:345). One moment fairgoers could amble through displays of the latest mechanical technology housed in pavilions designed by the era's visionary urban architects. A few steps more would take the curious into mock villages of Samoans, Kwakiutls, Lapps, and Dahomians. And somewhere in this vast assemblage an immigrant entrepreneur, Otto Georgi, displayed and demonstrated the virtues of the German concertina.

Nearly a century later, on Labor Day weekend 1992, roughly a hundred devotees of the German concertina congregated in the tiny village of Allenton, Wisconsin. Over a three-day span concertina makers, sellers, and arrangers peddled their wares; new members ascended into the "Concertina Hall of Fame"; and musicians chiefly from the Upper Midwest (the northern parts of Indiana and Illinois as well as Michigan, Minnesota, and Wisconsin) played the concertina continuously in a stylistic babel that ranged from the German, Polish, Czech, and Slovenian polka legacy of Central Europe to the sounds of American pop, jazz, and country. The eighteenth World Concertina Congress was in session

These two events—separated by a century, linked by the concertina's presence—tease speculations regarding the evolving relationships between music, ethnicity, class, region, and culture in American life. With regard to Otto Georgi's involvement in the 1893 Columbian Exposition, we know little for certain beyond the

Figure 1. DJ Scott Lopas of WTKM radio in Hartford, Wisconsin, approaches the bandstand as that city's "Push and Pull Orchestra" plays for the 1992 World Concertina Congress in Allenton. Photo by James P. Leary.

testimony, offered sixty-two years later by a fellow concertina promoter, that he was there (Watters 1955). From what we know about the Exposition and about Georgi's subsequent career, however, we can guess that he was an occupant of that seventy-thousand square-foot section of the Hall of Manufacturers devoted to musical instruments. Here were "organs and pianos," "stringed instruments played with fingers and the bow" and "wind instruments." Russia and Austria were the only "foreign powers" represented by displays, but the

> exhibits of the United States cover the entire range of musical appliances, including not only all modern instruments, but their accessories, and the materials of which they are made. (Bancroft 1893:231–232)

Georgi was likely among this throng, championing the German concertina to the world, or at least to a broad stratum of the American citizenry.

That Georgi made a scant impression on the cosmopolitan crowd may be inferred from his absence in any printed accounts of the Exposition. Neither an exotic tribal drummer nor a familiar European violinist, Georgi and his concertina would have looked inescapably "foreign" amidst other purveyors of American musical wares. And although his playing might well have mixed the classical pieces favored by a European-American elite with the couple dances beloved by rural and working- class immigrants, Georgi was likely associated with the latter. To be foreign and working-class in late nineteenth-century America was to be embattled.

The rise of white Anglo-Saxon Protestant (WASP) capitalists; the influx of Jewish, Slavic, and Italian workers; the struggles of fledgling labor unions; the military expansion of the American empire; the emergence of racist anthropological theories linking intelligence with ethnicity; and myriad other factors contributed variously to a powerful nativist movement in the 1890s that stressed assimilation to a decidedly Anglo-American identity (Higham 1963:68–105). Even midwestern German communities of long standing were assailed by legislation seeking to restrict their language, patterns of worship, and fondness for sociable drink. Music and dance were similarly ridiculed by the WASP press.

In 1885, for example, the *Chicago Tribune* reported on a dance sponsored by a workers' association. The largely foreign-born couples doubtless executed the polka, the waltz and the schottische, with perhaps an occasional Ländler, oberek, krakowiak, or hambo. But the *Tribune* tells us:

> Every step might have been witnessed yesterday. The "Bohemian dip," the "German lunge," the "Austrian kick," the "Polish ramp," and the "Scandinavian trot." (Nelson 1986)

Such sneering xenophobia was only slightly tempered two decades later when W. A. Curtis toured Wisconsin to inform middle-class readers of the nationally popular *Century Magazine* that the state's hopelessly rustic ethnics "still polka and schottische in the country" (1907). Small wonder Otto Georgi's presence commanded little or no public acknowledgment at Chicago's Columbian Exposition.

Yet Georgi and others like him clearly had appreciative followers. The 1992 Allenton, Wisconsin, gathering is an indication of their limitations and accomplishments over a century of American life. In contrast to the extended duration, urban setting, varied content, and diverse clientele of the Columbian Exposition, the Allenton event was a brief small-town affair with a single purpose. Its narrow constituency not only hailed chiefly from the rural and working-class Central European ethnic enclaves of the Upper Midwest, but also relied on an Old World repertoire pronounced outmoded a century before by arbiters of American taste.

Bound together by their cultural conservatism and by the intermingling forces of musical taste, ethnicity, class, and region, the Allenton devotees nonetheless gathered under the nominal banner of the *World* Concertina Congress; they continued to assert Georgi's entrepreneurial internationalism. Meanwhile their establishment of a Hall of Fame argued a concern with upward mobility, with status, with commanding a measure of respect within the context of American life.

This essay will chronicle the cultural odyssey of the German concertina in American life, with particular attention to the instrument's presence in what has become its New-World *Heimat*—the Upper Midwest. In this region rural and working-class immigrants and ethnics have not only played the concertina as an extension of Old World heritage, but they have also promoted it, albeit with lesser success, as an instrument compatible with any modern musical style and accessible to everyone. Their dual stance toward the concertina, at once insular and evangelical, is also emblematic of their ongoing assertion, often in the face of powerful assimilative forces, of pluralistic cultural identities as rural and working-class, ethnic, Upper Midwestern Americans.

An Overlooked Instrument

But where to begin?

There is a curious gap between scholars' knowledge and grassroots reality. Walter Maurer's standard history of the accordion and related "squeezeboxes," for example, gives short shrift to the German concertina, while offering no mention of its presence in America (Maurer 1983:131–138). *The New Grove Dictionary of Musical Instruments* likewise ignores the instrument's New World status, excepting brief mention of "the much larger Bandoneon [sic] . . . particularly favoured in [the tango orchestras of] South America" (Romani and Beynon 1984:460).

The lack of attention to the concertina is far more attributable to the quirky evolution of academic disciplines than it is to the relative worth of concertinists. In the late twentieth century scholars have begun to reexamine the ideological underpinnings of their disciplines to the extent that artificial barriers to intellectual inquiry have been diminishing briskly (Bohlman 1988; Greene 1992; Keil, Keil, and Blau 1992; Slobin 1992). But until quite recently musicologists have favored the West's classical music over its folk counterpart, ethnomusicologists have been preoccupied with the performances of non-Western cultures, and folklorists have concentrated on Anglo-Celtic and African-derived expressions in America and on the traditions of peasants in Europe. That division of labor has hardly favored systematic inquiries into the eclectic vernacular music of Central European ethnics in the American Midwest. By extension, academic custom has implicitly confined testimonies regarding the concertina's importance to the oral tradition and scattered ephemeral publications of the instrument's aficionados. The scholars, the librarians, the archivists upon whom I have drawn are chiefly the players, composers, makers, and repairers whose filing cabinets, shoeboxes, instrument cases, and memories swell with the concertina's story.

From Chemnitz to Chicago

"Squeezeboxes" of various names and designs flourished in the first half of the nineteenth century as increased urbanization offered both market and means to musical inventors inclined toward the mass-production of instruments. Prototypical accordions, bandonions, English concertinas, and German concertinas had not only been created by the 1840s, but had also begun a rapid diffusion into the street and parlor traditions of Europe and, subsequently, the world. Their popularity is hardly surprising. These instruments, all of the portable free reed family, are distinguished by treble and bass reed chambers joined by a bellows. The bellows' push-pull forces air through select reeds controlled by players who raise dampers via the fingering of buttons or keys. Thus, a single player can produce melody, harmony, and rhythm; a soloist can become a "one-man band"; a small ensemble can become an "orchestra."

Although resembling other bellows-driven free reed instruments, the German concertina has distinct features. Like the button accordion, its reeds give a different note on the compression and extension—the push and pull—of the bellows. Yet the concertina's square shape, its chromatic capabilities, and the set of its buttons on the side of each reed chamber contrast with the rectangular diatonic button accordion whose buttons are set in a panel appended at right angles to the reed chamber. And although it shares partial designation with the better known English concertina, the German concertina's large size, square shape, and two-notes-to-a-button distinguish it from its nominal counterpart which is small, hexagonal, and features the same note on the push and the pull. Finally, the reeds of the German concertina are not organized sequentially as tonal steps in musical scales; rather they are scattered about, like letters on a typewriter's keyboard, in accordance with their frequency of use.[1]

---

[1] The bandonion is the closest "squeezebox" relative of the German concertina. The bandonion was likely developed by C. Zimmermann of Carlsfeld, Saxony, around 1849. Its name, however, appears to have derived from that of another Carlsfelder, Heinrich Band (1821–1860), a musician and purveyor of musical instruments (Román 1988). Dissatisfied with the limited tonal range of the concertina, Band developed an instrument which altered and expanded the key arrangement of the concertina. Put simply, the bandonion is an enlarged German concertina (Roth 1954). Many players in the Upper Midwest are adept with either instrument.

This unique design is generally attributed to Carl Friedrich Uhlig (1789–1874), a former accordion maker, who produced the first German concertina in 1834.[2] Operating out of Chemnitz in Saxony, Uhlig was soon joined by a handful of other manufacturers, each of whom put an idiosyncratic stamp on the instrument. In 1854, Uhlig convened a meeting with eleven other German concertina-makers for the dual purpose of developing a standard keyboard and a system of notation for the concertina. Beyond burgeoning in Germany, the instrument's popularity extended to neighboring Czechs and Poles and to Central European immigrants to the United States.[3]

We do not know precisely when the German concertina took hold in the United States, but its vigorous presence in the Midwest has been evident since the 1880s—particularly in Chicago and Milwaukee, but also in the region's hinterlands. Otto Georgi, the instrument's first significant American exponent, had settled in Chicago by the 1880s. Although we lack precise information, it is likely that he emigrated from Chemnitz where he was affiliated with Friedrich Lange, the son-in-law of Carl Uhlig. Georgi was a player, a teacher, an importer, a publisher, an all-around promoter. In the 1880s he established a shop at 4663 Gross Avenue, the corner of Ashland and Forty-seventh Street, on Chicago's South Side. He sold Lange concertinas; initiated a sheet-music series (*Collection of Popular Music for Concertina*); taught local players; and, by 1889, organized the Chicago Concertina Club. When the Columbian Exposition of 1893 opened in Chicago, Georgi was there, as we have seen, with a display of German concertinas. Around 1902 Georgi went into partnership with Louis Vitak, a Czech music publisher. Besides selling concertinas, the firm of Georgi and Vitak "turned out scores of polkas, marches, and waltzes and was becoming the genre's leading American publisher" by the mid-1920s when the partners had a falling out. Little is known of Georgi's subsequent career, but Vitak continued as an ethnic music publisher in partnership with his nephew Joseph P. Elsnic (Greene 1992:54–55).

---

[2] Although most sources credit Uhlig as the concertina's inventor, Henry Silberhorn, in his *Booster* 1:5–6 (1928), states:

> The first German Concertina, consisting of 40 keys and having 10 buttons on each side, was first made by Herr Zimmerman at Carlsfeld, Saxony in 1832. This instrument was received with great favor and from this time the Concertina was gradually improved and modified to its present qualifications. C. F. Uhlig improved the original to 38 buttons or 76 keys with a compass of 3 1/2 octaves.

[3] Pat Watters (1955) reports, without offering any sources, that the mysterious Herr Zimmermann of Carlsfeld "manufactured the first concertinas that were exported to the United States" in 1850; Brown (ca. 1970) echoes this claim. In 1854, Watters continues, "Mr. Zimmerman . . . emigrated to Philadelphia." No mention is made of his further involvement with concertinas.

Georgi's career overlapped with that of Henry Silberhorn, the most important apostle of the concertina to the American Midwest. Silberhorn (1868–1962) was born in Bavaria and emigrated to Chicago at age seventeen in 1885 (*Music and Dance News* 19:46, 1977). A fine concertina player and a student of music theory, Silberhorn began producing arrangements for the concertina under the imprint of Georgi. By at least 1890 he was teaching the instrument, and in 1910 he authored the first of many publications: *Henry Silberhorn's Instructor for the Concertina*. Like Georgi, Silberhorn established a music store, at various locations on Milwaukee Avenue, where he sold sheet music, concertinas, and accessories. Beyond importing Lange concertinas from Germany, Silberhorn developed his own Clarion line. Silberhorn tirelessly supported the formation of concertina clubs and, in 1927, initiated a "concertina players magazine," *Silberhorn's Booster for the Advancement of the Concertina*.

Together Georgi and Silberhorn helped establish an infrastructure that allowed the German concertina to flourish in the American Midwest. They set a pattern for other clubs, teachers, importers, manufacturers, and publishers. Their efforts at promotion, meanwhile, were augmented by touring concertina players and by artists who made commercial recordings and performed over the radio. Each of these overlapping segments deserves brief illumination.

Concertina Clubs

Around 1880 Saxon industrial workers and Rhine Valley miners established concertina clubs or circles, with American counterparts soon following (Román 1988:44). The Chicago Concertina Club's formation in 1889 was echoed by the emergence of the Milwaukee Concertina Circle in 1890 and by Chicago's Czech-American Concertina Club Band in 1893. Others soon followed. Indeed clubs involving numerous players of a single instrument or a family of instruments were common in late nineteenth-century Europe and America for a number of reasons. By then both new instruments and standardized versions of older instruments were mass-produced; thus they were not only readily and often cheaply available but also sonically compatible. Astute music merchants who could supply customers with instruments, teach them to play, and offer them new tunes had a vested interest in fostering the development of clubs. Clubs were also a consequence of city life, especially among immigrant Americans. Displaced from the old country's close-knit agrarian villages, newcomers to the urban Midwest sought community by forming countless fraternal and cultural organizations, most of which encouraged musical performances. Europe's slow political transformation from a continent of royal principalities to one of democratic republics likewise spawned a romantic nationalism that venerated certain instruments regarded as indigenous: the Italian mandolin, the *tamburitza* of Croatians and Serbians, the Greek *balalaika*. These factors all contributed to the rise of German concertina clubs in America's Midwest. The broad popularity of such parallel free reed instruments as the harmonica and the accordion and the proliferation of harmonica and accordion clubs may also have inspired a friendly rivalry.[4]

Early photographs of the Chicago Concertina Club reveal more than a score of concertinists, as well as players of the cornet, trombone, violin, and snare and bass drums. Georgi stands in the center with a conductor's baton. The club's poses on the curtained stage of some "opera house" (see Figure 2) and against a photographer's rustic backdrop suggest both formal concert programs and informal dance jobs for outdoor picnics or beer gardens (see Figure 4). Certainly these speculations are in keeping with the activities of concertina clubs in the twentieth century.

Harvey Lemke of Milwaukee encountered concertina clubs as early as 1899 and was playing with them regularly by 1911. His daughter Mildred's recollections from the 1930s describe a pattern established decades prior. The club's leader, Al Giese, taught the fine points of playing, while introducing new tunes. The club "used to have doings at a barn with the kids sleeping over and the men playing." Besides concertinas, there were "drums, a few horns" to fill out the sound for Sunday afternoon dances at Milwaukee's Jefferson and Bohemian Halls. "Big dances, a lot of people went to those" (Kaminski 1989).

The Clarion Concertina Club of Tinley Park, Illinois, attracted a similarly enthusiastic public for their first dance.

> The Club being young, the members did not expect a very large crowd and engaged a medium-sized hall for the occasion. But before dancing began there was already a large number of people there and by eleven o'clock several hundred people were stepping on each others toes in an effort to dance. It was necessary to discontinue the sale of tickets and no one was admitted after eleven o'clock. The dancers liked the music so well that the club members soon found it necessary to play in relays to keep the crowd satisfied. The entire community talked about the success of the dance and many who came too late to gain admission are looking forward to the next dance which will be held in a large and modern dance hall. (*Booster* Christmas 1930)

---

[4] We still lack full studies regarding the accordion and the harmonica in America folk and vernacular music and far less has been written concerning accordion and harmonica clubs. The best preliminary treatments are Charuhas (1955) and Licht (1984).

Figure 2. Sheet music published by Otto Georgi, with Georgi and members of the Chicago Concertina Club, ca. 1895. Courtesy of Jerry Minar.

Figure 3. Henry Silberhorn from his *Instructor*, Chicago, 1910. Wisconsin Folk Museum Collection.

Figure 4. Chicago Concertina Club, ca. 1895. Courtesy of Jack Zimmerman.

The Hustisford Concertina Club of Dodge County, Wisconsin, adopted a variety show format in the late 1930s and early 40s. In the manner of vaudevillians, the club performed against specially painted backdrops while in western attire or "gay nineties" regalia. The entire ensemble would open with several numbers, but nearly "everyone in the club had something special they could do." One played the xylophone, another the musical saw and an especially small child climbed atop a box to play the string bass (DeWitz 1985). A poster from 1942 lured spectators to the Hustisford Town Hall where, for 35 cents (20 for children), they could:

> See Concertina Robert: playing two concertinas at one time!
> THE ONE-MAN BAND—Six instruments played by one man!
> ALSO featuring LITTLE WONDER GOLDIE on the Marimba. The smallest known Bass Player, and a song by that "Little Sweetheart of the West."

As recently as the late 1980s concertina clubs could be found throughout the Midwest, extending from the greater Chicago area to the east (South Bend, Indiana; Union and Manistee, Michigan) and the northwest (Milwaukee and Wausau in Wisconsin; Minneapolis, St. Joseph, and Duluth in Minnesota). Several of these remain active, while others have declined. To some extent the concertina club has been supplanted by the "concertina jamboree."

Concertina jamborees have their roots in informal jam sessions that might occur when a traveling concertina salesman descended upon a community, or at a tavern or music store that served as a hangout for musicians, or when amateur players gathered on the fringes of weekend polka festivals. By the 1960s more formalized jamborees emerged as promoters supplied a sound system and backup musicians for all comers. The flier for a five-day polka festival in Gibbon, Minnesota, in 1993 claims invention while outlining a typical format:

> The big concertina jamboree starts at noon in the boom room. A drummer and bass horn player will be present and concertina players will register as they arrive for their playing time. Each will play about four tunes and receive five dollars. Gibbon Ballroom was the originator of this in 1964—remember!!!

Gibbon's annual jamboree, like the yearly gathering of the World Concertina Congress, attracts hundreds of players from throughout the Upper Midwest.

Figure 5. Art Altenburg entertains from behind the bar at his Concertina Bar in Milwaukee, 1985. Photo by Lewis Koch.

Art Altenburg's Concertina Bar on South Thirty-seventh Street in Milwaukee draws a similar, albeit more local, parade of concertina players for a weekly Thursday night jamboree. Born in the German farming community of Knowlton, Wisconsin, in 1929, Altenburg learned to play the concertina as a young man before coming to Milwaukee in 1953 where he sold Chevrolet trucks for twenty-two years. Not surprisingly, he continued to play the concertina. Small bands based around the instrument were common in Milwaukee taverns on weekends, the Continental and Cream City Concertina Clubs were active and players would also gather regularly at Karpek's music store on South Sixteenth Street and at a succession of taverns like the Hideaway Bar on South Thirteenth where concertinist Stan Nowicki held forth. Altenburg purchased his bar in 1979, about the time the Hideaway shut down. His jamborees have been going ever since (Altenburg 1988).

Teachers

There were no concertina teachers in Art Altenburg's rural community. He learned to play by ear, with a few tips from an uncle and from barnstorming professionals like Minnesota's Whoopee John Wilfahrt. Nonetheless, from the days of Georgi and Silberhorn, concertina teachers have had a profound effect on the instrument's popularity. Indeed Silberhorn's influence remains strong forty years after his death.

The concertina's aforementioned peculiar arrangement of notes rendered the instrument baffling to other squeezebox players. The logic of the button accordion, the piano accordion, or the English concertina simply did not apply to the German concertina. Nor was it an easy matter for even the musically literate to play a new tune by scanning a sheet of music. Even today concertina players hope that someone will invent a "converter" to turn standard musical notation into arrangements for the concertina. Silberhorn's *Instructor for the Concertina* (1910) strove "to establish the Concertina as the Ideal Home Instrument" by enabling people "To Learn to Play the Concertina without having Previous Knowledge of Music." Toward this end, Silberhorn offered a tablature system of notation. A number corresponded to each button, and since each button had a different tone depending on the compression or extension of the bellows, a circumflex over the number indicated "push," while a dash meant "pull."[5]

Silberhorn revised his instruction book periodically, while supplementing it with a vast trove of tunes in tablature: Central European dances, classical pieces, children's game songs, American popular music, and college anthems. Eventually his catalogue swelled to four thousand titles.

Beyond attracting students from afar with his instruction book and sheet music, Silberhorn inspired other teachers and arrangers throughout the Upper Midwest. Irving DeWitz was one such disciple. DeWitz was born in 1896 on a farm near the village of Hustisford in heavily German Dodge County, Wisconsin. His father played a bit of violin at home and at house parties. At one party when Irving was thirteen, he heard a man named Griebe play the concertina: "The music stayed in my head two–three days" (DeWitz 1985). DeWitz had a chance to get a used concertina but insisted on a new one. Soon he was walking three miles round trip, in all seasons, to take lessons from Ernst Hauke, a watchmaker and musician who "could play any instrument."

Once he had learned a waltz, a two-step, and a square dance, DeWitz played for his first dance: "a woman flew out the window during the square dance." In his first year of playing, young Irving earned enough for a new wardrobe; in the second he was able to buy a new car. Soon he opened a music store on Hustisford's Main Street. Although DeWitz also sold and repaired farm machinery and pumps, he is best remembered for teaching over five hundred local students to play the concertina.

DeWitz's music business was highly dependent on trips to Chicago:

> Henry Silberhorn was a music man, see, he sold concertinas. And I sold concertinas. I would go in, even in Chicago, I would go in and buy a dozen

---

[5] With regard to the origin and evolution of concertina notation, Jack Zimmerman observes:

> The circumflex and dash were, I think, borrowed from bow direction of the violin. Modern concertina arrangements use only the circumflex for press—no notation at all for pull, except in bass a dash means to repeat (Zimmerman 1992).

> concertinas at one time. But I wanted to play them, because some of them played hard, and I didn't like that for giving lessons. So I played them, and then I had them shipped out, see, and then I gave lessons.

DeWitz is remembered as a demanding yet patient teacher. Fred Kaulitz recalls progressively more difficult lessons and periodic examinations (Kaulitz 1985). Although serious about music, DeWitz had a playful side. Once Herbie Zuilsdorf left his concertina in DeWitz's shop. DeWitz opened the case, removed the concertina, and inserted a battery of comparable weight (Neuenschwander 1985).

Like Kaulitz and Zuilsdorf, DeWitz's students were mostly youthful. Some were drawn to the instrument on their own, others were encouraged by their parents. While a teen in nearby Lebanon Township, Ed Peirick and his brother purchased a concertina from DeWitz and paid for lessons (Peirick 1985). Mel Knaack's dad, Arthur, liked polka music and, when Mel was seven, the elder Knaack bought him and his sister Marian a concertina. Although times were hard and busy on the farm, Arthur Knaack drove his children to Hustisford each Thursday for an hour's lesson. The instrument's grip had to be shifted to accommodate their small hands, yet Marian soon rewarded her dad's investment by playing for public programs with DeWitz's Hustisford Concertina Club (Knaack 1985).

From the 1920s through the 1960s, as DeWitz was instructing his charges, other concertina teachers were doing the same. A few of the notable include: in Illinois, Henry Bobzien of Des Plaines, George Hrica, Rudy Patek, Frank Schmidt, Henry Schuckert, Joe Stacey, Wally Stark (all of Chicago), and Edward "Star" Starzynski of West Dundee; in Wisconsin, Dan Gruetzmacher of Wausau, John Bondowski, Stanley Nowicki, Thomas Smigielski and Ed Teikowski (all of Milwaukee); in Minnesota, Bill Brown of New Ulm, Joe Czerniak of Duluth, George Servatius of Melrose, and Tony and Betty Wolf of St. Joseph (*The Booster*; Stark 1993; Watters ca. 1972; Zimmerman 1992). All of them owed something to Silberhorn. Schmidt was Silberhorn's student and Bobzien, in turn, learned the concertina from Schmidt. Starzynski relied on the "Silberhorn method," while the Wolfs and Brown simplified Silberhorn. Both Brown and Gruetzmacher presently maintain large portions of the Silberhorn catalogue of arrangements.

Importers and Manufacturers

Concertina teachers and players, predictably, needed a continuous and reliable source of new instruments. In the late nineteenth and early twentieth centuries, concertina enthusiasts, like DeWitz, looked to Chicago. Georgi, Silberhorn, and others relied initially on concertinas imported chiefly from Saxony: the Uhlig and Lange com-

Figure 6. Irving DeWitz and his daughter Lucille, Hustisford, ca. 1928. Courtesy of Robert DeWitz.

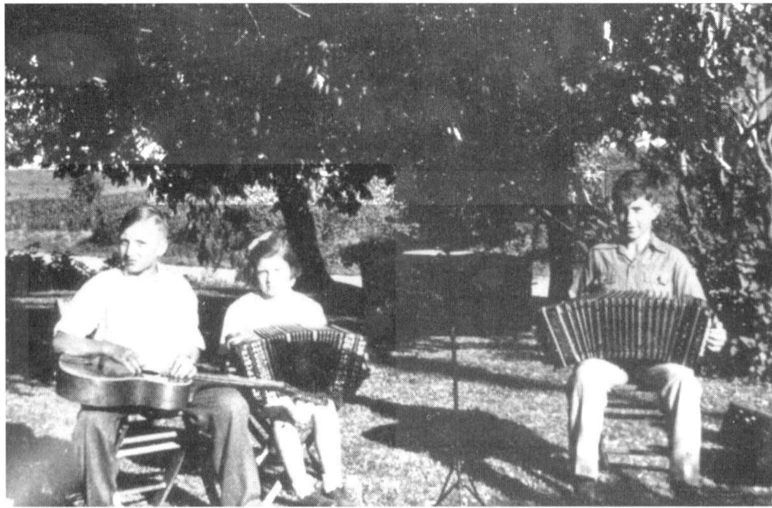

Figure 7. Mel and Marian Knaack on concertinas, with an unidentified lap steel guitar player, Watertown, 1930s. Courtesy of Mel Knaack.

panies in Chemnitz, the Alfred Arnold and the Ernst Louis Arnold companies in Carlsfield, and the Wunderlich company of Siebenbrunn. As early as 1896, Silberhorn published a catalogue of his Old Country wares: *Price List of Concertinas and Bandonions and Furnishings*. Not surprisingly, the necessity of servicing instruments and refurbishing used models for resale attracted craftsmen. By the mid-1890s Otto Schicht, a German immigrant, was gaining a wide reputation as Chicago's leading "repair and service man" for the concertina (Watters 1955).

Meanwhile the preferences of American concertinists and the peculiarities of the American market prompted entrepreneurs to recommend new designs to German manufacturers. One result was "Silberhorn's Clarion Concertina . . . [b]uilt According to the Plans and Specifications of a Concertina Specialist." Writing in his *Booster* in 1930, Silberhorn described the Clarion as "An Ideal Realized."

> Looking back 40 years—what great changes have occurred; then—we simply accepted a Concertina as it was made and let it go at that; as time went on, adding new experiences from year-to-year, partly through repairing and tuning, and partly through the ever more apparent need of a real reliable Concertina, a great desire grew within me, a determination to be able to sell the best quality in tone and wear that could be made; through suggestions, plans, drawings, etc., new improvements were made—until the war retarded the advance of the Concertina. But during the last ten years this wonderful instrument not only came back to its own prestige, but new laurels were added; through tireless efforts I have succeeded in offering a Concertina which has truly reached the highest point of perfection of the day; viz.: a strong and yet mild tone—a real Concertina tone—which becomes richer, the longer it is being played; and its name is: The "Clarion."

Amidst touting the innovations of his Clarion concertina, Silberhorn alludes to World War I. The war effectively stopped the importing of German concertinas. While this development may have temporarily "halted the advance of the Concertina," Americans had already been producing the instrument in small quantities.

Around 1900 Otto Schlicht, the renowned technician, introduced the "Pearl Queen" concertina for Chicago's Georgi and Vitak Company—erstwhile publishers of Czech, German and other "foreign" sheet music. By the close of World War I, Schlicht's shop was also making concertinas for Rudy Patek's Patek Music Company—located at 769, then 835 Milwaukee Avenue in Chicago, just blocks from Silberhorn's establishment. A catalogue from the period lauds Schlicht as the "Master

Builder of the World's Finest Concertinas," while denigrating "foreign Concertinas so lacking in tone, efficiency, and beauty." On the other hand:

> Every craftsman engaged in the building of a Patek Concertina has served many years of apprenticeship under Otto Schlicht, and no doubt this explains why a PATEK Concertina is the proud possession of its owner, and a wonderful thrill to those who listen to it.

Who would doubt that in the immediate postwar climate of "100% Americanism" the Patek's catalogue's anti-foreign bias was also a means of asserting the all-American pedigree of his German concertinas.

Several other Midwestern companies followed suit in the 1920s. In Chicago, they included both the Glass brothers and Walter Kadlubowski, who launched the Star Concertina and Accordion Manufacturing Company in 1925 at 2351 Milwaukee Avenue.[6] In Milwaukee, ninety miles to the north, the Karpek Accordion Manufacturing Company, begun in 1915 by Andrew Karpek, a Russian immigrant, soon added concertinas to its line of piano and button accordions (Leary and Teske 1990:30–31).

The importing of German concertinas resumed briefly in the late 1920s and the 1930s. Helmut and Max Peters, virtuoso musicians about whom more will be said, made periodic trips to Germany where they purchased concertinas from the Arnold Concertina-Bandonion factory. Back in the Midwest Helmut opened a concertina sales and repair shop in Belleville, Illinois, while Max operated a Milwaukee tavern. The pair also worked the vaudeville circuit, peddling concertinas as a sideline, with particular success in Illinois, Michigan, Minnesota, and Wisconsin (Roll 1980).

In the late 1930s, as sentiment mounted against Adolf Hitler's Nazi regime, the Peters Brothers fell victim to ugly and preposterous rumors that they were German spies who exchanged secret information in the housings of concertinas. Whoopee John Wilfahrt, the noted Minnesota concertinist, was similarly beleaguered by ludicrous stories suggesting that his band's tours were a cover for espionage and that his drumming son tapped coded messages to German agents. In Wilfahrt's case, rumors escalated to the extent that the Federal Bureau of Investigation issued a public denial (Rippley 1992:7).

---

[6] Information on Otto Schlicht, the Patek Music Company and Star Concertina is drawn from the files of the Star Concertina Company and from information provided by Wally Stark (1993).

The availability of German concertinas to America's Midwest ceased once more with the onset of World War II. Nor did it resume quickly in peacetime. Beyond the devastation wrought by war on the German economy, the concertina manufacturing companies of Saxony were in East Germany—cut off from trade with the West. It was not until the early 1950s that Arno Arnold emigrated to West Germany to reestablish the Arnold Concertina Company. His wares found American customers, like Chicago's Vitak-Elsnic Company and especially Pat Watters, the Minneapolis entrepreneur, who "furnished Arno Arnold with designs for seventeen models of concertinas ranging from low-priced student models through progressively amateur, semi-professional and professional instruments" (Arnold ca. 1960, Watters ca. 1972).

Despite Arnold's resurgence, German companies had ceased to be major manufacturers of the German concertina for the American market. After the closing of Schlicht's Chicago factory in the early 1950s, neighboring Star Concertina, which persists to the present, had become the most prominent American supplier. Other American companies—like Baldoni and Karpek, both of Milwaukee—relied on their long-standing relationship with Italian accordion factories to have concertinas produced in Italy to their specifications and under their names. For a time even Star Concertinas were made in Italy. Meanwhile in the hinterlands, far from Chicago and Milwaukee but amidst throngs of concertinists, Christy Hengel and Anton Wolfe each began crafting instruments in one-man shops.

Wolfe in particular regards his work as being in contradistinction to concertinas made in Italian factories. Because of their prior and continued experience with the piano accordion, Wolfe contends, they have fostered "the piano accordionisation of the concertina." His commitment is to the "true concertina tone" of prior Patek and German-made concertinas.

Wolfe began tinkering with concertinas in the early 1940s when his own instrument, a Wunderlich, broke, and he could not acquire replacement parts from Germany. He was born in 1922 on a farm near Moquah in Bayfield County, Wisconsin. As a "little shaver" in the 1930s, Wolfe caught what he called the "concertina disease" by listening to old time bands on the radio: Omaha Czech bands, Joe Fischer out of Cedar Rapids, Iowa, and Whoopee John over WTCN in St. Paul. There were also concertina players nearby like Louis Kolonko and Bob Mathiowetz (Wolfe 1985).

In 1967, shortly after his mother's death, Wolfe gave up farming and purchased concertina stock and equipment from Patek. Patek, who had retained materials from his years of collaboration with Schlicht, had retired by then to Weyawauga, Wisconsin. At the same time, Wolfe also moved to nearby Stevens Point, an area where concertina players have been plentiful for more than a century. He has been making concertinas ever since. The promotional flier for Wolfe's Old Style Concertina aptly proclaims:

> I have made all of my own dies, punches and broaches to make reed plates, and dies and cutters to make reeds. . . . A few of the other things I make and do: reeds, reed plates, tuning, reed blocks, action boards, action support, rails, valves, frames, celluloiding, engraving, bellows (fold my own), hand rails, hand straps, and much more. Plus doing the complete assembly of the concertina.

In the mid-1970s Jerry Minar of New Prague, Minnesota, a concertina player, teacher, tuner, and repairman, joined with Wolfe to become his exclusive dealer-distributor. They developed the Wolfe "Deluxe" concertina in 1982 and, in 1989, fashioned the "Accordina": a concertina with the keyboards of a three-row button accordion.

Christy Hengel, Wolfe's contemporary, was born on a farm near Wanda, Minnesota, in 1922, not far from New Ulm—the home of Whoopee John Wilfahrt and a host of stellar concertinists. Wilfahrt's playing and showmanship captivated ten-year-old Hengel. Money was scarce in the depression, but Hengel trapped weasels and skunks to earn enough for his first concertina in 1939. In 1947 he started the Christy Hengel Band. From 1951–1953, Hengel played with Harold Loeffelmacher's Six Fat Dutchmen, one of the finest bands in an era when polka music commanded a national audience (Leary and March 1991; Spottswood 1982).

Like many players, Hengel tinkered with, tuned, and rebuilt various concertinas. Toward the end of his stint with Loeffelmacher, he decided to purchase concertina-making equipment from Otto Schlicht's Chicago shop. He produced the first Hengel Concertina in 1955, eventually introducing innovations that resulted in a concertina that was lighter and easier to play yet retained a full sound. Today, Hengel Concertinas are so sought after that players must wait years to receive one (Nusbaum 1986).

Publications

The ephemeral fliers and catalogues of concertina makers and distributors offer occasional shards of information regarding the instrument's cultural history in America's Midwest. The handful of concertina and polka periodicals issued since the 1920s are far richer sources, although sometimes no less ephemeral.

In November 1927 Silberhorn published the first volume of a "Concertina Players Magazine." A series of question marks topped the masthead, while the lead article offered "$10.00 in concertina music of your own selection" to the reader who would suggest the "most appropriate name." "The Concertinist," "Concert-Tone," "Voice of the Concertina," "Silberhorn's Music Box," "Concertina Broadcaster," "Buttonettes," "United Concertinists," "Concertination," "Melody," and "Squeezebox Educator" were all proposed to a panel of judges, but they settled on a name sent in by Phil Beitel of Norway, Michigan: "Booster." *Silberhorn's Booster for the Advancement of the Concertina* ran to at least twenty-two issues from November 1927 through New Year's Day 1934.[7]

The first issue presented a four-point statement of purpose. The third and fourth points were familiar extensions of Silberhorn's prior efforts as an educator:

> 3. To constantly improve the Concertina and its method of instruction.
> 4. To help every concertina player become an expert player.

Beyond recurrent articles on topics like "The Experience of a Teacher" and "Dirt—The Concertina's Worst Enemy," the *Booster* provided a pair of pedagogical columns with each installment. "Hints, Helps, and Advice" offered players exercises for the right and left hands, tips on volume and dynamics, and methods of concertina maintenance and repair. "Questions? Answers!" responded to readers' queries that ranged from matters technical ("Can you make a full triple Concertina out of my double by adding extra plates?") to logistical ("How soon can I get my music after sending in an order?") to philosophical ("Why do large music stores advertise 'Everything in Music' when they do not sell Concertinas?").

With his platform's second point, Silberhorn vowed "To make the Concertina popular as a high grade instrument." Indeed the publication's first issue lauded the concertina as "The World's Most Complete Instrument." Bristling at notions that the concertina is merely a "push and pull box," Silberhorn reckoned that not only does the concertina deserve respect, but that "there is no instrument that compares" with it for fullness of sound, accessibility, affordability, and portability.

> The violin is considered the world's nearest perfect instrument, but it must be accompanied with piano, it is not complete in itself, and it takes years of study to master. The piano and pipe organ are the most nearly complete musical instruments but they can't be carried from place to place and are

[7] My count of *Booster* issues is based upon copies provided by Jerry Minar, Wally Stark, and Jack Zimmerman. After the first few years Silberhorn abandoned both a regular schedule of publication and an indication of volume and issue numbers.

> very expensive. All other wind and string instruments are specialties and are ineffectual when played without accompaniment.

The concertina, however, is a veritable "organ upon your lap."

While clearly an egalitarian attack on instrumental canons that excluded the concertina, such praise was also aligned with Silberhorn's economic interests. In keeping with the name *Booster*, he repeatedly presented an image of the German concertina that was congruent with the optimistic, self-promoting, imaginative, capitalist spirit that characterizes the public face of American business. In his most visionary effusions, Silberhorn touted the concertina, especially his "Clarion" concertina, as the means by which players could rise—like sellers of *Grit* or Amway products, like Horatio Alger's heroes—from rags to riches. The juxtaposition "Concertina or Automobile?" recurred frequently.

> An automobile costs a great deal more than a Concertina, and you can't have any more fun with it. Besides the initial cost, you must spend money for gas, oil, and tires and you can't use your car to make more money. If you buy a Concertina you are making an investment that will pay you high interest. One player made $400 in six months with his Concertina—in six months an automobile drops over $400.00 in value! Another player paid off the mortgage on his home, playing on jobs—you can't do that with an automobile! Look here, you can have both a Concertina and a motor car—but, buy the Concertina first and you can earn the price of an auto. Furthermore your Concertina can buy the gas, oil, and tires to keep your car going. A Concertina is a sound investment in **Music, Pleasure, and Profit**.

The foregoing suggestion was typically followed by testimonies from such enterprising concertinists as Merton Birmingham of Hortonville, Wisconsin, who "bought a Clarion Full Triple ($175) from us in March of this year and so far has made over $400.00."

Would-be Birminghams were given advice on how to get paying musical jobs and how to hold their audiences. They were offered discounts on the "Latest Popular Concertina Music." They were treated to plentiful ads for new and used instruments and for concertina accessories that included cases, straps, music stands, and folios and concertina club banners. Not surprisingly, the ads were all for products carried by Silberhorn.

Even stories intended to inspire were framed with a booster's rhetoric. In "Traveled 461 Miles To Play," Herman Waller's epic journey from Webster, South Dakota, to Green, Iowa—dramatized by muddy roads that twice required "teams to drag them out"—is prefaced by the sentiment that "The Concertina is becoming more popular every day in the city as well as in the country." "Saved By Concertina" —regarding a missionary couple from Willmar, Minnesota, who were able to save themselves from Chinese bandits by "singing hymns and playing on a battered concertina"—is followed immediately with a "SPECIAL HOLIDAY OFFER" of the latest popular music.

Although often a glorified commercial catalogue masquerading as a magazine, the *Booster* nonetheless demonstrated a firm commitment to the first point in Silberhorn's statement of purpose: "To unite all players into one big family." The "family" may not have extended to rivals Vitak and Elsnic and, just down the street, Rudy Patek, but it did include scores of concertina players who contributed letters and photographs to a regular feature. "Concertina Orchestra and Radio News" is our most vivid glimpse of the culture revolving around the German concertina fifty years after its introduction to America's Midwest.

Beyond teaching and participating in clubs, many of Silberhorn's correspondents were active, semi-professional public performers. The top of a representative page from the February 1928 *Booster* featured a studio photograph of a "Bonduel Orchestra" that included:

> Emil Berkhahn, Concertina and Saxophone; Walter Richter, Concertina; William Froemming, Cornet; Walter Froemming, Clarinet; Wado Krueger, Drums. Under the able management of Mr. Berkhahn this orchestra has been playing, for the citizens of Bonduel, Wisconsin, for a number of years. Although they make a specialty of "old time" music, they are able to furnish the best of popular music as well.

Entries regarding five other bands filled a column below.

> Otto C. Rettke of Fairmont, Minnesota, is manager of the S&R Concertina Orchestra. This is a combination of three pieces: Concertina, violin, and banjo. They have four or five dance jobs a week and attract large crowds at every dance. The other night they had 215 couples on the floor. Mr. Rettke says that if his Concertina was not loud and clear their music would have been drowned out. With the temperature often 40 degrees below zero, it takes a good orchestra to draw the crowds.

> John Papa, well-known Chicago player, broadcasted over radio station WKBI on February 6th. This station has a wave length of 215. Mr. Papa often broadcasts from this station and would be pleased to have you send your requests in to same.
>
> Alfred Schultz of Chief, Michigan, is the leader of a three piece orchestra consisting of Violin, Concertina and drums. The other members are his brother and father. This is a busy orchestra and a good one for, they had an average of two jobs a week last year and already have a dance hall engaged for next summer.
>
> John Stypa of Kansas City, Kansas, has been enjoying a successful season with an orchestra combination of the Concertina and a violin, saxophone and drum. More power to you and a busy 1928.
>
> Zims Novelty Orchestra announce an engagement on February 21st. This Concertina Orchestra will play for the American Citizens Society at their hall at 3143 Brighton Road, N.S. Pittsburgh, Pa. If you live in Pittsburgh be sure to attend.

The collective testimony of these and similar excerpts reveal an occasional solo concertinist, but more commonly a three- to five-piece band that provides some combination of "foreign" and "American" dance music for a somewhat diverse yet mostly ethnic local crowd in community halls and over the radio.

Excerpts in the "Concertina Orchestra and Radio News" also suggest the extent of a musical network revolving around Chicago. Of the 114 contributors to this column, 94 were from the Upper Midwest: 44 from Illinois (half from Chicago), 23 from Wisconsin, 11 from Minnesota, 10 from Michigan, and 6 from northern Indiana. Pennsylvania, with six (all from Pittsburgh and environs) was the only other state registering more than two. This dispersion supports subsequent claims that: "The concertina became most popular in the Middle West of the United States, radiating from Chicago, whence most of the European players of the instrument emigrated" (Watters 1955).

Beyond encouraging unity among active bandleaders by providing them with a forum, *Silberhorn's Booster* offered sketches like "The History of the Concertina," "Concertina Clubs in Germany," and "Argentina Tango Bands" that placed the concertina in a broader context. High-minded illumination was balanced with low comedy through a regular column on "Squeezebox Humor." While some entries were standard "Dutchman," "Negro," "Irish," "Hebrew," and "rube" dialect jokes of the era, many were tailored to the concertina. "Repasz Band," a popular old-time march, figured in several.[8]

> "Weakened Too Soon"
> Angry Neighbor—Look here can't you play any other piece except Repasz Band. You kept me awake until 1:00 o'clock playing that one piece.
> Concertina Player—You should have stuck it out a little longer. I finally mastered it about 1:30.
>
> "Deathless Music"
> Scientists excavating a city that was covered by an erupting volcano many centuries ago, found a mummified figure of a man, sitting erect with a musical instrument similar to the Concertina upon his knees. From the position of his hands when uncovered the scientists state positively that he was playing Repasz Band.
>
> "Getting It Right"
> Two fellows were listening to a Concertina orchestra. One insisted they were playing Repasz Band and the other was sure they were playing Over There. Finally one fellow agreed to go up to the stage and look back at the announcement board. He came back and said, "We're both wrong. It is the 'Refrain from Spitting.'"

Silberhorn's readers occasionally responded in kind with witty poems, quips, and cartoons, including a sketch of a bucksaw-driven concertina (see Figure 8).

Perhaps because of his desire to unite concertina players into "one big family," Henry Silberhorn avoided political issues that might have affected his readers—with a single exception. Temperance-minded Chicago mayors, convinced by WASP church groups that music in combination with alcohol fostered promiscuity, had tried to enforce bans since the turn of the century, "but German saloons on the North Side refused to silence their beer garden bands and plugged the courts with

---

[8] Recordings of "Repasz Band March," in chronological order, include: Henry Magnuson and Einar Holt (Swedish), Victor trial, Camden, New Jersey, October 29, 1919; Victor Lisjak's Orchestra (Slovenian), Columbia 25004-F, New York, ca. 1923; Henry Schuckert and Henry Schepp (German), Odeon 1073, Chicago, January 29, 1924; Dominic Bartol (Italian), Victor 77415, New York, March 11, 1924; Kosatka Concertina Quartette (Czech), Columbia 12034-F, Chicago, ca. February 1926; Louis Spehek and son (Slovenian), Columbia 25103-F, New York, September 1928 (Spottswood 1990).

My daughter in Benton Harbor, Mich. sent this sketch and writes; Dear Pa: I think this would be an excellent idea for you to spend some week-ends in the country. - Gretchen.

Figure 8: A Concertinist cuts wood, a cartoon sent in by a Benton Harbor, Michigan, reader of the *Booster*, 1927. Courtesy of Jerry Minar and Jack Zimmerman.

lawsuits" (Duis 1983:253). The Volstead Act, establishing Prohibition in 1919, not only outlawed alcoholic beverages but also eliminated the tavern as a site for music. Prohibition was lampooned periodically in the *Booster*'s pages. The Christmas 1932 edition, on the eve of Prohibition's repeal, announced "Better Days Are Coming." Proclaiming "Nazdrowie" and "Prosit" to his Polish- and German-American readers, Silberhorn declared:

> We probably won't have beer by Christmas but we'll have it soon—so they tell us. And all of you who remember the good old times B.P. (before Prohibition) know that there'll be more parties and more dances that will look to the Concertina player for music.

The editorial concluded predictably with a plug for a new composition, "Beer Waltz Medley."

There were few subsequent issues of the *Booster,* although Henry Silberhorn continued with his concertina business for another three decades. Perhaps he felt he had delivered on his platform. Nor has there been a publication since devoted exclusively to the German concertina, although concertina devotees have figured regularly in a succession of publications treating the larger polka scene in the Upper Midwest.

C. B. Brown of Minneapolis published seventeen issues of *Polka and Old Time News*, beginning on a monthly basis in November 1963. Brown was a partner in a commercial printing company and the founder of both the "Pleasant Peasant" polka record label and the Lingua-Musica publishing company. His magazine was chiefly aimed at readers in Minnesota, Wisconsin, and northern Iowa. It included profiles of band leaders ("Polka Personalities"), regular columnists who commented on the musical scene in their locales, editorials, a "Family File" of humor and recipes, photographs of bands, sheet music, and letters from readers—along with advertisements from record companies, radio stations, dance halls, and concertina manufacturers.

Although his magazine was not overtly oriented toward the concertina, Brown was clearly aware of the instrument's importance in his region. The monthly inclusions of polka, waltz and schottische sheet music—most of them Brown compositions—were outfitted with tablature for concertinists. Brown even aided one reader's search for the elusive concertina converter:

> CONVERTER ANYONE?
> Calvin H. Reuter, RFD 2, Wisner, Nebraska, asks "Can you tell me how to convert regular music to concertina music?"
> This question came up before and response indicated that there is at least one device by which this can be done. Anyone having one available should write Mr. Reuter directly. (*Polka and Old Time News*, January 1965)

Nine of the fifteen "Polka Personalities," meanwhile, featured concertinas as central instruments in their bands: John Check, Ernie Coopman, Ray Dorschner, Christy Hengel, Ray Konkol, Harold Loeffelmacher, Dick Rodgers, Elmer Scheid, and Norm Wilke. There were also such occasional features as the "Echo Concertina" (POTN August 1964)—concerning an instrument made by Stanley Uhlig of Montgomery, Minnesota—and "A Brief History of the Concertina's Development" (POTN May 1964) by Pat Watters.

Financial woes caused Brown to shift from a magazine to a newsletter format for two final issues before ceasing publication altogether in March 1965. Pat Watters of Minneapolis took up the paper thereafter, changing its name to *Music and Dance News*, giving even greater attention to the concertina and eventually expanding the readership to "46 states, Canada, England, France, Austria, and Italy" (*Music and Dance News* 15:4, 1979:4).

A veteran piano accordion educator and salesman, Watters (1903–1983) established Watters Music Center in downtown Minneapolis in 1942. That year he also purchased a stock of used concertinas and began to apply teaching techniques to the concertina that he had developed previously with the piano accordion. Eventually Watters would become a dealer for Silberhorn's sheet music, collaborator with concertina manufacturer Arno Arnold, sponsor of concertina jamborees, supporter of concertina clubs, and charter member of the World Concertina Congress.

Music and Dance News promoted all of these activities through photographs, pages of sheet music, advertising, and features. The latter included valuable profiles of deceased giants of the concertina world (C. F. Uhlig, Henry Silberhorn, Rudy Patek, Andrew Karpek), along with biographical sketches of contemporary players in both the United States and Germany. Citing age and declining health, Watters ceased fifteen years of publication in 1980.

The name *Music and Dance News* was revived in 1992 by the Minnesota Ballroom Operator's Association as a titular replacement for twenty-year-old *Entertainment Bits*. The paper covers the country, rock, and polka dance hall scene in Minnesota and contiguous states, with regular features on concertina players. *The Polka News*, begun in 1971 as *The Michigan Polka News*, has expanded to cover the polka scene nationally. Its Upper Midwestern emphasis is particularly strong, and it likewise commonly features concertinists.

Touring Artists

The concertinists commanding media attention today are no longer the chiefly local players profiled in *Silberhorn's Booster*. Rather, they are touring artists who play nearly every weekend over an area that often spans several states.

The Peters Brothers were perhaps the first concertina players to barnstorm the country. Max Peters (1895–1983) and his brother Helmut (b. 1897) were two of eight children in the Paul and Anna Hager Peters family. Their home in Leipzig was a scant fifty miles from Chemnitz, birthplace of the German concertina.

At the age of nine, Max Peters was earning money by carrying luggage for train passengers, selling papers, and delivering baked goods. One day he spied a concertina in a shop and heard a dozen students playing the concertina and bandonion. With his mother's help, he bought an instrument: "I took it to bed with me that night" (Peters 1981). Soon Max, Helmut, and another brother, Wilhelm, were playing.

The Peters family immigrated to the United States in 1912, settling in Henryetta, Oklahoma, where young Max labored briefly and reluctantly in a coal mine. A local theater owner heard the brothers playing at a birthday party and offered them five dollars each to perform on stage that night. Max was thrilled by the chance to earn money without dirt and danger (Christopulos 1983). His father, however, was skeptical, discounting his sons' music as frivolous, but when he heard a packed audience clap for them, he rose and declared: "Those are my boys!" Nearly seventy years later Max recalled that incident as the "best time of my life."

Figure 9. The Peters Brothers—Helmut, Wilhelm, and Max—pose on stage at the onset of their vaudeville careers, ca. 1914. Courtesy of Dorothy Peters Bertolas.

The one-night engagement in Henryetta led to twenty years of touring in theaters and dance halls in the waning days of vaudeville. Playing initially in Oklahoma and Kansas, the brothers branched out to Missouri and Texas. There were enough Germans and curious ethnic outsiders to sustain Mid-South audiences for a time. Excepting the occasional jaunts to New York and Florida, however, the Peters Brothers soon turned to an Upper Midwestern circuit (Illinois, Wisconsin, Michigan, Minnesota, and the Dakotas) where locals in considerable numbers hungered for concertina virtuosity.

Clad like rustic Bavarians—in plumed alpine hats, lederhosen, and knee socks—the Peters billed themselves as "Players from Germany" and "World's Famous Concertina Troupe from Germany." Although the phrase "from Germany" might be construed as implying that the Peters were touring America directly from an Old World base, the German-born brothers did maintain constant ties with the Old Country. Max and Helmut frequently returned to Germany to purchase concertinas for sale in the United States and to sustain friendships with fellow musicians—including the German concertina and bandonion virtuoso, Walter Porschmann (1901–1959), who played at Max Peters' wedding in 1922.

In America the Peters "troupe" ranged from two to five players and typically commenced an evening's entertainment with a formal concert. Beyond offering German folk-dance medleys and brisk marches, Max and Helmut Peters executed complex classical pieces in a manner that combined subtle musicianship with a showman's flair (Bertolas 1985). Irving DeWitz recalls them playing "like nobody's business" while "twisting around their concertinas." After an evening's concert, the Peters might provide a short film (one was a "30 Minute Talkie—A Trip Through Germany"), but a dance always followed. The brothers often stayed with and inspired local concertinists as, in the wee hours, they made still more music.

The Great Depression and the conversion of "opera houses" to "movie houses" in the early 1930s contributed to the demise of vaudeville. The Peters Brothers settled in Illinois and Wisconsin, respectively, where they continued as active but local musicians until the early 1980s.

Records

While one emergent form of mass media, the motion picture, contributed to the decline of concertina players on the stage, another, sound recording, provided new opportunities. In June 1926 the Peters Brothers made their only 78 rpm recording—a march ("Unter der Flagge von Hamburg") and a medley of "Alte deutsche Melodien"—on the Okeh label in Chicago (Spottswood 1990:227). Others would be more prolific.

By the second decade of the twentieth century, recording companies had begun to realize there was a vast untapped market among America's "foreign" population (Greene 1992; Gronow 1982; Spottswood 1982). Pioneering labels like Columbia, Okeh, and Victor initially recorded ethnic artists in New York City. In 1911, accordingly, a contingent of Chicagoans traveled to the Big Apple's Columbia studios. In keeping with the Upper Midwest's ethnic eclecticism—and in parallel with the Central European concertina scene—the first Americans to make commercial recordings on the German concertina were Czechs or Bohemians whose repertoire relied in part on Polish tunes.

On August 1, Charles Blim, Louis Solar, James Sidlo, and Thomas Kosatka recorded six sides as the Bohemian Concertina Quartet. Over the next two days, Blim and Solar, working as a duet, set down another fourteen sides. Sidlo and Kosatka likewise contributed six duets on August 2 (Spottswood 1990: vol. 2). That the four traveled from Chicago to New York suggests enterprise and organization. Indeed, Thomas Kosatka is likely the "T. Kosatka" shown in 1893 as a member of Chicago's Czech-American Concertina Band Club (see photographs in Greene 1992). Clearly the concertina veteran Kosatka and his fellows were not only confident in their own playing, but were also able to convince a record company that there was a market for their performances. Louis Solar must have made a particular impression.

Four years later, in August 1915, Columbia invited Solar to record—this time in Chicago—where he waxed another ten sides (Spottswood 1990:665). By the mid-1920s Chicago concertinists recorded regularly in Chicago studios. Louis Solar's 1911 session mate Thomas Kosatka recorded again for Columbia as the Kosatka Concertina Trio, while Charles Blim, with whom Solar performed duets, went on to team with concertina promoter Rudy Patek on more than forty sides for Okeh (Spottswood 1990:641, 657–659). Patek likewise provided an occasional third concertina to recordings by Henry Schuckert and Henry Schepp on Victor in 1926 (Spottswood 1990:241–242).

While quartets, trios, and duets dominated recordings on the German concertina in the 1920s, an occasional soloist found his way into the studio. Bruno Rudzinski was foremost among them. Born in Chicago in 1900, Rudzniski learned to speak Polish, English, Czech, and Italian while growing up in an ethnically diverse neighborhood. Richard Spottswood informs us that in the 1920s Rudzinski was

> well known in the taverns on Division Street as "Wild Bruno" and "Crazy Bruno." He recorded six songs in 1928, a few days after meeting at a party a Victor representative who invited him to audition. Shortly afterwards his windpipe was injured, damaging his singing and he did not record again.[9]

Rudzinski's recordings contrast markedly with those of fellow concertinists. While other players emphasized a controlled musical attack, with strict tempos and clear notes, Rudzinski altered the beat and slurred the tone. The strictly instrumental conventions of other concertinists were likewise abandoned by Rudzinski who slid from raucous vocals into wordless scatting. Although somewhat idiosyncratic, Rudzinski's style also bent toward the improvisatory exuberance, dissonance, and syncopation that Polish village orchestras favored in urban Chicago.

Concertinists and the Polka Scene

Concertina players who made records in the years following Rudzinski's 1928 session were, almost without exception, contributors to a regional ensemble sound that became known as "polka music." A lively couple dance in 2/4 time that originated in the late 1830s in northwestern Bohemia near the German and Polish borders, the polka was already a pan-European dance when immigrant musicians began holding forth in the Upper Midwest. In the 1930s, as second-generation ethnic Americans

---

[9] Richard K. Spottswood, notes to Spiew Juchasa/*Song of the Shepherd: Songs of Slavic Americans* LP (1977). This recording reissues Rudzinski's "Na Obie Nogi Polka" (On Both Feet). Rudzinski's "Pawel Walc" (Paul's Waltz) is reissued on *Polish-American Dance Music, The Early Recordings: 1927–1933* LP (1979). Another Rudzinski reissue, "Przeszedl Chlop do Karczmy" (A Man Came to the Saloon), is reissued on an LP in the Archive of American Folksong's *Folk Music in America* series (1976).

began to merge their parents' Old World sound with elements of their era's American popular music, "polka" emerged as a generic term for the synthesis. In Chicago the polka bands incorporating the concertina were chiefly Polish, while concertina players in the hinterlands generally worked in a German-Bohemian concertina style.

Wojciech Dzialowy, among others, sustained the concertina's presence in Chicago's Polish polka circles. An immigrant from the village of Makow in southwestern Poland, Dzialowy teamed with a violinist around 1914 to play for weddings and dances. He added a clarinetist in 1922 and, two years later, filled out the band to six pieces. The "Makowska Orkiestra Dzialwego" recorded roughly a hundred sides for Vocalion and Victor while enjoying a career that extended through 1938 (Spottswood 1990:703–706; Makowska Orkiestra LP liner notes ca. 1978).

Essentially an updated village orchestra, with a concertina/violin duet at its melodic center, the Makowska Orchestra's polka sound was challenged throughout the 1930s by the more polished and urbane "eastern" Polish style that eschewed concertina altogether. But in Chicago's working-class Polish neighborhoods, local players still favored the concertina. Dzialowy inspired them and they still remembered Rudzinski. In the late 1930s and throughout the 1940s Eddie Zima and Walter "Li'l Wally" Jagiello began performing at ethnic picnics and in the Polish taverns along Chicago's Division Street. Their slow tempos, swirling concertina improvisations and heartfelt vocals launched the modern Polish polka sound that dominates America's Polonia today (Kleeman 1982; Keil, Keil, and Blau 1992:46–60).

Whoopee John Wilfahrt likewise inspired scores of concertinists in Minnesota, Wisconsin, northern Iowa, and the Dakotas. Born in 1893 on a farm near New Ulm, Minnesota, Wilfahrt was of Bohemian German background, his grandparents having come from German villages in Czechoslovakia. Steeped in old country folk music, Wilfahrt began playing the button accordion as a young boy. The crisp tones of the concertina were more compelling, however, and Wilfahrt purchased his first of many concertinas from a neighbor in 1911 (Rippley 1992:12; see also generally Brown 1991; Lornell 1985). The Wilfahrt trio, which had already begun to play for local dances, expanded to six pieces by the early 1920s.

Whoopee John won the admiration of New Ulm audiences with his repertoire of Old-Country dance tunes and his showmanship on the concertina: he stretched the bellows to their limit, twirled his instrument, and even tossed it in the air. But he did not begin to capture a larger following until the mid-1920s. Radio was a new medium and stations like WLAG (soon to become WCCO) in Minneapolis sought live performers to entertain listeners in a five-state area. Whoopee John's 1924 debut launched a career that extended until his death in 1961 and crossed over from radio into television. Wilfahrt also began making records in 1927. His sales for the

DECCA label would rival those of pop crooner Bing Crosby in the late 1930s. In tandem with this media success, the Whoopee John band traversed the Upper Midwest's ballrooms, playing for enthusiastic crowds nearly every day of the year from the 1920s through the 1950s.

Indeed the Wilfahrt band inspired other players and a regional musical style was born. The "New Ulm" or "Minnesota" or "Dutchman" sound—that continues to maintain the concertina as its central instrument (Leary and March 1991:21–43). John Wilfahrt's deceptively simple yet ebullient musicianship, meanwhile, has been built upon by successive generations of concertina innovators: Elmer Scheid, whose sustained notes and flowing solos defined the "Dutchman" genre in the 1950s; Syl Liebl, whose deft mastery of sixteenth notes, triplets, and trills dazzled players in the 1960s; and Karl Hartwich, whose inventive improvisations and rapid chromatic runs astonish today (Leary 1990:2–3).

Thanks to its persistence in the Upper Midwest's evolving polka scene, the German concertina is as vital as it has ever been. Indeed, as concertinist and recording studio proprietor Jerry Minar (1993) attests, "There is more concertina music being recorded nowadays than ever before."

The World Concertina Congress

The German concertina's longevity and regional popularity in America's Upper Midwest have, not surprisingly, sparked pride and a sense of history in the instrument's devotees. Sharing Georgi's internationalist vision and Silberhorn's desire "to unite all players into one big family," the World Concertina Congress has striven since 1975 "to elevate the image of the concertina as a musical instrument" and to honor those, living and dead, who have "labored and contributed unselfishly toward the Production, Preservation, and Promotion of the Concertina" (World Concertina Congress, Constitution and By-Laws 1984).

Begun by a handful of players and promoters (including Pat Watters; Harold Zimmerman of Union, Michigan; and Harold's son Jack of South Bend, Indiana), the World Concertina Congress has grown to more than a thousand members. Jack Zimmerman, whose small den overflows with concertinalia, maintains a mailing list in his official capacity as the organization's secretary. He is also the group's de facto historian and archivist.

While its name, logo, and vision span continents, the World Concertina Congress is strongest in the Upper Midwestern region that has always been the instrument's American home. Several of its most active regional affiliates are in Wisconsin, as is Allenton, the site in recent years of the Congress's annual Labor Day "Jamboree." While the Jamboree functions as a social and promotional event,

Figure 10. Whoopee John Wilfahrt (left) with DECCA A&R (artists and repertoire) man Leonard Joy, 1950s. Courtesy of Jerry Minar.

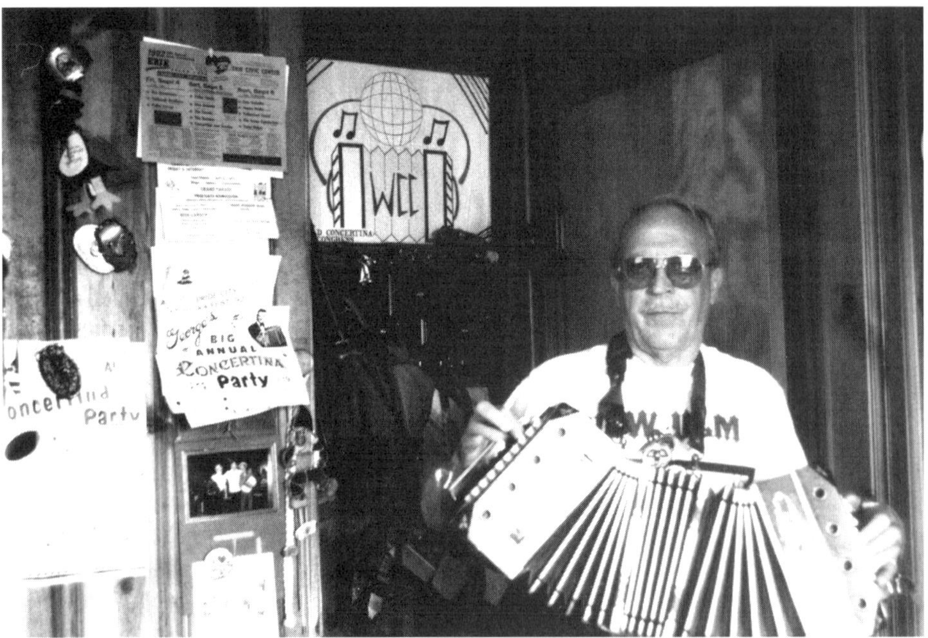

Figure 11. Jack Zimmerman, secretary of the World Concertina Congress, performs in his music room, South Bend, Indiana, 1992. Photo by James P. Leary.

it is also the occasion for inducting new members into the "World Concertina Congress Hall of Fame."

Unlike, say, the Country Music Hall of Fame—which attracts tourists to an impressive museum, issues documentary recordings of the genre's pioneers, and maintains a substantial archives—the Concertina Hall of Fame is not a place but a collective idea, a means by which the instrument's aficionados honor their exemplary peers. The Hall's phantom status stems partly from the concertina's existence outside the popular music mainstream: there is neither the money nor the audience for a physical hall of fame. But there is also something egalitarian about the concertina and its supporters that runs contrary to hierarchical trappings. A handful of the eighty-two concertina inductees (1976–1992) are international, national, and regional figures, but even they are uniformly "apostles to the common man." The bulk are chiefly local practitioners who have kept the instrument vital at the grassroots. Like few halls of fame, the Concertina Congress's version not only praises lofty "stars," but also recognizes "down-to-earth" players.

The Germanness of the German Concertina

While nearly all the inductees to the Concertina Hall of Fame are ethnic Americans, less than half are of German origin (my count numbers thirty-six Germans, twenty-nine Poles, nine Czechs, and eight others). The players listed in Silberhorn's *Booster* of the 1920s indicate a similar range of Central European heritage, with the addition of a few Italians. The instrument's players likewise have favored a broad stylistic and ethnic range of music for more than a century. And they have been playing chiefly in America's Upper Midwest. What then can we say is "German" about the German concertina? And what does the cultural complex surrounding the instrument tell us about Old World musical traditions in America?

Like the concertina, the accordion and the harmonica were initially developed and manufactured by Germans (as well as by German-speaking Austrians). Despite the continued international prominence of the German Hohner company as a producer of accordions and harmonicas, however, few in either the general public or the fellowship of musicians are likely to regard those instruments as exclusively, or even primarily, German. In the American context, the harmonica has often been called the "French harp," while the accordion, particularly the piano accordion, has been associated with Italians. In contrast, while the accordion and, to a lesser extent, the harmonica are integral to a broad range of the world's folk musical styles (from Louisiana *Cajun* to Brazilian *forro* to Nigerian *jùjú*), the concertina's diffusion has been far more limited—probably because of the peculiarity of its note-to-button arrangement and the necessity of learning through teachers and tablature. Apart from the kindred bandonion's place in Argentine tango music, the concertina has been confined chiefly to the musical traditions of Germans, Poles, and Czechs in the Old World and the New. The concertina, consequently, retains its German association in America because its lineage is relatively limited and easily traced.

In addition, the musicians who play the instrument often assert its origin as a defense against the general public's repeated false assumptions that: 1. all "squeezeboxes" are accordions, 2. "accordion" and "concertina" are different names for the same instrument, or 3. to the extent that concertinas exist, they are small hexagonal instruments popularized by English sailors. "No!" the concertina players assert: we play the concertina, not the accordion, and the kind of concertina we play is not the English concertina but the German (or, even more specifically, the Chemnitzer) concertina. Put another way, the ethnic pedigree of the German concertina is maintained by players in reaction to the forces of historical ignorance and cultural homogenization in American life.

Germanness persists in other ways. Henry Silberhorn and various purveyors of sheet music have always offered a wide ethnic and stylistic array of tunes, yet some German tunes—marches, polkas, waltzes, Ländlers, schottisches—are part of the core of nearly every player's repertoire: "Ach, du lieber Augustin"; "Du, du liegst mir im Herzen"; "Du kannst nicht treu sein"; "Herr Schmidt"; "Immer noch ein Tröpfchen"; and "Unter dem Doppeladler." Moreover there is a German style that remains pervasive, especially among those active in concertina clubs. As one member of the Concertina Hall of Fame put it:

> Germans have a *real* old way of playing [i.e., an "authentic" as opposed to a "very" old way], with an old time repertoire you can sing German to. Germans set the standard. They emphasize the melody, they accent the basses more, their notes are clearer. A real concertina player goes for the Dutchman or German style.

German-American himself, the player continued in an ethnocentric vein: "The poorer concertina players, they go for the Polish style. The Polish drag notes and blur melodies."[10] Although this observation fails to recognize the exuberant, improvisatory aesthetic of concertinists working within the Polish-American polka tradition, it does articulate a widely shared notion that the German concertina style is the "*real* old way." With the exception of Rudzinski, the Czechs, Poles, and Germans who made the first concertina recordings between 1911 and the late 1920s relied—

---

[10] In deference to his friendly relations with Polish-American players, the speaker and his Upper Midwestern whereabouts shall remain anonymous.

whether playing German, Czech, or Polish tunes—on the German preference for an orderly presentation of clear notes, distinct melodies, and an even-tempoed bass accompaniment. In the late twentieth century many concertinists of non-German heritage continue to perform in what they regard as a German style (Leary and March 1991:31). Characterized by the instrument's historical and nominal pedigree, by consistent elements of a core repertoire, and by a prevailing style deemed authentic, the "Germanness" of the German concertina is accessible, like the Germanness of German food, to anyone who wants to taste it—at least in theory. In fact, the "tasters" in America have been chiefly rural and working class German-Americans and their New and Old World neighbors: Czechs and Poles. Within the context of America's Upper Midwest, the concertina served initially as a familiar sign of pan-ethnic and class commonality among newcomers of Central European heritage. Dispersion and differences notwithstanding, players might regard themselves, in Silberhorn's phrase, as "one big family." As concertinists began to cross stylistic boundaries between their shared ethnic traditions and such American musical forms as pop, jazz, and country, the concertina became an Old Country means of encountering the New World. Rather than reject the instrument and repertoire of prior generations, players rendered new musical idioms in their own evolving ethnic American dialect.

By embracing both the old and the new, by maintaining a hybridizing or synthesizing stance toward their instrument and its tradition, concertinists have contributed mightily to the larger culture of the Upper Midwest, a regional culture distinguished by pluralism and by the preference of common folks descended from Central European stock for beer, sausage, polka dancing, and the crisp voice of the German concertina.

Notes

This essay could not have been written without the extraordinary generosity of the Upper Midwest's concertina players, makers, and promoters. I wish to thank them all. The many who permitted me to interview them are cited in the list of sources. Some lent or gave me photographs, sheet music, periodicals, and other rare materials. They include Art Altenburg, John Bernhardt, Dorothy Bertolas, Robert DeWitz, Dan Gruetzmacher, "Concertina Millie" Kaminski, Jerry Minar, Wally Stark, Elmer Stillman, Anton Wolfe, and Jack Zimmerman. Minar, Stark, and Zimmerman were especially kind in offering comments as this essay evolved. On the academic side, Victor Greene, Philip Bohlman, and especially Christoph Wagner offered perceptive criticisms. I hope the finished version is some recompense for their essential contributions. Any errors are entirely my own.

Bibliography

Interviews, Field Notes, and Correspondence

All interviews, field notes, and correspondence are deposited in the archive of the Wisconsin Folk Museum.

Altenburg, Arthur. Tape recorded interview with author and Richard March. Milwaukee, Wisconsin, 17 May 1988.

Bernhardt, John. Correspondence with the author. Chicago, Illinois, September 1992.

Bertolas, Dorothy Peters. Correspondence with the author. Menomonee Falls, Wisconsin, March 1985.

DeWitz, Irving. Tape recorded interview with the author. Hustisford, Wisconsin, 15 February 1985.

Gruetzmacher, Daniel. Tape recorded interview with Philip V. Bohlman. Wausau, Wisconsin, 28 February 1985.

Kaminski, Mildred ("Concertina Millie") Lemke. Tape recorded interview with the author. Muskego, Wisconsin, 12 October 1989.

Kaulitz, Frederick. Tape recorded interview with the author. Watertown, Wisconsin, 5 February 1985.

Knaack, Melvin. Tape recorded interview with the author. Watertown, Wisconsin, 27 March 1985.

Neuenschwander, Herbert. Field notes. Hustisford, Wisconsin, March 1985.

Minar, Jerry. Tape recorded interview with the author. New Prague, Wisconsin, 6 February 1990. Original in the archive of the Minnesota Historical Society, St. Paul; copy in the archive of the WFM.

Minar, Jerry. Correspondence with the author. New Prague, Minnesota. September, November, January 1992–1993.

Peirick, Edward. Tape recorded interview with the author. Watertown, Wisconsin, 8 February 1985.

Peters, Max. Tape recorded interview with Andrew H. Roll. St. Louis, Missouri, Fall 1981.

Stark, Wally. Correspondence with the author. Garland, Texas, January 1993.

Stillman, Elmer. Correspondence with the author. Rockford, Illinois, May–June 1992.

Wolf, Betty. Tape recorded interview with the author. St. Joseph, Minnesota, 8 February 1990. Original in the archive of the Minnesota Historical Society, St. Paul; copy in archive of WFM.

Wolfe, Anton. Field notes. Stevens Point, Wisconsin, 19 April 1985.

Zimmerman, Jack. Tape recorded interview with the author. South Bend, Indiana, 17 August 1992.

Books and Articles

Bancroft, Hubert H. *The Book of the Fair: An Historical and Descriptive Presentation of the World's Science, Art, and Industry, as Viewed through the Columbian Exposition at Chicago in 1893*. 2 vols. Chicago: The Bancroft Company, 1893.

Bohlman, Philip V. *The Study of Folk Music in the Modern World*. Bloomington: Indiana University Press, 1988.

Brown, Dennis. *Whoopee John: His Musical Story*. New Ulm, MN: privately published, 1991.

Charuhas, Toni. *The Accordion*. New York City: Accordion Music Publishing Company, 1955.

Christopulos, Mike. "Ex-Vaudevillian Plays Concertina into Hall of Fame." *Milwaukee Sentinel*, May 1983.

Curtis, W. A. "The Light Fantastic in the Central West: Country Dances of Many Nationalities in Wisconsin." *Century Magazine* 73 (1907): 570–579.

Duis, Perry R. *The Saloon: Public Drinking in Chicago and Boston, 1880–1920*. Urbana: University of Illinois Press, 1983.

Greene, Victor. *A Passion for Polka: Old-Time Ethnic Music in America*. Berkeley: University of California Press, 1992.

Gronow, Pekka. "Ethnic Recordings: An Introduction." In *Ethnic Recordings in America: A Neglected Heritage*, 1–49. Washington, DC: American Folklife Center, 1982.

Higham, John. *Strangers in the Land: Patterns of American Nativism 1860–1925*. New York: Atheneum, 1963.

Hinsley, Curtis M. "The World as Marketplace: Commodification of the Exotic at the World's Columbian Exposition, Chicago, 1893." In *Exhibiting Cultures: The Poetics and Politics of Museum Display*, edited by Ivan Karp and

Steven D. Lavine, 344–365. Washington, DC: Smithsonian Institution Press, 1991.

Keil, Charles, Angeliki V. Keil, and Dick Blau. *Polka Happiness*. Philadelphia: Temple University Press, 1992.

Kleeman, Janice Ellen. *The Origins and Stylistic Development of Polish-American Polka Music*. Ann Arbor, MI: University Microfilms International, 1982.

Leary, James P. *Minnesota Polka: Dance Music From Four Traditions.* St. Paul: Minnesota Historical Society Press, 1990. 20-page booklet and accompanying sound recording.

Leary, James P. and Richard March. "Dutchman Bands: Genre, Ethnicity, and Pluralism." In Creative *Ethnicity: Symbols and Strategies of Contemporary Ethnic Life*, edited by Stephen Stern and John Alan Cicala, 22–43. Logan: Utah State University Press, 1991.

Leary, James P. and Robert T. Teske. *In Tune With Tradition: Wisconsin Folk Musical Instruments*. Cedarburg, WI: Cedarburg Cultural Center, 1990.

Licht, Michael. "America's Harp." *Folklife Center News* 7/3 (1984): 6–9.

Lornell, Kip. "The Early Career of Whoopee John Wilfahrt." *JEMF Quarterly* 21/75–76 (1985): 51–53.

Maurer, Walter. Accordion: *Handbuch eines Instruments, seiner historischen Entwicklung und seiner Literatur*. Vienna: Edition Harmonia, 1983.

Nelson, Bruce C. "Dancing and Picnicking Anarchists? The Movement below the Martyred Leadership." In *Haymarket Scrapbook*, edited by Dave Roediger and Franklin Rosemont, 76–79. Chicago: Charles Kerr, 1986.

Román, Manuel. "Notes on the History of the Bandonion." In *The Bandonion: A Tango History*, edited by Javier Garciá Méndez and Arturo Penón, 39–47. London, ON: Nightwood, 1988.

Romani, G. and Ivor Beynon. "Concertina." In *The New Grove Dictionary of Musical Instruments*, edited by Stanley Sadie, 459–460. London and New York: Macmillan Press, 1984.

Rippley, LaVern J. *The Whoopee John Wilfahrt Dance Band: His Bohemian-German Roots*. Northfield, MN: St. Olaf College German Department, 1992.

Roth, August. *Geschichte der Harmonika Volksmusikinstrumente*. Essen, 1954.

Silberhorn, Henry. *Henry Silberhorn's Instructor for the Concertina*. Chicago: Henry Silberhorn, 1910.

Slobin, Mark. "Micromusics of the West: A Comparative Approach." *Ethnomusicology* 36/1 (1992): 1–87.

Spottswood, Richard K. "Commercial Ethnic Recordings in the United States." In *Ethnic Recordings in America: A Neglected Heritage*, 51–66. Washington, DC: American Folklife Center, 1982.

______. *Ethnic Music on Records: A Discography of Ethnic Recordings in the United States, 1893 to 1942*. 7 vols., esp. vols. 1 (Western Europe) and 2 (Slavic). Urbana: University of Illinois Press, 1990.

Watters, Pat. "A Brief History of the Concertina's Development." *Music Trades Magazine*, October 1955. Reprinted in *Polka and Old Time News*, May 1964.

Periodicals

Entertainment Bits (renamed *Music and Dance News*, October/November 1992). Minneapolis: Minnesota Ballroom Operators, 1973–present. Published every two months. Volumes 10–20 in the archive of the Wisconsin Folk Museum (WFM).

Music and Dance News. Mosinee, WI: Pat Watters, editor and publisher, 1965–1980. Published quarterly. A few random copies in the archive of the WFM.

The Polka News (formerly *The Michigan Polka News*). St. Charles, Michigan: Carl Rohwetter, editor and publisher, 1971–present. Published every two weeks. Volumes 15–22 in the archive of the WFM.

Polka and Old Time News. Minneapolis: Lindstrom-Brown Publications, C. B. Brown, editor, 1963–1965. Published monthly. Photocopies of all issues are in the archive of the WFM.

Silberhorn's Booster for the Advancement of the Concertina. Chicago: Henry Silberhorn, 1927–1934. Photocopies of all issues are in the archive of the WFM.

Printed Ephemera

Originals or copies of all materials are in the archive of the Wisconsin Folk Museum.

Arnold's Concertinas. Illustrated flier for Arno Arnold concertinas. Minneapolis: Watters Distributing Company, ca. 1960. "World's Largest Concertina Handler" (copy).

______. Illustrated flier for Arno Arnold "German Made" concertinas. Chicago: Vitak-Elsnic, ca. 1960 (copy).

______. Illustrated catalogue for Arno Arnold "German Made" concertinas, published in English for the American market, ca. 1950 (partial copy).

Brown, William W. "Brief History of the Concertina." New Ulm, MN: typescript, 1 p., ca. 1970 (copy).

Elmer's Concertina Music. Concertina sheet music in tablature format and listing of available titles, arranged by Elmer Stillman, Rockford, Illinois, 1990–1992 (originals).

Georgi, Otto. *Collection of Popular Music for Concertina.* Chicago: Otto Georgi, ca. 1895. Georgi used a standard cover—with a picture of F. Lange of Chemnitz, Germany—for various sheet music arrangements (copy).

______. Sheet music for the "Fest March," arranged by Henry Silberhorn. Chicago: Otto Georgi, ca. 1906. Picture of the Chicago Concertina Club on the cover (copy).

Gibbon Polka Fest. Promotional flier for events at the Gibbon Ballroom, MN, with a listing of bands and activities for Fall 1992, and Spring and Summer 1993 (original).

Hengel Concertinas. Illustrated flier for the Hengel Concertina line, New Ulm, MN, 1970s (copy).

Hustisford Concertina Club. Flier for a community concert, April 1942 (original).

Milwaukee Concertina Circle. Sheet music for "A Summer Dream," a mazurka composed by F. H. Brinker, director of the Milwaukee Concertina Circle, 1890 (partial copy).

Nusbaum, Philip. Nomination of Christy Hengel for Heritage Fellowship from the Folk Arts Program of the National Endowment for the Arts, 1986 (copy).

Patek Concertinas. Illustrated flier for concertinas sold by the Patek Music Company, Chicago, 1920s (partial copy). Includes photographs of Rudy Patek and Otto Schlicht.

Pearl Queen Concertinas. Illustrated flier for concertinas sold by the Vitak-Elsnic Company, Chicago, 1950 (partial copy).

Roll, Andrew H. Nomination of Max and Helmut Peters to the Concertina Hall of Fame of the World Concertina Congress, 1980 (copy).

Silberhorn, Henry. *Price List of Concertinas and Bandonions and Furnishings*. Chicago: Henry Silberhorn, ca. 1896 (partial copy).

Star Concertinas. Illustrated fliers of Star Concertinas, Chicago, 1950 (partial copy), 1975 (original).

Stradivarius Concertinas. Illustrated catalogue. N. p., ca. 1970 (partial copy).

Watters, Pat. "A Brief History of Concertina and Music Promotion by Pat Watters." Mosinee, WI, ca. 1972: typescript, 2 pp. (original).

Wolfe Concertinas. Illustrated flier for concertinas made by Anton Wolf, ca. 1970 (original).

World Concertina Congress. "Constitution and By-Laws," 1984 (copy).

________. Programs for the Concertina Hall of Fame "Awards Banquet," 1987–1990 (copies).

Sound Recordings

The text of this essay refers to appropriate pages in Spottswood's *Ethnic Music on Records*. That essential discography includes a full listing of 78 rpm recordings by the concertina artists I have mentioned. Only the handful of reissues of 78 rpm recordings fall below.

Makowska Orkiestra Dzia ego. "Polska Zabawa." Chicago Polkas Collectors Series LP 4101, ca. 1978.

Miscellaneous Artists. *Folk Music in America*, Volume 11. Library of Congress LP LBC-11, 1976. Includes "Na Obie Nogi Polka" (On Two Feet) by Bruno Rudzinski.

Miscellaneous Polish Artists. *Polish-American Dance Music: The Early Recordings, 1927–1933*. Folklyric LP 9026, 1979. Includes "Zbojnicy w Karcmie" (Outlaws in the Roadhouse) by the Makowska Orkiestra Dzia ego, and "Pawel Walc" (Paul's Waltz) by Bruno Rudzinski.

______. *From the Tatra Mountains: Classic Polish-American Recordings from the 1920s*. Morning Star LP 45007, 1983. Includes "Krakowiak z Marcharza" (Krakowiak from Mucharza) by the Makowska Orkiestra Dzia wgo.

Miscellaneous Polish and Ukrainian Artists. *Spiew Juchasa (Song of the Shepherd): Songs of the Slavic Americans*. New World Records LP 283,

1977. Includes “Przysezed Chłop do Karczmy” (A Man Came to the Saloon) by Bruno Rudzinski.

9

"EIN PROSIT DER GEMÜTLICHKEIT": THE TRADITIONALIZATION PROCESS IN A GERMAN-AMERICAN SINGING SOCIETY

Alan R. Burdette

Introduction: The Gift of Tradition

In the music library of the Germania Männerchor in Evansville, Indiana, there is a well-thumbed partbook from the turn of the century. On the inside of its hard cover a table of contents is handwritten in a flowing script. Eighteen songs, printed by a variety of publishers, are taped into the book. The book raises issues that are just as relevant to club members now as they were to club members at the turn of the century. Among the pieces the book contains is "Wie hab' ich sie geliebt" (Oh, How I Loved Her), a song about crossing the sea and bidding farewell to both sweetheart and Fatherland. A few pages earlier, one finds "Mein Alt-Kentucky Heim" (My Old Kentucky Home). While the sentiments of Stephen Foster and the legions of *Heimatlieder* (literally, songs of the homeland) are remarkably congruent, it seems obvious that Kentucky is not likely to have the same kind of resonance for German-Americans as Germany for the immigrant and ethnic generations.[1] Its presence, alongside two other Foster songs, "Old Black Joe" and "Das alte Heim" (Old Folks at Home), tells us that it is not an isolated indulgence in American culture. The

[1] With the possible exception of the large number of Germans who settled there, *Heimatlieder* have always constituted a large part of the repertory of *Gesangvereine* in the United States, referring generally to Germany as a whole. In Germany, *Heimatlieder* are often more localized in their references, often referring to a region and employing stylized forms of dialect.

"homemade" construction of this partbook lets us know that these popular American songs from the nineteenth century are not there by the whim of some publisher.

Ethnomusicologists frequently take the items of tradition as the objects of their study, but determining what is traditional is very rarely simple. This old German songbook was lent to me on my very first evening of fieldwork, as if it were an icon or as an emblem of the club's oldness and its Germanness. Beyond its worn exterior and fraktur-scripted lyrics, however, it demonstrates the simultaneous gestures early twentieth-century members were making to their contemporary German and American musical culture. When certain members learned I was present to learn about their club, I was given a small paper sack containing the book and two other old volumes of music. From the very beginning, club life was presented to me by situating it in the past. While certain actions and objects may bear all the qualities of what we know as tradition, it may not be identified as such for particular reasons. It is unlikely that anyone in this club would categorize "Das alte Heim" as part of their tradition, even though it was popular before and after World War I, was sung at the 1952 National Sängerfest in Cincinnati, and seems to express the same kinds of sentiments found in *Heimatlieder*. In reality, the choir performs a higher percentage of songs in German than it ever did in the past, despite the dwindling number of current members who speak German. Such seeming contradictions are not a new problem for ethnomusicologists, but they emphasize the fact that tradition is clearly a category with a particular ideological significance transcending age, content, and aesthetics. For choir members today, choosing music for their performances involves balancing the realities of audiences and singers who generally do not understand German and the need to fulfill ideas about who they are as a German singing society. To sing everything in English would negate one of their fundamental reasons for existing, yet they must accommodate the fact that few among their own ranks speak German.

How far members of the Germania Männerchor lean in one direction or the other—do we sing in German for symbolic and historical reasons, or do we sing in English for listeners who understand no German?—is always up for negotiation, and one key to these negotiations is the rhetorical strategies that give weight to particular objects or actions by connecting them to the past. In this article I examine these processes by looking into the traditionalization process within this German-American singing society, with a particular emphasis on an expressed ideal of interaction known as *Gemütlichkeit*.[2] By examining how members talk about their socio-

---

[2] Literally, *Gemütlichkeit* describes a sense of feeling good or having a pleasant sensation. That the meanings of *Gemütlichkeit* are more complex than this will emerge as I examine its significance for and use by the Germania Männerchor.

musical experiences, I intend to illuminate how some members of the Germania Männerchor give meaning to their actions by connecting them to the past.

It has been a long time now that folklorists have moved the notion of tradition from one of static entity to one of process. Though older notions of tradition permeate what we do and motivate the choices we make about the objects we study, there is in the discipline itself a general acceptance of tradition as a rhetorical stance and strategy. The present article aligns itself with these strategies, but, instead of concerning myself with traditionalization in the grand scheme of nationalism (Handler and Linnekin 1984, Williams 1977), I examine the traditionalization process at work on a human and individual level, in the interaction among people. What does the traditionalization process look or sound like? The primary location of this process is in the discourse that frames texts or attempts to explain a worldview.

The emblematic partbook I received when beginning fieldwork was among several that were given to the Evansville Germania Männerchor during World War I by the Concordia Gesangverein, which closed because of the anti-German pressure of the time. The Germania Männerchor survived this turbulent period through sheer determination and by taking a generally lower public profile.[3] Today the club faces not animosity but indifference, and the means by which a German experience is made meaningful is all the more important when fewer and fewer members have a direct experience of Germany and the German language.

Even a strong connection to Germany does not eliminate the incongruities presented to a scholar searching for the items of tradition or ethnic identity. In the summer of 1991 at the grave of a former immigrant who had joined the singers immediately after he arrived in 1939, the Männerchor gathered to sing his favorite song: "I've Been Working on the Railroad." At club dances, when "My Wild Irish Rose" draws participation from the audience equal to that of "The Beer Barrel Polka" (Rosemunde), it becomes clear that ethnic identity cannot always be located in the content of texts of performance or items of signification themselves.

Gemütlichkeit: Traditionalizing Culture

The creation and maintenance of a German-American identity in this case is a complex combination of music, foodways, family background, values, and a sense of place. The designation has as much to do with Evansville as a place as it does Germany. Most important for members, being German-American means partici-

---

[3] Although the United States did not enter World War I until 1917, anti-German sentiment quickly became virulent, and public attacks on institutions of German-American culture multiplied. One response to such attacks was to erase aspects of surface identity; for example, to Americanize a German name.

pating in a type of interaction in which the performers and the participants are focused on a singular goal—musical and/or social—that leads to a feeling of union with fellow club members. At Germania Männerchor and in many other German-American communities, this feeling has a name: *Gemütlichkeit*. For many members of Evansville's Germania Männerchor, *Gemütlichkeit* embodies a rich and complex index of identity that affirms their local community while simultaneously connecting them to a larger German and German-American culture.[4]

Gemütlichkeit is an orienting ideal of social and musical activity as well as a conceptual context that participants create, experience, and inscribe through performance. In short, *Gemütlichkeit* allows the creation of a particular context of interaction that has powerful implications for personal and group identity. The sensation of "heightened experience" often associated with *Gemütlichkeit* may be due to the successful creation of a context freed from the paradigm of the "everyday."

The nature of *Gemütlichkeit* in Evansville and German-American society does not lend itself easily to translation, and there is no direct English equivalent for the word. It is translated in the *Collins German Dictionary* as "comfortableness, friendliness, coziness, snugness, leisure, unhurriedness" (Terrell et al. 1980). While this captures a certain spirit of the word, it conveys none of the richness and depth of feeling evident in the interactions within the Germania Männerchor. Members have described it to me as an experience involving one or more of the following aspects: synergy, "going for the gusto," relaxation, congeniality, an expansive welcome, social harmony, wholesome fun, extraordinary group competence in performance, a feeling of unity, and an atmosphere in which criticism is suspended. Enactments can entail anything from casual conversation to eating, drinking, singing, and dancing. To synthesize what some of my collaborators have said, *Gemütlichkeit* is an important part of good socializing and good musical performance. Ideally, they are one and the same phenomenon. The result is a kind of euphoria in affinity with others much like what ethnomusicologists have described in diverse musical expe-

---

[4] I am using the designation "German-American" emically, as it is used at Germania Männerchor. On the one hand, the members use the term very loosely, without determining just how German or how American members are. On the other, they use "German-American" to refer to themselves and what they do within their club. In the context of this club it refers to persons who lived part of their life in Germany but are now United States citizens, as well as to people whose familial link to Germany is as distant as a great-grandparent. For a few members, the roots of their family tree do not go back to Germany but to Ireland. As a result, contact with any sort of "homeland" varies widely among members. A few make an occasional trip to Germany to visit relatives; others have traveled to see the country from which they claim their heritage. Many more have never been to Germany, nor do they feel any great need to connect their identity to Germany with a European trip. Contacts with a larger German-American community consist of the strong presence in the Evansville area and association with other German-American singing societies through regional and national Sängerfeste.

riences of many cultures. Indeed, what Charles Keil has described as "polka happiness" is remarkably similar to what Evansville's German-Americans call *Gemütlichkeit* (Keil, et al. 1992).

From my observations and discussions with Germania Männerchor members, there seem to be three different kinds of *Gemütlichkeit*. The following descriptive categories are my own, created out of observation and the distinctions made by members about the different types of events in which *Gemütlichkeit* occurs. In reality, *Gemütlichkeit* does not fall into such neat divisions, but I think it is useful to distinguish the different ways activity is organized in the production of *Gemütlichkeit*. The first is a low-level *Gemütlichkeit* that occurs between people engaged in conversation or face-to-face interaction. It refers to an extended, pleasant exchange within a small group. The second takes on a musical dimension and occurs, for example, in the singing of German songs with a group of people. Today, this is an activity in which members rarely engage, although as recently as 1980 it had been a vital part of after-rehearsal activities. In the third category are dances where German music is performed. The production of *Gemütlichkeit* at dance events is perhaps most conscious and conspicuous, and it is likely to include activities of the first two types as well.[5] The song "Ein Prosit der Gemütlichkeit" (A Toast to Gemütlichkeit) is performed numerous times in the course of such occasions, punctuating them with a litany of identity. Members of the audience raise their mugs of beer into the air and sing:

> Ein Prosit, ein Prosit, der Gemütlichkeit!
> Ein Prosit, ein Prosit, der Gemütlichkeit!
> Prost, Prost, Prost!
> Eins! Zwei! g'suffe![6]

Invariably, it follows dances that have encouraged group participation, such as "Schneewalzer," "The Chicken," or "Roll Out the Barrel," thus framing and enhancing the processes of group identity.[7]

---

[5] For example, at the Männerchor's Volksfest there may be four thousand people; some in small groups talking, and some in groups singing along to German songs being played by the band. Others, however, dance. As some of my collaborators have pointed out, it is also possible to be present at such large activities and experience *Gemütlichkeit* by merely observing it.

[6] A Toast, a toast to Gemütlichkeit! A Toast, a toast to Gemütlichkeit! Cheers! Cheers! Cheers! One! Two! We drink!

[7] Audience involvement in the "Schneewalzer" (Snow Waltz) includes standing up from one's chair and giving a yell at the appropriate time. "The Chicken" (known in Germany as "Die Ente," [The

Many members closely associate the practice of spontaneous group singing after rehearsal with the notion of *Gemütlichkeit*. The spontaneous singing of German "folksongs"[8] at gatherings was a regular activity of members until roughly twenty years ago. The spontaneous singing—which fosters *Gemütlichkeit*—has been contrasted by some members with the rehearsed singing—which does not usually foster *Gemütlichkeit*—that has been a regular activity of the organization since its inception.

> One of the things what I miss the most is, years ago when I first started, up to a few years ago . . . before all of the [German] members passed away, after singing we all the time had a little get together either when somebody left for vacation in Germany, that was a reason to celebrate. The whole singing room had beer together and all of us, what they call "kommersing"—sing old songs, somebody knew a little harmony to it and the other guys learned what didn't speak German . . . they picked it up. And since some of these older members been gone, it has died out. And I have tried to revitalize it, and when Jim Haygood was one of our directors, and he started again, it died out again. I have contacted our present director and he said too, it's a good idea, and to get interested in this again. I mean, after all, it's a German club and you're singing there in stiff rehearsals—there's no fun to it. There also should be fun to it, huh? And fun comes after the rehearsal rather than sitting on the bar and having a few beers together. Why not sing with the group and keep that old German heritage of singing, huh? (Interview with Bernie Resing, 1991)

Gemütlichkeit is a concept that is imagined, communicated, and performed, and events are structured to encourage its occurrence. For example, all concerts are followed by a dance, and choir rehearsals adjourn to the adjoining bar. *Gemütlichkeit* allows participants to establish local affiliations and social world boundaries, as

---

Duck]) is a dance that requires the audience to make clucking, flapping, and waddling gestures with various parts of the body. It is a favorite among visitors and establishes a rapport. "Roll Out the Barrel" is a song whose text most people know and is, furthermore, a polka that often brings reluctant dancers onto the floor.

[8] "Folksong" is the terminology of club members, and it generally refers to those songs of German heritage, whether popular *Schlager* (hits) or folk in the more traditional usage of that term. These were the songs that were part of individual members' repertoire that over time were shared with others and became a shared competence; in short, what we typically call tradition.

well as to enact larger ideas of what it means to be "German." Frequent in discussions with members is a description of the past when *Gemütlichkeit* was more common and identity clearer. The pursuit of *Gemütlichkeit* is perhaps one of the primary reasons for the formation of the club, and it has remained at the center of club life through the changing social and political realities that members have faced in larger contexts.

History of the Germania Männerchor

The Germania Männerchor was founded in 1900 by fourteen German residents of the city of Evansville. They began to hold concerts and *Abendunterhaltungen*[9] almost immediately, and within a year the choir had grown to twenty-one singers, with over fifty "passive" or social members.[10] Early on the club participated in the well-established network of German organizations in the Ohio River valley. Two other singing clubs, the Liederkranz and the Concordia, as well as non-singing German clubs such as the Deutsche Gesellschaft, the West End Harmonie, and the Ben Hur Society existed in the city already. These organizations were important supporters and collaborators in the concerts, plays, *Weihnachtsfeiern*, *Stiftungsfeste*, *Maskenbälle*, *Sommernachtsfeste*, *Maifeste*, *Narrensitzungen*, *Waldfeste*, *Bismarck-Feiern*, *Abendunterhaltungen*, and German Day celebrations held before the war. In 1902 they joined the Nordamerikanischer Sängerbund (North American Singers' Union) and took part in the Sängerfest in St. Louis that same year. The Germania Männerchor also traveled to the nearby cities of Henderson and Louisville in Kentucky and Tell City, Indiana, to participate in activities with singing clubs there.

By 1914, Germania had 32 singers and 620 passive members. In a few short years, these numbers would drop dramatically when America entered World War I and anti-German sentiments increased. The war had a tremendous impact on the culture of German-Americans throughout the United States. Cities and streets that sounded remotely German were renamed, and in 1918, for example, the governor of Iowa banned the speaking of any foreign language "in train cars, in telephone conversations, in public addresses, in public and private schools and in churches" (Kirschbaum 1986:121). Evansville had a high concentration of Germans, and though they were not immune from ethnic slurs, it seems they did not experience as much of the harassment that occurred in other places.[11] Thirty-eight members of Germania

---

[9] *Abendunterhaltungen* are evening entertainments, which sometimes included skits with a humorous or moral theme.

[10] Passive or social members help support activities but do not sing in the choir.

[11] According to an 1889 history of the city, 50% of Evansville's residents were of German birth or descent (*Evansville Illustrated* 1889).

Figure 1. Germania Männerchor Hall was built in 1913 and remains the locus of club life and activity.

fought in the war on the American side. Many others left the club out of fear or patriotism. A 1925 Anniversary booklet describing the club's history makes no attempt to hide its disdain for those members who had abandoned the club calling them "knieschwach" —"weak in the knees" (Dreisch 1925:28). The sharp decline in membership meant a proportional decrease in funds, and the club was forced drastically to cut the hours it was open in order to stay solvent.

In an era of ethnic uncertainty that saw sauerkraut become "liberty cabbage," Germania sought to maintain its basic social and cultural framework but under different names. Social events were still held, but under names such as the "Washington Festival" or the "Thanksgiving Ball." A large number of members also participated in the citizenship classes offered by the club, where, in preparation for naturalization, they learned about the laws and government of the United States. The other two local singing societies, however, were not able to adjust to the new social circumstances and folded before the war was over.

World War I undermined one of the primary emblems of ethnic identification for the club—language—and Prohibition undermined another—social drinking. Singing in German and drinking beer were fundamentally related in the socio-cultural activities of the club, and both were essential to notions of *Gemütlichkeit*. During the 1920s there was covert violation of the new restrictions. "Home brew" was made at the club as it was in many German households of the time. German plays, such as *In Tiroler Bergen*, *Im weißen Roß'l*, and *Der Herrgottschnitzer von Ammergau*, which had been so popular at the club, could not be staged in the early

1920s, and they were replaced by *The Lamasco Minstrels*, thereby demonstrating the unassailable Americanness of the minstrel tradition. The choir, which had dwindled to sixteen singers, painted themselves in blackface and sang the songs of Stephen Foster in English. It was not until 1923 that club members began to notice that verbal harassment from the outside had begun to subside.

After Prohibition, the club experienced an increase in membership and a resurgence of German cultural activities. They participated in the national Sängerfests, gave plays, and purchased a picnic grounds. Germania, nevertheless, continued to hold citizenship classes. Many immigrant members from the post-World War I wave also learned to speak English through classes taught at the club. World War II subjected Germania again to scrutiny and criticism, but it responded publicly by actively participating in the American Legion and donating to the Red Cross Canteen. Once again, many members enlisted or were drafted to serve on the American side. Older members believed that the FBI kept a close watch on Germania during these years, with agents showing up at dances and recruiting informants ("stool pigeons" as some members describe them) from the membership. No trouble ever came from the federal government, however, in part because there was an unwritten rule in the club to avoid politics as a topic for discussion. For most members, the war was senseless from either perspective.[12]

Though the name and formal structure of the club identifies it as a men's organization, women and families have always been a crucial part of club life. A "ladies auxiliary" was started in 1910, and in 1954 a *Damenchor* (women's chorus) was initiated. The auxiliary has been extremely important because of its fund-raising efforts, as well as the individual contributions necessary to ensure the success of club events. Both groups are still active. The Damenchor usually performs a few pieces with the Männerchor, but the groups remain distinct, rehearsing at different times and with different directors. In the face of declining memberships, many other clubs have moved to only a mixed chorus, a trend Germania Männerchor has staunchly avoided.[13]

Depending on the historical moment, political expedience affected the maintenance of the club's distinctively "traditional" activities. Public events were discontinued, only to be resurrected in different forms depending on the pressures from

---

[12] By taking this stance, however, the Germania Männerchor distinguished itself from many other Midwestern German social organizations that often exhibited exaggerated forms of patriotism. Accounting for the somewhat more reserved ambivalence of the Evansville club may be the rather high percentage of more recent immigrants, especially those arriving in the wake of World War I.

[13] German-American mixed choruses, however, usually maintain the distinctive repertoires for men and women. Typically, a concert will include a group of songs for men followed by a group for women.

the outside and the needs from within. Plays were an important part of club life during its first forty years. These were suspended for almost thirty-five years, only to return recently in the form of the St. Nikolaus Grandfest, for which a group of members write a new play every year.

Germania club meetings maintained the use of the German language until 1962, when members recognized that it was necessary to accommodate the needs of a growing number of new members who did not speak German. Today only a few members speak German, and even fewer were actually born in Germany. In 1992, the men's choir has just two German-born singers. Only a few of the other members speak German fluently. As a result, the German language is only occasionally heard in the club. For the most part, the choirs hold to the practice of singing in German, but the understanding and proper pronunciation of German song texts present a problem for many singers. Too few members understand the words of the songs, and even fewer know the songs well enough to sustain the lengthy singing sessions that were common in the past.

Traditionalization

The transformation of German from functional to symbolic functions in the repertoire has led several members to express concern about the cultural identity of the club in the present and its survival into the future. The organization is an "intended community"—they are members by choice. Most members have lives outside of the club that do not involve the same kind of enactment of German identity occurring during club functions. Division in the community often results from different visions of what the group is, and how they attempt to maintain a balance between these different visions is critical to the group's survival. The building of ideas about community through discourse and musical performance are an important means of maintaining their ideas about who they are as a group and community. In an organization with a long history, it is not surprising that the past is used as a means to validate the present.

Tradition is still a concept that focuses much ethnographic description and discourse, and it continues to be the defining element for the objects we submit to ethnomusicological analysis, that is, we generally study those things we consider "traditional." In recent years some ethnomusicologists have offered alternative ways to look at tradition (Coplan 1991, Seeger 1991), and they have challenged the monolithic and static view of tradition itself. Dell Hymes, in his reformulation, suggests that we look at tradition as more than a particular kind of lore or legacy, but rather as a particular kind of legitimating process.

Figure 2. Cletus Muensterman, Bernie Resing, and Bill Greer of Germania Männerchor in the mass choir rehearsal at the 1991 District Sängerfest in Dayton, Ohio.

> Let us root the notion not in time but in social life. Let us postulate that the traditional is a functional prerequisite of social life. Let us consider the notion, not simply as naming objects, traditions, but also, and more fundamentally, as a naming process. It seems in fact the case that every person, and group, makes some effort to "traditionalize" aspects of its experience. To "traditionalize" would seem to be a universal need. Groups and persons differ, then, not in presence or absence of the traditional—there are none which do not "traditionalize"—but in the degree, and the form, of success in satisfying the universal need (1975:353).

By looking at context and what people say about their music, it becomes possible to examine processes by which people *make* their music traditional. Viewed in this way, traditionalization can be seen as a process that exists not in the past, but as one in which people are engaged in the present.

The traditionalization process occurs when the past is brought into the present as an example of a favorable pattern of interaction. A group or community claims continuity as the overriding way actions form through performance. Traditionalization is a process through which an object or activity is given a positive valence by connecting it with selective aspects of the past and one's personal history. We generally use the word tradition to mean "to hand something down," but traditionalization implies that an object or activity is "handed down" or created with a particular kind of symbolic weight attached to it. By relating what we do to that which preceded it, we establish validity and authority. Traditionalization has less to do with lengthy periods of customary actions than it has to do with rhetorical strategies of legitimation. This is not to say that a traditionalized object or action cannot have a lengthy relationship with a particular community, but rather that they acquire a heightened ideological status when traditionalized.

Folklorist Richard Bauman stresses the importance of traditionalization as a strategy of contextualization by noting that it is "part of the process of endowing the story with situated meaning," and that tradition begins "not with some objective quality of pastness that inheres in a cultural object but with the active construction of connections that link the present with a meaningful past" (1991:15). Ethnomusicologists such as Béhague (1984) have called for an awareness of the contextualization process and its importance in imparting meaning to the event at hand. Traditionalization not only contextualizes the activity by referring to the past, but also places a positive valence on it within a social world of the present. Traditionalization, as Bauman states, does not just link the object or activity with *the* past but with a *meaningful* past. In so doing, it not only gives immediate, situated meaning to the activity through the contextualization process, but also creates a larger conceptual context with which members of the group interpret and guide action. Accordingly, the traditionalized objects and activities become part of their identity. These objects and activities, which are then symbolically charged with personal and corporate identity, become the kinds of things ethnomusicologists commonly refer to as a "canon."

Philip Bohlman points out that traditionalization plays a key role in the formation of musical canons, as members of a group attempt to define the content that generates group cohesiveness. He states that the folk music canon always remains a process because of the continually changing social base of a community. The canon responds "creatively to new texts and changing contexts" (1988:104). He has postulated a suggestive theoretical framework that was, for me, congruent with my observations of musical processes in a German-American singing club. Bohlman's position also implies that there are dialogues in which people negotiate those aspects of their musical practice that they endeavor to consider as traditional.

I now turn to several examples well suited to explore what Bohlman has called the dialectic between text and context (1988:xviii). I take a micro-view and focus on the *discourse* that guides and surrounds the idea of *Gemütlichkeit* in order to discover the rhetorical strategies that give this idea meaning. The formation and maintenance of canons depend on the ability of individuals to give items authority and validity. By connecting the object or action to a shared past (or the idea of one), they push it into the collective memory, the "imagined community" (Anderson 1983), the *text*ure of that group of people. For many years now, work in folklore, ethnomusicology, and anthropology has shown that our deeply held ideas about the homogeneous community do not usually hold up under scrutiny. As I pointed out at the beginning of this essay, human beings draw from a wide variety of expressive resources to construct cultural identity. However, we know from experience and observation that people do create some idea of belonging to a particular group or groups. Somehow, the "texts" or actions with which they identify themselves achieve a status in the community that is recognized and sanctioned by some as representative of that community.

Examples from Evansville's Germania Männerchor make it possible to explore the process of giving weight to certain texts or ideas in performance, which gives those forms an advantage in the community's repertoire of appropriate expressive forms. In other words, what we refer to as "the canon" may vary from individual to individual, but it is only a useful analytical designation in that people share some ideas about its content. In order for this canon formation to occur, people must interact with the canon, with each other, and with their context. Verbal discourse plays a vital role in this process of negotiation.

Many of the objects and actions that are traditionalized may be of the kind Hobsbawm and Ranger (1983) have called "invented traditions." However, the important point for me is not the validity of a particular "tradition," but rather the manner in which this tradition—be it genuine or spurious (see Handler and Linnekin 1984)—is maintained and *why* it is maintained. I posit here that it is more important to ask how a German-American singing club maintains activities they consider to be traditional or authentic, rather than to debate the "Germanness" of what they do. Traditionalization as a study object should then yield information about those features a group attempts to make salient. Because this is a negotiated process, not all efforts to traditionalize are successful. However, if we observe this process closely, it is possible to reach some conclusions about why certain aspects are maintained and others are not. For members of Evansville's German-American singing club, music is an expressive form that is a very important part of their identity as a community. More important, the *singing* of songs indexes their ideas about an ideal of interaction—*Gemütlichkeit*. As I asked several members to describe *Gemütlichkeit* to me, I was struck by how often it was associated with the past and ideas about Germany. The informal singing with which it was so strongly identified was also significant to members' ideas about what the club is, therefore allowing one to see how the idea of *Gemütlichkeit* is deeply connected with past activities.

If we are to understand the ways in which German-American music is given meaning and gives meaning to the members of Germania, it becomes necessary to listen to and examine the discourse that surrounds it—not so much for what it says but for what it does. Thus, when a choir member turned to me during rehearsal just before we were to sing "Zwei Blümchen" and remarked, "this is the first song the club ever sang and we've sung it at the Stiftungsfest [founding-day festival] every year for ninety years," he was engaging in a process of meaning-creation for himself, for me, and for the club. At an informal singing session in the spring of 1992, a veteran member told a young man who had come to rehearsal for the first time that "we used to always do this after rehearsal in the old days." In so doing, he was passing on ideas about who they are in relation to their past. Such statements present newer members and outsiders with ideas about a collective past and "imagined community" that as new members, they cannot experience directly.

Entering Tradition

Through a series of examples from fieldwork with the Germania Männerchor, the discourse that makes it possible to traditionalize German-American musical culture in Evansville can begin to take shape. The first two examples come from a musical event in which a group of members gathered at the bar to sing old folksongs "for old time's sake." As they flip through a songbook choosing songs, they take turns leading them and suggesting new ones. A few of the songs are highlighted by connecting them to the past, even to specific moments shared by the historical community of the club members. Sung passages are indicated with italics. Remarks locate the singing experience in the past, but connect it discursively to the present, when it may or may not take place.

> **Elsbeth:** Oh my God I know all those songs, "Hoch auf dem gelben Wagen." I used to sing all those when I was a kid. (Interview with Elsbeth Mathews, 1991)

Though the other participants do not share her personal experiences, such statements help give more importance to this song. The following response to this statement is the encouragement by others to sing this song.

> **Elsbeth:** "Ein Jäger aus Kurpfalz," I used to sing that all the time for singing lessons, you know we had to sing, you know I'd sing "Ein Jäger aus Kurpfalz."
> **Gene:** How's it go?
> **Eddie:** Yeah! Sing it! Sing it!
> **Elsbeth:** Oh God!
> **Tony:** *Ein Jäger aus Kurpfalz, die hatten. . . .* (Interview with Elsbeth Mathews, Tony Hollaender, Gene Lutterbach, and Eddie Sellars, 1991)

Germania members entered more directly into a confrontation with the processes of their own traditionalization as the conversations during fieldwork unfolded, which is to say, as they represented the symbols of tradition through conversation. In the following exchange, I asked a question that had arisen from comments made before the group started singing. My presence as someone interested in "folk" music had provided just the excuse one member needed to instigate an informal singing event. The resulting responses to my question both connect what they are doing to the past and critique the lapse of this activity in the present. Whereas it is true that in this case I was deliberately drawing attention to the past, the question arose from statements members had made moments earlier, thereby remaining consistent with the members' own discourse about tradition. What is important about these statements is that they are placing what they are doing within a larger context of activity—a continuum, but in this case a continuum that had been broken and for the sake of identity must be revived. Though not explicitly stated, the *Kommers*[14] is closely associated with *Gemütlichkeit.*

> **Alan:** Did Germania used to do more informal singing, like at the bar?
> **Tony:** Always. Years ago we always did after singing. Today they don't do that anymore.
> **Gene:** Here in the bar? It's called the "kommers."
> **Tony:** When Charlie was playing the piano (**Gene:** yeah), we were singing in there!
> **Gene:** Yeah, we used to do that. Now we've got to get back to doing it.
> **Alan:** So you'd rehearse and then you'd sing some more?
> **Gene:** Yeah, we *used* to, but now we're kind of getting away from it. We're going to have to get back to it. That's why—
> **Tony:** Yeah, we *went* away from it.
> **Gene:** That's why I'm the librarian; we're going to get this shit going again. (Interview with Tony Hollaender and Gene Lutterbach, 1991)

Prior to the following comments, I had asked Steve Rode about the large festival the club puts on every year, which is attended by over thirteen thousand people over a three-day period. His response connects what club members do today, that is, in the context of the festival, to their own past and to the club's concept of what is authentically German.

> **Steve:** So I think it's probably just the fact . . . that it's the same festival now that it was then, except we're bigger obviously and more organized. From our standpoint the festival itself is the same and maybe the continuity has kept the German—and it hasn't ever veered from that. So, it's not as if we have to kind of come back to—pull back into being German, it's more or less still the same German festival it's always been. That would be my estimation. I, I've told this when I was chairman and newspapers ask me that, you know, and I used to go, until the last couple years, I used to go every summer to Germany, you know, four, five, six weeks. And every time

[14] The *Allgemeines Deutsches Commersbuch* is the most common and widely used collection of popular German folksongs from the nineteenth century. With sections devoted to "student songs," "songs of the homeland," "love songs," and other categories, the *Kommers* links genre to history, and immigrant culture to imagined homeland. Reprinted in hundreds of editions since the mid-nineteenth century, the *Kommers* provides a musical symbol connecting German organizations throughout the world.

I'd go through, either they'd be getting ready for a festival or having one or getting ready for one or whatever, and I went to a lot of them, and our festival is exactly like anything over there. I mean it's the exact same atmosphere—music, food, you know, the clothes everybody is wearing, you know, it's just identical. I mean, you can take off — well you can look at our festival, you can look at like, say St. Wendel's or Haubstadt's and you can definitely see ours is different. And it's identical to anything you would find in any German city. So, I don't think there's a problem having to correct back to it, because the festival hasn't veered from it. (Interview with Steve Rode, 1991)

The following transcriptions all come from interviews with members, in which the conscious focal point was a discussion of *Gemütlichkeit*. I have also presented these transcriptions in a way that highlights the parallel nature of the discourse as well as the use of quoted speech and paraphrase. Though I will not be analyzing them in poetic detail, the poetics work to increase the rhetorical and performative nature of this discourse. My questions were not about the past, but *Gemütlichkeit* was empowered by linking it to past activities and the ways these represented a further connection to Germany. In this example, Germany is invoked again, this time in an explanation of *Gemütlichkeit*. I asked Bill Greer to explain *Gemütlichkeit*, pushing him toward a definition that would be as explicit as possible, and he provided the following response:

Alan: I was wondering if you could explain, uh, not really a definition but what the word *Gemütlichkeit* means to you—how would you describe it?
Bill: Right, there is no English word, as you are well aware.
When I do the publicity for the Volksfest every year,
I explain this.
I spell it out phonetically for the TV,
and we say
it has to be observed.
It has to be felt,
or participated in to be understood.
It's what one sees at Volksfest.
It's the, everybody having a good time singing,
dancing,
eating,
drinking

> and the big expansive welcome in the old German tradition.
> Uh, it's not conviviality.
> It's just "let it all out and have fun," in a wholesome way.
> The Germans ethnically play hard,
> and they work hard,
> and play hard again.
> They have festivals
> to plan festivals,
> and this is a real part of their lives.
> Originally, these things were
> a way of celebrating a successful harvest,
> whether it was corn,
> whether it was wheat,
> or grapes,
> or hops,
> a successful vintage.
> In every German city or town
> there's some kind of festival
> that has gone on for hundreds of years.
> And people then get out their costumes
> that are hundreds of years old in design,
> and they welcome all their neighbors—
> there are no enemies.
> There's a saying in Munich during Oktoberfest,
> there [chuckles] are no divorce laws,
> that they're suspended for that time,
> and everyone has a wonderful good feeling.
> This is *Gemütlichkeit*. (Interview with Bill Greer, 1992)

Describing what *Gemütlichkeit* means to him, Bill refers to "the old German tradition." It is more than just having a good time and is conceptually linked to Romantic visions of Germany and the past.

In the following extended example, two male club members engage in an exchange to explain *Gemütlichkeit*. Once again, traditionalization comes into play. In this case, it is part of a narrative of a past event that both men had experienced. Narrative is used to present an example of *Gemütlichkeit* and functions to create a past landscape (see indented section). It is significant that this example from the past is used to critique a present where people, according to the speakers, seem to have forgotten how to create *Gemütlichkeit*. This conversation is rich in its use of metaphors that make this abstract conception more concrete, as well as the delineation of interactional boundaries that work to define the German as distinct from the American and *Gemütlichkeit* from the everyday (cf. Burdette 1992).

Gene: *Gemütlichkeit* is almost like
when everybody's singing in harmony.
And you hear that little, [holds his thumb and forefinger together as if to indicate some point in space] and you say,
"*God*, that sounds good."
You know.
The—
Alan: Where it locks—
it kind of *rings* up there at the top
and the basses
and the baritones
and everything—
it all comes together,
and sometimes you're out walking around
at some of these Sängerfests,
and all of a sudden you have that feeling like
"God, isn't this great?"
You know?
The breeze is blowing,
and you see people,
and they're nice to you,
and everybody's smiling,
and everybody's dancing,
and everybody's—
and you think,
"That doesn't exist all the time."
But that's what you're going for, is that, that,
I don't know what that word is but, that, uh,
where everything comes together. . . .
Steve: Harmony's a good word.
Gene: That harmony.
That harmony all comes together
and you can hear that ring,

and you see that on TV
where the glass breaks, [gestures and makes the sound][15]
well that's the epitome of *Gemütlichkeit*—
you know, the glass breaking.
But when everybody's having a good time.
And I, I know of—
when I was at Fort Wayne,
Uh, several years back.
Steve: '81.
Gene: And that guy had that—
Steve: You're right, that was a good example. '81.
Gene: Damn squeezebox.
God!
We got back in that damn wine room—
they had the wine room
and the beer room
and all that kind of stuff
and that guy back in the wine room,
and they started singing those songs,
and there was,
there wasn't anybody
that knew what the word *critical* meant.
Nobody was critical of anybody.
Steve: No.
Gene: And they started singing,
and they were hugging each other
and holding on
and all this kind of stuff,
and if (**Steve:** It was fun, man.) somebody stumbled they didn't say,
"Hey, you screwed up." You know,
they didn't say that.
They said,
"C'mon, that's great," you know,
"Keep going."
Steve: We were all standing in a big circle (**Gene:** Yeah)

---

[15] He is referring to a well-known commercial, "Is it live or is it Memorex?" in which a woman sings a high note that shatters a wine glass.

and arms around each other singing. . . .
Gene: Boy, to me,
I'll never forget that—
I mean it was the glass breaking, you know,
everybody had had a few drinks,
everybody was happy,
everybody was in harmony with everybody,
everybody had smiles.
You notice (**Steve:** Yeah. . . .) when you go to those things,
people got smiles on their faces.
They're not, "Yeah, goddamn,
let me tell you about *my* goddamn troubles.
You want to tell me one?
I'll tell you one better," you know.
They're just having a good time.
Leave your troubles behind, you know.
Good music,
a little booze,
and you know,
and when they sing they go up
and dance
and all that
and all that shit.
You're just *happy*.
And it's hard to get that.
Really. (Interview with Gene Lutterbach and Steve Rode, 1992)

The highly poetic nature of this example is indicative of its rhetorical intent. Not only is Gene validating *Gemütlichkeit* by associating it with a good time in the past, but he also has an ax to grind: the club needs to return to the ideals of socializing that made this organization appealing for German-Americans in search of a community that brings them pleasure.

The preceding examples have shown one way in which ethnomusicologists and others interested in the construction of ethnic meaning and community can look at traditionalization as process. In so doing, we recognize that people actively create meaning in their present by referring to their past—or *a* past. Issues of contextualization, canon formation, and rhetorical strategies of legitimation are a part of how people talk about the music they perform—"Ein Prosit der Gemütlichkeit."

Figure 3. Rosemary Muensterman teachers visitors to the 1991 Volksfest how to do "The Chicken."

Figure 4. Revelers and dancers at Germania Maennerchor's 1993 Volksfest raise their glasses as they sing "Ein Prosit der Gemütlichkeit" to the accompaniment of the Rhein Valley Brass.

Sometimes thought only to be banal or an embarrassing reference to excessive beer consumption, this toast, which punctuates German-American social gatherings, is a powerful idea, an idea that is part of the draw for the thousands of people who visit this club's Volksfest every year to experience "Germanness," each in her or his own way, yet each in a way symbolically connected to the ways others enter into the culture at that time and place. For members, associating *Gemütlichkeit* with the past is an important way to give it a deeper and richer meaning. It is a process of making this idea a part of how they encounter and organize their social world. Traditionalization can serve to situate actions within an immediate context of personal experience as well as connect experience with larger ideas about personal identity. By examining situated examples of this process in action we can not only become increasingly aware of the motivations behind the actions of these music- and community-makers, but can also add another dimension to our understanding of the use of the past in the present.

By examining the ways in which the members of Evansville's Germania Männerchor traditionalize the complex German-American culture that gives meaning to their lives at the beginning of the twenty-first century, I by no means intend to diminish what they do. Nor do I wish to suggest that it is somehow inauthentic by arguing for the rhetorical nature of tradition. The fact that *Gemütlichkeit* has been important in club life for almost one hundred years is, in fact, only of secondary importance. Unlike the partbooks that collect dust in the darkness of the Germania Männerchor music library, the traditionalized text and the Germania community continuously acquire new life when members make them old.

Bibliography

Anderson, Benedict. *Imagined Communities: Reflections on the Origin and Spread of Nationalism*. London: Verso, 1983.

Bauman, Richard. "Contextualization, Tradition, and the Dialogue of Genres: Icelandic Legends of the *Kraftaskáld*." In *Rethinking Context*, edited by Charles Goodwin and A. Duranti. Cambridge: Cambridge University Press, 1991.

Béhague, Gerard, ed. *Performance Practice: Ethnomusicological Perspectives*. Westport, CO: Greenwood Press, 1984.

Blum, Stephen, Philip Bohlman and Daniel Neuman, eds. *Ethnomusicology and Modern Music History*. Urbana: University of Illinois Press, 1991.

Bohlman, Philip V. *The Study of Folk Music in the Modern World*. Bloomington: Indiana University Press, 1988.

Burdette, Alan. "'Ein Prosit der Gemütlichkeit': Heightened Experience and the Creation of Context in a German American Singing Society." M.A. Thesis, Indiana University, Bloomington, 1992.

Coplan, David B. "Ethnomusicology and the Meaning of Tradition." In Blum, Bohlman, and Neuman, 35–48.

Dreisch, Carl. "Geschichte des Vereins." *Gedenkbuch zum Silbernen Jubiläum des Germania Männerchor*. Evansville, IN: 1925.

Evansville Illustrated. Evansville, IN: H.R. Page & Company, 1889.

Handler, Richard and Jocelyn Linnekin. "Tradition, Genuine or Spurious." *Journal of American Folklore* 97 (1984):273–290.

Hobsbawm, Eric and Terrence Ranger, eds. *The Invention of Tradition*. Cambridge: Cambridge University Press, 1984.

Hymes, Dell. "Folklore's Nature and the Sun's Myth." *Journal of American Folklore* 88 (1975): 345–69.

Keil, Charles, Angeliki Keil, and Dick Blau. *Polka Happiness*. Philadelphia: Temple University Press, 1992.

Kirschbaum, Erik. *The Eradication of German Culture in the United States 1917–1918*. Stuttgart: Hans-Dieter Heinz, 1986.

Seeger, Anthony. "When Music Makes History." In Blum, Bohlman, and Neuman, 23–24.

Terrell, Peter, et al. *Collins German–English, English–German Dictionary*. London: Collins, 1980.

Williams, Raymond. *Marxism and Literature*. Oxford: Oxford University Press, 1977.

10

BURGENLAND-AMERICAN MUSIC AND THE "ETHNIC MAINSTREAM"

Rudolf Pietsch

Introduction

This article is not about German-American music. It is also not about the musical culture of German-Americans. This article is, however, about a music that depends on the presence of German musics in America, and about a musical culture whose identity results from complex relations with German America. In other words, if there were not a German-American musical culture with complex and contested popular ethnic musics, the music of Americans from Burgenland would be very different from what it is today.

Burgenland is not in Germany, but in Austria, in fact in that part of Austria that is at the greatest distance from Germany. Whereas there are regions and regional cultures whose musical traditions overlap with German, especially Bavarian traditions, this is not so much the case in Burgenland, which borders on Hungary and Slovakia and has musical traditions that overlap with those of Eastern, as well as Central, Europe. For most of its history, Burgenland belonged to Central Europe neither politically nor culturally, but rather depended on the political conditions of Eastern European countries, notably Hungary. Geographically, too, Burgenland belongs to the Pannonian Region, the great Hungarian Plain that stretches eastward, eventually into Serbia, Slovakia, and Romania. Burgenland's culture — its architecture, agricultural economy, and music—bears witness to the regional traditions of the Pannonian east, and these are the traditions that by and large ascribe ethnic identity to Burgenland music up to the present (Deutsch 1990).

The emigration of Burgenlanders to North America is also not a German-American phenomenon. Burgenlanders left their homeland for reasons unrelated to the large waves of German emigration; indeed, the largest immigrations of Germans had subsided before those from Burgenland began. The first wave of emigrant Burgenlanders left their home because of the collapse of the Habsburg Empire in

Eastern Europe, whose border they had historically embodied; the identity of these Burgenlanders is today no longer a part of the larger identity of Burgenland-Americans. When the new border of a reduced Austria replaced the imperial border, Burgenlanders responded to the radical economic and cultural changes that resulted by emigrating in large numbers (cf. the essays in Baumgartner, Müllner, and Münz 1989).

And yet, Burgenland's history is inseparable from questions of Germanness; indeed, questions about just what type of identity German language and music can bring to regions far removed from the usual bastions of German culture. In Burgenland itself, issues of German identity formed around the presence of the Heanzen, the German-speaking ethnic group in middle and southern Burgenland. The Heanzen have represented one part of a larger ethnic multiculturalism, albeit a part that in many ways serves as the core for cultural and musical diversity. The folk music of the Heanzen cannot be understood as dominating that of other ethnic groups, say, the Hungarians or Croatians in Burgenland, but rather complementing them in the history of the province as a whole.[1]

The relation of parts to the whole is central to the history of ethnic music that I examine in this article. Burgenland's musical traditions, so I wish to suggest, consist of many parts that represent a larger identity for Burgenland in a constantly changing history. Sometimes that change is gradual, but more often it is radical, the product of sweeping and dramatic historical events, most especially for the twentieth century, the immigration of Burgenlanders to North America. In the New World, the parts that constitute Burgenland music have been reassembled, and a new whole has emerged. That whole is today overwhelmingly American, and it is the identity of that whole in relation to American ethnicity that I examine in this article. For Burgenlanders in America, music has been a means of choosing how they relate to certain aspects of American ethnicity, that is to say, how they retain the identifiably Burgenland as a tributary of what I call here the "ethnic mainstream" of American music.

Burgenland's Ethnic Diversity in Europe and North America

Burgenland, which as German West Hungary belonged to the Hungarian part of the Habsburg Empire until 1921, is the youngest of all Austrian provinces. With a popu-

[1] Of German-speaking Burgenland ancestry on my mother's side and Czech on my father's, I lead two ensembles that perform the music of Burgenland both specifically and generally. The Heanzenquartett specializes in the music of the German ethnic group, while the Tanzgeiger consciously incorporates Hungarian and Croatian pieces. For musical cross-sections of the folk-music culture of Burgenland, listen to the CDs *Burgenländische Volkmusik* and *Burgenland.*

lation of about 250,000, Burgenland has a demographic identity that has been profoundly shaped by emigration, which began about 150 years ago and only began to subside substantially in the 1950s. There were three major waves of emigration, totaling at least 100,000, of which an estimated 66,000 emigrants left Burgenland as young adults for purely financial reasons. For the most part, Burgenlanders immigrated to the American Midwest and the East Coast. My own research has focused primarily on the Burgenland-American population of the Lehigh Valley in eastern Pennsylvania, where today one can still speak of a relatively "closed" area of approximately fourteen thousand residents either from Burgenland or with direct ancestry from Burgenland.[2] The major wave of immigrants to the Lehigh Valley took place immediately after World War I, with the peak actually during the period 1923–1930. The immigrants who arrived after World War II came largely as "German" (i.e., German-speaking) minorities from Hungarian villages in Burgenland (e.g., Rabfidish/Rabafüszes and Radling/Rönök). In the first immigrant waves, most Burgenlanders found jobs in cement factories or other manufacturing trades, such as silk mills or cigar manufacturing (Dujmovits 1992).

The culture of Burgenlanders is historically that of diaspora on numerous levels. Burgenland itself has been multicultural, indeed, in the modern use of that term, since at least the Early Modern Era, or, more specifically, since the defeat of the Ottoman Empire in East-Central Europe. On the border between Austria and Hungary, the market cities and courts were constantly shifting between royal families and changing political affiliations. There was already a substantial population of Jewish Burgenlanders in the fifteenth century, making the province the most intensively Jewish rural area of Central Europe (see, e.g., Ernst 1987:233–237 and Bohlman 1997). Roma and Croatian settlement dates to at least the sixteenth century, and the large number of Roma and Croatian residents in Burgenland today live in distinctively Burgenland Roma and Croatian cultures. In the wake of the Ottoman retreat from Hungary in the late seventeenth century, so-called "Saxons" and Swabians settled in large numbers, and Jewish communities, particularly the "Seven Holy Communities" that form a ring around Sopron/Ödenburg, grew in number and population. Hungarians constituted an administrative class, consisting largely of civil servants, teachers, and other government officials.

The multicultural and diasporic culture of Burgenland is, furthermore, a result of the province's economic history, for even today many Burgenlanders must travel

[2] I have also conducted fieldwork in Chicago in 1988 and 1996, which many Austrians regard as the "largest city in Burgenland," because it counts a Burgenland population of between thirty and forty thousand.

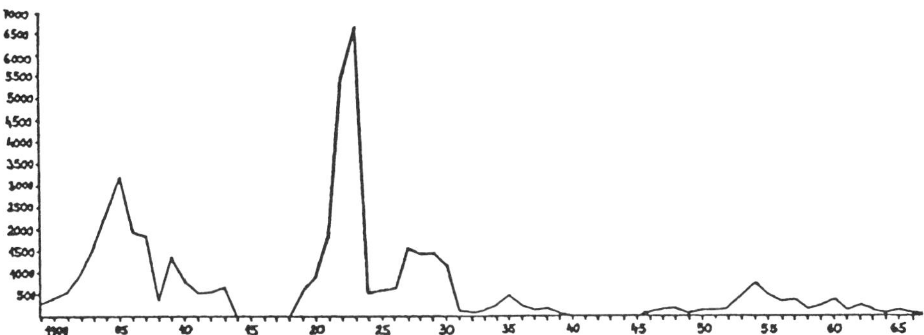

Figure 1. Overview of Immigration Patterns from Burgenland to the United States.

to Vienna to work during the week, returning home only on weekends. The dispersed Burgenland communities of North America, it might be argued, have benefited from this history of diaspora, insofar as there are extensive socio-cultural networks among and within the communities, connecting those communities in North America but also to Burgenland itself.

Because of this diasporic framework, one might argue that the living conditions of the first immigrant generation already differed sharply from those of the village culture in Burgenland itself. Only in the second generation were Burgenlanders really able to establish their own distinctive culture. This generational difference is evident in the family structure itself, for families were by and large founded only in North America. It was, moreover, relatively common for an immigrant to spend some years alone working in North America before returning to Burgenland in order to bring back a wife to the immigrant culture.

The immigrants quickly established organizations and institutions that strengthened their cultural networks. Far more important than socio-cultural institutions (e.g., *Gesangvereine* or singing societies) were those that offered a sort of insurance, that is, mutual-aid societies. As a member, one paid a certain amount monthly in case of death or injury, at which time one would receive necessary financial support. The socio-cultural institutions, in fact, were formed in order to support these mutual-aid societies, which sponsored many different kinds of dances, such as the women's balls, masked balls, Fasching balls (see Figure 2), or farmers' balls (*Bauernbälle*) (see Figure 3). In the fall, dances to celebrate the wine harvest

(*Traubentanz* and *Weinlesefest*) were especially popular.[3] Musical organizations, especially dance bands, developed as a means of supporting the network of social connections in the immigrant culture, and they came to require the flexibility and mobility necessitated by such connections.

Many folkways in the immigrant culture of Pennsylvania, nonetheless, were similar to those in Burgenland, producing many dialect sayings such as "gråd so wia dahoam draußt" —"it's just like at home out there." Well into the postwar period, many Burgenlanders in North America baked bread at home and kept small animals and pigs, if not occasionally a cow. During Prohibition, many Burgenlanders, who worked in disproportionately large numbers in breweries or operated taverns, were especially hard hit and lost their jobs. Still, many Burgenlanders continued to produce a certain quantity of wine for their own consumption, relocating the traditions associated with the consumption of alcohol to the basement, which even today is an important site for the performance and maintenance of Burgenland-American identity.

Church and tavern were and still are centers of village life. In the immigrant areas of the United States, however, the tavern lost this function during Prohibition and has regained it only to a limited degree. If one did not meet with others at home or did not use the home for social functions, then one turned to the hall of the local mutual-aid society, or other fraternal organizations, for social gatherings of all kinds. These serve, until the present, as the real "place of the homeland"—"Ort der Heimat"—where virtually all cultural activities take place. Every Friday and Saturday, there is a dance at these social clubs, for which all members have free admission, and where the many Burgenland bands play dance music. Together with language, music serves as the clearest characteristic for measuring the degree of assimilation in an ethnic group (see Martschin 1993). For Burgenland-Americans, the musical activities of the social organizations, especially in the weekly dances and the dances for special occasions, have an even more heightened degree of undergirding identity.

Instrumental Music

Although the music of Burgenland exhibits a complex multiculturalism, and the music of Burgenland-Americans multiplies the regional and ethnic diversity through diaspora, there are still certain genres and practices that represent a distinctively Burgenland identity. The nature of this identity is recognized both emically and

[3] Burgenland is a major wine-producing region of Austria. These wine-harvest dances, it follows, were traditions imported from Austria, with no calendric functions in North America, where Burgenlanders did not settle in areas that supported vineyards.

Figure 2. Masked Ball and Fasching Dance of the First Burgenland Society for Aiding the Sick, Chicago, 1933.

Figure 3. Farmers' Ball, Lehigh Valley, Pennsylvania, 1938.

Figure 4. The Schanta Band playing at the Austrian-Hungarian Veterans' Society, Allentown, Pennsylvania, 1988.

etically, and it manifests specific functions when used inside and outside the Burgenland-American community. The identity, nonetheless, achieves its character by drawing upon many traditions and assembling selected elements of these in distinctive ways. At a very fundamental level, Burgenland-American music draws on the two larger traditions that the hyphenated parts of its name symbolize. "Burgenland" traditions center around local and folk-music practices, a core repertory of button-box tunes, for example. The "American" components are those that come from the ethnic mainstream, especially traditions and elements whose origins are from southern German and Austrian or Slavic music.[4] Instrumental music symbolizes these different histories and musical traditions in easily distinguishable ways, and I now wish to examine the larger domain of instrumental music by focusing on two of its most pronounced aspects: (1) techniques used to play the *diatonic button accordion*, usually called "button box" (German, *Knopfharmonika*, though in Burgenland often with a localized name, such as *Steirische*, literally a Styrian); (2) musical and functional contexts of *ensemble music*.

[4]Southern Germany, especially Bavaria, and Austria share a common region of cultural, linguistic, and religious traditions, and folk musicians often perform widely on both sides of the Austro-German border. The long history of cultural exchange with surrounding Slavic- and Hungarian-speaking cultures, in contrast, serves as a level of musical style and repertory that distinguishes Austrian from southern German folk music.

Figure 5. Franz "Frank" Unger, Burgenland immigrant in Allentown, Pennsylvania.

The Button Box (Diatonic Button Accordion)

Because it was primarily new immigrants who brought their instruments with them, the *Steirische* often jokingly received the name, "greenhorn instrument" (see Figure 5). In the earliest waves of immigration, button boxes[5] were important to the musical culture of Burgenland-Americans, but after World War II the tradition began to die down a bit. In recent decades, however, it has enjoyed a resurgence in popularity. Today, the button box enjoys high status as an instrument that expresses identity (see Figure 6). One plays the button box because one is a Burgenlander, even when one is "only at home," among friends, or playing in the kitchen or basement (see Figure 7).[6]

The chart in Figure 8 summarizes the different occasions on which musicians play the button box and represents the ways in which these occasions bring about certain types of interaction between musicians and public. On the vertical coordinate, we see a listening public that stretches from the private circle to the public sphere.[7] The horizontal coordinate represents the musical groups that are associ-

[5] Henceforth, I refer to the instrument only as a "button box" because this is by far the most common name in the vernacular.

[6] See Proulx (1996) for an interesting fictional portrayal of the button box in ethnic North America.

[7] This range, however, should not be interpreted as representing the public as a whole.

Figure 6. The Josef Krobuth Orchestra, appearing with the Copley Sängerbund, February, 1988.

Figure 7. Private party at a Burgenland house, New York, soon after World War II.

ated with certain types of musical occasions. Other fields on the graph represent the occasions for music-making during the year or life cycle, as well as everyday occasions. As in the case of annual and life cycles, there are also occasions that achieve a heightened significance for one reason or another, though this may not be conceived from the outset because of their connection to everyday occasions. When they occur, nonetheless, they require an extra level of performance from the musicians, who therefore transform them so as to make them transcend the everyday.

With an example from Figure 8 it is possible to refer to characteristic functions to illustrate historical change. Today, musicians regard a wedding as an extremely formal setting—they are engaged for a very specific period of time; they receive a respectable fee, at least in comparison to other occasions; and they have specific tasks to fulfill and a certain order of events to follow. Several years ago, the situation was completely different—a wedding could last several days, though it did not have to, and the musicians were always present, which meant that there were increased demands on them to fill out the time in the wedding. The specific events taking place during a wedding were much more diverse than today. Everything else that took place during the wedding ranged from moments of informal exchange to those of extreme excess. Musicians were paid according to their ability to respond to these changing moments in the wedding. In principle, the situation is the same today; however, the performance of the musicians at each moment is highly regulated, fixed already in the contract they sign prior to the wedding. We witness, therefore, a transformation from weddings that depended on a constant shift between informal and formal music-making to a contemporary situation in which each type of performance must respond to normative restrictions.

At the same time, the structure of the listening public underwent changes. Between the world wars, one invited not just members of the family circle to the wedding, but as many friends from the neighborhood as possible, whereas today one limits the invitations to the immediate family, with a few close friends. The wedding, therefore, has undergone a transformation from a public to a private event.

At the most private and informal level we find the musical culture of the *basement*. A few friends might be present at such events, but for the most part the musicians—the *kitchen players* or the *down-home players*—play primarily for themselves. When this is the case, ethnicity is entirely taken for granted because the musicians depend not at all on a public to consume their music. The transcription in Figure 9 represents a "Steirischer Ländler" performed without conscious attention to projecting ethnicity beyond the private sphere.

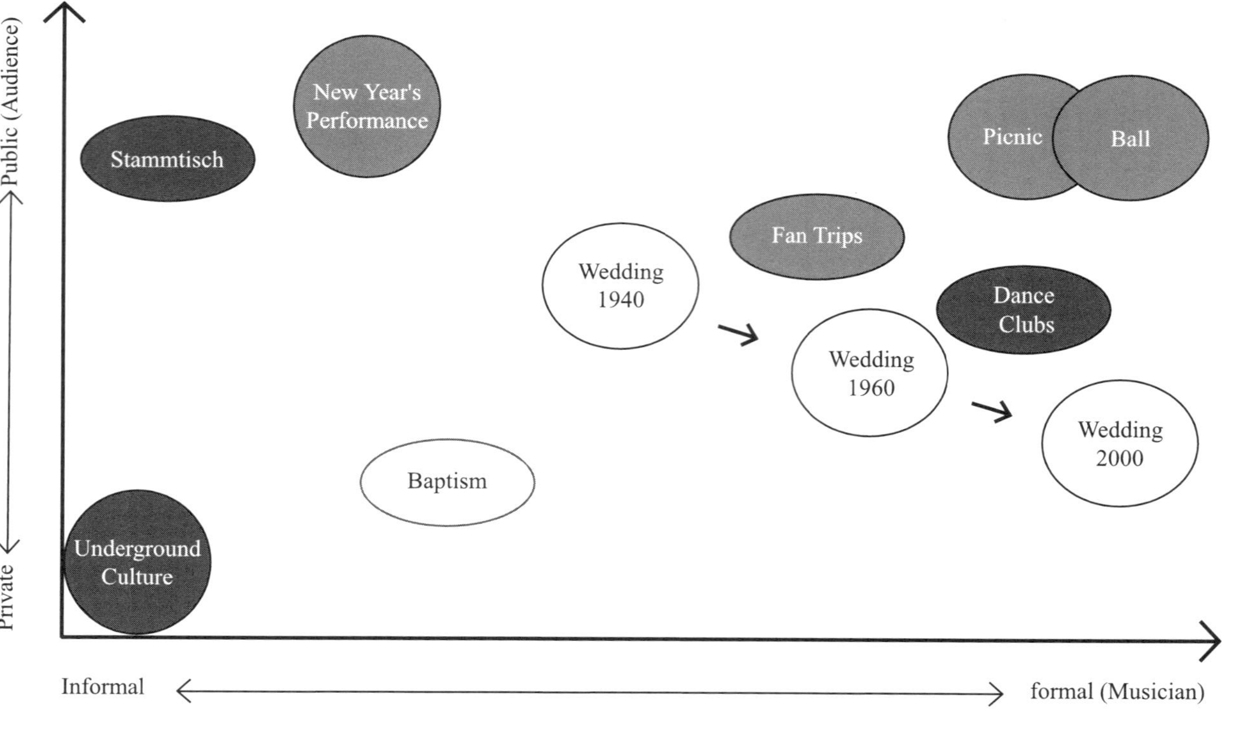

Figure 8. Musical Occasions and Ensembles.

MM 𝅗𝅥. = 45
A1 Fm F C C F F C C F Cm
9 A'1 F C C A F F C C F Cm
17 CO1 A A G F D (A) D C A F F F F
23 B9 Cm F C C F A G Fm F C C C A F Fm
31 B'1 F C C F A G F F C C A F Fm
39 B$^{Q}_{1}$ B♭ F F B♭ B♭ B♭ F F B♭ Cm
47 B"1 F C C F F C C F
55 CO2 F A F D D 3 C F Cm Cm F F F
61 C9 Cm F Cm Cm C Dm A C C A F F Cm Cm C C F Cm
69 C'1 F Cm Cm C C A C C A F F Cm Cm C C C A F Fm
77 C$^{Q}_{1}$ B♭ Fm Fm F F E♭ C B♭ B♭ Fm Fm F F E♭ C B♭ Cm
85 CO3 F Cm Cm C C A C C A F F Cm Cm C C A C F Cm

Figure 9. “Steirischer Ländler”—Frank Spitzer, Northampton, Pennsylvania; button box.

Ethnic Multilingualism

The button box also lends itself to musical styles and repertories that cross the borders between private and public spheres in the Burgenland-American musical culture. Performers, who most frequently play in their basements or under more familiar circumstances in the community, also play in public at dances where Burgenland-Americans and other ethnic groups mix. Dance tunes that reflect both Burgenland and popular American traditions evolve; the mixture that results manifests itself both in the identity of the melodic and dance material itself—the tune or tunes—and in the style of performance. A performance that crosses stylistic boundaries and mixes repertories in this way often takes the form of a medley, a piece that unfolds as a set of discrete tunes that may or may not demonstrate close stylistic unity. Such medleys, however, are not necessarily less Austrian, for the tradition of cobbling together different dance tunes for a medley has precedents in Austrian folk dance. The *Ländler*, for example, unfolds as a series of sections, with new tunes spinning out as the *Ländler* grows in length. [8] In American culture, button-box players simply drew upon different stocks to create their medleys, as in the case of Ed-

[8] Arguably, this is one of the reasons that composers such as Franz Schubert and Gustav Mahler employed the *Ländler* in their compositions. Especially in the case of Schubert (e.g., in his *Atzenbrügger Tänze*, “Acht Ländler in B,” D. 378), *Ländler* were conceived with real dancing in mind. For Mahler, the *Ländler* provided an opportunity for juxtaposing different, sometimes jarringly so, melodies.

die Kemeter's "Golden Slippers Hoedown," in which the movement between Burgenland and popular American styles takes place almost seamlessly in a style Kemeter simply calls "Western" (for the Hoedown and its contexts, see *New Grove* [1980] 8:612). Compare the original arrangement of "Oh, Them Golden Slippers" in Figure 10 with the recording of Kemeter's adaptation of it on the companion CD.

At yet another level, ethnic stylistic mixtures are even more complex than just Old Country versus New World combinations. Polkas, for example, may contain elements of style that ascribe group identity, on one hand, but borrow an entire bricolage of traits from the mainstream. The purpose of this borrowing is to mark a polka as "ethnic," that is, to create a sense that there are other ethnic groups and communities that dance our music, albeit in their own ways or dialects. I employ the metaphors of language quite deliberately in this case, because the mixture I am describing is multilingual, indeed, in the most practical sense of applying this concept. For the ethnic musician, it may be necessary to play for a Burgenland club on Friday night, a German Fasching Dance on Saturday, and on the stage of an ethnic festival on Sunday afternoon. Rather than performing or even drawing from three different repertories, I wish to suggest that many ethnic musicians actually depend upon an ability to remix a single repertory, that is, to draw on their multilingualism. Figure 11 illustrates this multilingual remixing with a well-known polka transcribed from a performance by Frankie Yankovic, the most famous Slovenian-American ethnic popular musician. Mixing takes place in very direct ways, so as to communicate to dancers and record consumers upon first hearing. Although obviously not a Burgenlander, Yankovic has served as a model for many Burgenland-American musicians, whose audiences were equally as diverse as those to whom Yankovic appealed. Like Yankovic, many Burgenlanders relied on this musical multilingualism as a means of crossing the border into the ethnic mainstream.

The text of Yankovic's recorded version of "She's Too Fat for Me" polka stretches the mixed languages of American polka culture over a formal template, transforming the text into an expressive performance of Americanness, while at the same time indexing the ethnic landscape of a European dance form. The following scheme represents the form of the polka, indicating the relation between melodic parts and language of text.

A1 – English
A2 – Croatian
B1 – English
A3 – English, with accent, which leads into a linguistic mix of
English, Croatian, and Italian

Oh, Them Golden Slippers

Figure 10. James A. Bland "Oh, Them Golden Slippers"

Instrumental Introduction
IT
9
A1
Here's a sil - ly dit - ty you can sing it right a - way Now
13
here is what you say so sing it while you may
17
Here's a sil - ly jin - gle you can sing it night or noon
21
Here's the words that's all you need 'cause I just sang the tune Yoy!
25
A2
Ja ju ne - ću, ti ju ze - mi on - a de - be - la,
29
on - a de - be - la yoy! on - a de - be - la
33
ja ju ne - ću, ti ju ze - mi on - a de - be - la
37
de - be - la de - be - la on - a de - be - la I get
41
B1
diz - zy I get num - bo when I'm dan - cing with my Jum - Jum Jum - bo -
49
A3
I'm go wan' 'er you can have 'er she's too fat for me,
53
too too fat for me do - kon fat for me Yo!
57
I don' wan' 'er, you can have 'er she's too fat for me
61
ros too fat two too fat she's too fat for me!

Figure 11. Frankie Yankovic, "She's Too Fat for Me."

C – English
A4 – Instrumental
B2 – English
A5 – English, followed by a linguistic mix of English,
Croatian, and Italian

In the printed version of "She's Too Fat for Me" polka, attributed to Ross MacLean and Arthur Richardson and first printed in 1947, the text is English alone, and it contains no C section as in Yankovic's performance. In the printed version the melodic sections unfold thus: A1–B1–A2–A1–B2–A2. The A sections make up a refrain, and there is little textual variation therefore between A1 and A2. Sections B1 and B2 are identical with those in Yankovic's performance. Clearly, Yankovic knows how to rely on formal polka structures to make his performance both American and ethnic. His additional sections, surely also his personal stamp on the performance, range between extreme ethnic mixture (A3) and openly American (C).

For a Burgenland-American musician, such as Eddie Kemeter of Allentown, Pennsylvania, Yankovic's ethnic mix makes further variation and transformation possible. At first hearing, Kemeter's "She's Too Fat for Me" polka suggests a retreat back to Europe, as if he is simply substituting German text for English, Croatian, or Italian. But we should not forget that Yankovic made the polka more *American* by introducing ethnic variation. Kemeter makes the polka more *ethnic-American*.

The German text has no relation to the English text in the Yankovic version discussed above. Melodic similarities, moreover, point to a well-known Viennese popular song, "Heit iß i nix" (Today I'll Eat Nothing), which had recently been sung in the circle of ethnic Burgenlanders where Kemeter often played. There are connections to snippets from other well-known songs, often just refrains, such as those that would be known from marches played in Austrian wine gardens, or *Heurigen*. Formally, these snippets from a shared body of popular tunes lead to a transformation to the genre known as "potpourri." Kemeter's middle section, therefore, is based on the trio melody from the "Steinriegler March," known widely by rural musicians in Austria (indexing it in Kemeter's performance is the text part, "O, mei liaber Gottvåter," a song composed by Carl Por to a text by J. Hornig). When the English section begins, Kemeter underlays the performance with "Slovenian style," the afterbeats stressing a continuous "feeling of four." The middle section, sung in German, assumes the feeling of "European flair."[9]

[9] These are concepts that Kemeter relates to a shared musical vocabulary of Burgenland-American musicians.

Introduction
DH
Bb Bb C C Eb G Eb G Bb Bb Bb C Eb G Eb G
Bb Bb C C Eb G Eb Eb Cm Cm Bb Bb Eb B Eb Eb
Oh,
VOC
Bb Bb C C Eb Eb Eb
you can have 'er, I don' wan' 'er, she's too fat for me, oh,
Eb Eb Bb Bb Eb Eb Eb Eb
she's too fat for me, oh, she's too fat for me! Oh,
Bb Bb C C Eb Eb Eb Eb
you can have 'er, I don' wan' 'er, she's too fat for me, oh,
C C Bb Bb Eb Bb Eb Eb
she's too fat, she's too fat, she's too fat for me!
Interlude
C Bb Bb Bb Eb G Eb Bb Bb Bb Bb Bb Eb F Eb G
Bb Bb Bb Bb Eb G Eb G Bb Bb Bb Bb Eb Bb Eb Eb
Heut

49
VOC
DH
iß i nix, heut
trink i nix, heut
g'freu i mir's auf
d'Nacht, heut
53
g'freu i mir's auf
d'Nacht, heut
g'freu i mir's auf
d'Nacht. Heut
57
setz i mein greans
Hia - tl auf und
schaur - i's Dian - dl
nach, da
61
schaur - i's Dian - dl
nach, bei der
Nacht.
Interlude
65
DH
73
81
89

Figure 12: Eddie Kemeter, "She's Too Fat for Me" polka.

Whereas Yankovic's version is *multilingual*, it is multilingual in a personalized way: we witness Yankovic's multilingualism, which he uses in an ironic dialogue with his own ethnic experiences. The use of Croatian and Italian in the song text is almost random, which is to say, it would be possible to use other languages at these points, even English, in different, "ethnicized" ways, to underscore the humor of the polka itself. When Kemeter interprets these sections, he uses German and English—his own bilingualism—but the sense of the German is completely different from that of the original version. The irony that was so important to Yankovic now completely disappears, and the *multilingualism* becomes Austrian- or Burgenland-American, transforming the polka to a song that could be sung by those sitting around a *Stammtisch* in a tavern or bar, that is, a *Gstanzllied*.[10]

Currently, there are still about forty active button-box players in the Burgenland-American community of eastern Pennsylvania. They get together (not always all of them, however) on Friday nights at the Edelweißhaus in the city of Northampton, which itself contextualizes the ethnicity of the music. The Edelweißhaus was established in the 1950s by an immigrant in the post-World War II wave. He was the proprietor until the end of his life, when his wife took over the establishment. On Fridays beginning at about 10:00 P.M. and lasting well past 1:00 A.M., there is a jam session for the button-box players; before and during the jam session, other instruments are played, but it is the button box that closes up the tavern. Two frameworks and two ethnic-music functions emerge from this pattern. On one hand, music is present at the Edelweißhaus as entertainment for the other guests; on the other, the musicians use it as an opportunity to focus on a specific Burgenland tradition and to engage in the intensive exchange that keeps that tradition vital. In the Edelweißhaus, the button box negotiates between two traditions, one American and one from Burgenland, and it is the negotiation itself that creates a new context for the entry of Burgenland-American music into the ethnic mainstream.

Broadening the Ethnic Mainstream: When Hyphenated Ethnicity Is Not Enough

When an Austrian ethnomusicologist and musician hears the music of Burgenland-Americans, the hyphenated concepts of American ethnicity that pair Old and New World do little to address the musical and historical complexity of the music. For one thing, the "Austrian" musical components are already "ethnic." Not only is there an ethnic mix from Burgenland, but there are also streams of ethnic influence

---

[10] A *Gstanzllied* (literally, a song with little stanzas) results from a group performance in which individuals sing bits and pieces, back and forth, almost in call-and-response fashion, often teasingly, but always with humor and double entendre.

that have been flowing into popular and ethnic music from the centuries of national interaction in the Habsburg Empire. Dance and folk music inevitably reflect at least one non-Austrian influence, for example, a Bohemian (Czech) woodwind and brass sound or the *Oberkrainer* derive from twentieth-century Slovenian folk music. Austrian ethnicity, it follows, interacts with American ethnicity in the United States, which may mix Bohemian and Slovenian sounds in very different ways with German (Dutchman) and Polish traditions, whose presence in Austria is much less important than influences from Hungarian and Roma music.

European and Austrian theories of ethnicity, it follows, differ according to the very different cultural histories of the Old World. Terms such as *ethnic groups* are rarely used in Austria; the closest equivalent is *minorities*, a term that in Austria enjoys widespread use for both cultural and political reasons (see, e.g., Hemetek 1996). For Austrian scholars, moreover, *ethnicity* has a distinctly American resonance, which is to say, it can, at least in principle, be applied to every group claiming some form of common history and social connection. Such neutrality of application does not, in principle, exist in Austria or in most European countries where some minorities have a protected legal status and others do not. This may seem like a small point, but in multicultural provinces such as Burgenland it has practical ramifications quite unlike those in the United States. Language and language maintenance, for example, play a defining role. The fact that Croatian and Hungarian are primary languages of instruction in some Burgenland schools, but, for example, Romani is not, suggests that Croatian and Hungarian Burgenlanders have a different status from Roma Burgenlanders. We witness here a minority politics that is different from the ethnic politics of the United States, where, universally, the only legal language of instruction is English.

In European concepts of ethnicity, the term refers to a unified culture in a bounded or closely defined group whose members are not required for political reasons to live together. Georg Elwert defines ethnicity as "groups that are larger than families and that include families as a subcategory, which ascribe to themselves a collective, sometimes exclusive, identity" (Elwert 1989:447). The central and fundamental criterion, therefore, is the individual's choice to place him- or herself into a category of definable ethnicity. Because this definition borders on social groups bound together by special interests, it lends itself to misinterpretation. Were this the case, everyone who decided to play a button box in the Edelweißhaus of Northampton, Pennsylvania, would be participating in a group defined by its Burgenland ethnicity. There are, nonetheless, Pennsylvania Germans and Ukrainians who also play the button box under these circumstances, and no one ascribes Burgenland ethnicity to them because they are not of Burgenland descent, to use the most common qualifier. For the survival of Burgenland identity, however, it is extremely important that these non-Burgenlanders can play button box at the Edelweißhaus Stammtisch in order that Burgenland-American music not die out. In my opinion, definitions that limit ethnicity to common ancestry are, in fact, a form of ethnocentrism. In the case of the Burgenland-American musical culture, this is most definitely not the case.

For European immigrants to North America there are two elements that seemingly must be preserved, if even rudimentarily: language and a way of life they brought with them. When knowledge of the European language diminishes and for everyday purposes disappears, there develops a language referring to Burgenland that consists largely of clichés, albeit clichés that have very definite functions. These take the form of verbal interjections at dances, such as "Auf geht's!" or "Hiaz geht's los!" or the question asked to all, "Wia geht's da?" ("How are you?") after which the conversation switches entirely into English. Burgenland-American musicians, furthermore, who do not use the German language regularly or may not even know the language anymore, still retain German songs in their repertory, not simply to provide the appropriate response to the public's needs, but rather consciously to retain and demonstrate their sense of ethnic belonging.

The Burgenland-American example is by no means exceptional. Philip Bohlman observed a similar phenomenon in a Polish-American group performing for an ethnic festival in Pittsburgh: "A few songs in Polish are therefore important not because many of those in the audience understand the texts—not even the singers have any real sensitivity to the texts —but because language provides a readily recognizable icon of ethnicity" (Nettl et al. 1997:281–282).

In contradistinction to German-speaking Central Europe, the term *ethnic* exists in the United States not only as a sociological category but also in a generally understood field of meanings, where it is associated also with economic goals and political dynamics. Ethnic groups living in the United States respond to a wide variety of ethnic pressures from the outside, not only the need to acculturate and coexist with other ethnic groups, but also to establish relations to the "Mother Country" and to determine the relative role of such relations. Ethnicity is therefore a highly determined mechanism of adaptation rather than an intellectual motivation. They choose to be ethnic because ethnicity brings them a desirable connection to a group, the advantages and security of living in a "warm nest" in the midst of a gigantic country. They connect themselves not only to others like themselves but do so across regional boundaries.

Opposing ethnicity in the American sociological and folkloristic literature is the so-called "cultural mainstream." From the European perspective, the cultural mainstream seems to have been invented for inclusive reasons, with the result nevertheless that it could only be defined by exclusive criteria. In short, being part of the cultural mainstream was viewed as positive and desirable, whereas the alternative had negative implications. The cultural mainstream also results from criteria that are for many very difficult to fulfill without first abandoning the culture of the Old Country; the preferred Protestantism of the mainstream, for example, poses a challenge to Burgenland-Americans that immigrants from northern Germany do not face. On one hand, political motivations shape the mainstream; on the other, it is primarily connected to a way of life. What this means is that there is no single label that tells us unequivocally what it takes to be a part of the cultural mainstream. Nowhere, I might argue, is the concept of a cultural mainstream more problematic than in the multicultural United States where, in fact, the term is most widely used.

Music exhibits a dichotomy in relation to American notions of ethnicity. It is a conservative factor in the retention of ethnicity because, consciously or subconsciously, it slows down the loss of tradition. Music, moreover, makes ethnicity audible, that is, it makes the boundaries of the group identifiable. In its functions in modern American society, music can reflect all stages of acculturation (e.g., absorbing elements from popular, contemporary music) as well as of interethnic relations (e.g., absorbing repertory and playing techniques from other ethnic musical cultures). More than perhaps any other element with the exception of language, music has an extraordinary ability to determine ethnic identity (cf. Nettl 1965:194, and Grame 1976).

In such an operationally complex field of meanings, it no longer becomes possible to draw specific parallels to other forms of identity. "Ethnic folk music" is not synonomous with "folk music." Instead, it is the music of a group of human beings who seek to identify their sense of belonging in certain ways. The term *ethnic music*, I argue, lies outside the field referred to by the European concept of folk music.

The criticism by many in the countries of origin that ethnic music in the United States consists only of fragments, and that most important signifiers of culture have died out relies on concepts that measure only the distance from an original culture. The immigrant distances him- or herself, according to this criticism, although ethnic consciousness of the immigrant actually results from a sense of drawing closer to a desired cultural goal. The European notion, thus, rests on a concept of "otherness" that results from noting only the survival of what are imagined to be essential traces. An ethnic group would, therefore, want to demonstrate otherness so that it would not have to fit into American culture, but it can only achieve this with clichés such as Oktoberfest, beer-drinking, or Christmas concerts.

One aspect of ethnic music is, therefore, that it is always "other-sounding," no matter which side is listening. For Austrians, Burgenland-American sounds American; for Americans, it has that Old Country feel, making it therefore typically

Burgenland. Both sides are right, for one set of styles and symbols coexists with another. The button box is unquestionably Burgenland-American, though when it is played with extensive ornamentation, it is Slovenian-American, and when it has strong metric contrasts, it is distinctively Polish-American (Bohlman 1988:116). The button box is ethnically specific and ethnically American. [11]

In American usage, both lay and academic, the concept of ethnic music has many different definitions; or better, it seems to resist definition in order to retain a certain malleability. Each ethnic group, as I see it from my Austrian perspective, defines and uses ethnic music for its own purposes. If for no other reason, then, Burgenland-American music can no more be German-American than it can be, say, Norwegian-American. There is, nonetheless, a conceptual unity that cuts across differences of usage and community that one finds best by listing the predominant characteristics of ethnic music:

1. Ethnic music demonstrates some connection to a country of origin. The nearer this connection, the greater the authenticity of the music. Even if authenticity is not a primary concern, there are moments when special traits are called upon and stressed to persuade through authenticity.
2. Ethnic music is under pressure from the outside to acculturate or assimilate to some sort of notion of mainstream. Here we witness a function of resistance that is not associated with folk music in the European sense.
3. The musicians and the community themselves choose repertories and instruments consciously to ascribe identity to themselves.
4. Ethnic music in America almost always demonstrates institutional connections. On one hand, there are clubs and choirs. On the other, there are school programs—German clubs or ethnic radio shows at a college—at one end of a continuum and, at the other, ethnic programs at state and national arts councils, such as the National Endowment for the Arts.
5. There are regular commercial functions. These may take the form of ethnic recordings (see Spottswood 1990) or participation in Grammy Awards ceremonies and Oktoberfests around the Midwest. Certain types

[11] E. Annie Proulx's fictional narrative of button boxes in the ethnic history of North America is a remarkably sensitive and nuanced treatment of the ways in which the instrument is a mechanism for the invention and display of ethnicity. It becomes ethnic in the hands of its performers (Proulx 1996).

of souvenirs bear specific witness to ethnic music (e.g., videocassettes of polka clubs).

6. Ethnic music changes rapidly, usually to meet the needs of new performance media.
7. Ethnic music has no rural roots. Urban communities may even support it more extensively than rural communities.
8. It fulfills the need to experience the exotic or foreign. It plays a role in the ethnic worlds propagated at Disney World's Epcot Center, what I should like to call "ethnic voyeurism." It allows a few words of Hungarian to allow one to understand a dance as a *czárdás*.
9. There is no need for ethnic music to be old. Quite the contrary, newly composed pieces inject new life into a tradition.
10. Ethnic music is not bound to a specific region in the United States. Burgenland-American music in both Chicago and in eastern Pennsylvania draws from its surroundings.
11. Ethnic music indexes other aspects of ethnic culture: ethnic food and restaurants, ethnic clothing, and ethnic festivals.
12. Ethnic music is bound neither to specific genres nor to specific groups. A "polka," though ethnic, may have very different sounds, depending on whether it is Mexican, Cajun, or Polish.

It is many or all these characteristics that coalesce as the ethnic maintream. The musics that fill the ethnic mainstream are indeed distinct but always changing and always available for different ethnic functions. The Burgenland-Americans, both because they are a small ethnic group, and because they have historically constituted their identity from many different, even conflicting traits, navigate the ethnic mainstream with great skill. The existence of the ethnic mainstream, it follows, allows them to construct their own Burgenland-Americanness: the Burgenlanders in Pennsylvania, for example, have never felt themselves to be "High German,"[12] but they still use the High German repertory. In Chicago, the Austrian Mixed Chorus, which mixes its repertory from Austrian dialects, still uses the DANK-Haus (Deutsch-Amerikanischer National-Kongreß), a center for the promulgation of High-German culture, for its rehearsals and many social events.

---

[12] Their songs, for example, always have texts in dialect.

Figure 13. The Austrian Mixed Chorus of Chicago, rehearsal at the DANK-Haus, February 1992.

Because of the highly institutionalized nature of the ethnic mainstream, it has become possible for Burgenland-Americans to learn their tradition by first apprenticing in the mainstream institutions. Al Meixner from Coplay, Pennsylvania, is today one of the best known Burgenland-American musicians. Growing up in the Burgenland region of eastern Pennsylvania, he studied "ethnic music" at Duquesne University in Pittsburgh, home of the Duquesne Tamburitzans, one of the most highly organized, semi-professional programs for learning and performing instrumental and dance traditions from the former Yugoslavia. With his music education in Duquesne's Serbo-Croatian-American traditions, Meixner qualitatively increased his button-box skills and expanded the repertory of Burgenland-American music when he returned to eastern Pennsylvania. He also used his media experiences from Duquesne to initiate programs in ethnic broadcasting, such as the local "International Radio Show" (WNUH, 91.7 FM). Even though there are different musical traditions represented on this program, local Burgenland-Americans regard its success as a source for the promulgation of "their music." The ethnic mainstream, in this way, directly and indirectly enriched the Burgenland-American musical traditions of eastern Pennsylvania.

Polka, Ethnic, and Burgenland-American

Whereas my schematic discussion of ethnic music suggested the existence of a broader context of traditions that enabled musical change, there are genres that emerge within that context and form canons of their own. The characteristic of an ethnic musical canon is, in fact, the paradox of flexibility and the specificity of ownership. In other words, it is music that can become "our music," even when its entry into ethnic tradition was from the outside, that is, when it crossed the boundaries between ethnic traditions.

From an Austrian perspective, polka in North America mediates ethnicity and the ethnic mainstream in the following ways: [13]

1. Although it is unequivocally marked as ethnic, polka does not require knowledge of a foreign language.
2. Those who celebrate the polka do so thinking that it represents an American way of life, and there is little awareness of its history and distribution in Europe.
3. The polka replaces other genres in an ethnic community, for example, religious or life-cycle songs, freeing the community from needing to know the language to maintain these songs.
4. Polka can be adapted to many functions in the ethnic traditions of a community, ranging from dance (its original function) to special religious holidays celebrated in the social space of a church, such as its gymnasium.
5. Polka is performative, and it therefore empowers a community to perform its ethnicity.
6. Polka musicians may be amateur, professional, or semi-professional; by allowing musicians to "moonlight," polka also makes it possible to move across ethnic borders where other polka repertories are learned and performed.
7. Because it is a popular music, polka allows an ethnic group or community to compete culturally in the larger public spaces of American popular culture, for example, through the polka category of the Grammy Awards or through various polka halls of fame.
8. The instrumentarium for polka bands reflects the traditions acquired and learned through American music education: saxophones have largely

---

[13] My Austrian perspective differs in many ways from the American perspectives in the excellent monographs by Victor Greene (1992) and Charles Keil, Angeliki Keil, and Dick Blau (1992). Greene addresses the ways in which polka culture mediates ethnicity, transforming it in ways that allow ethnic Americans to possess it. The performance of ethnicity contributing to its ability to construct a feeling of group underlies the thesis of Keil, Keil, and Blau. My concern here is to draw attention to the ways in which the music itself becomes a text for ethnic identity.

replaced clarinets; the sousaphone has replaced European tubas and euphoniums; and the drum set has become standard, taking over and transforming rhythmic and metric functions performed by the second violin and viola.

9. The polka creates a flexibility that allows outsiders to enter the tradition and to feel as if they were part of the group.
10. The polka connects local identity to the larger identity of the Polka Belt (see Figure 14) that stretches from the Dakotas in the Upper Midwest to Pennsylvania in the East, while also indexing regional polka styles in the Southwest, especially Texas. A local Burgenland polka style, therefore, can derive identity from surrounding Slovenian and Polish styles, for example, in Chicago.

Polka plays an important role in Burgenland-American social and dance music, redefining Burgenland music as a tradition that one can learn and acquire in various ways. Those who do not play it or dance it can still purchase records, cassettes, and CDs whose covers borrow from the ethnic mainstream (e.g., when Burgenland musicians wear Bavarian *Lederhosen* or hunters' hats with goose feathers) but locate polka on a landscape indexing Burgenland (e.g., a landmark or street scene from Burgenland) (see Figure 15). By making it possible to cross the ethnic boundaries into Burgenland, polka expands those boundaries and musically recreates Burgenland in North America.

Approaching the German and the American in Burgenland-American Music

After beginning this essay by distancing Burgenland-American music from German-American music, I gradually closed the distance between the two. The music of Burgenland-Americans does belong, in part, to the larger musical culture of German-Americans, if for no other reason than Burgenland bands play at ethnic events marked as German—Oktoberfest, Fasching dances—and because there are Americans of German ancestry who participate in Austrian-American musical organizations in order to reinforce their German-American identity. At one end of a continuum, language serves to provide the common culture of this area of shared musical practices. Language, however, no longer has the functions that it once did for the Burgenland-Americans and the German-Americans. It is perhaps less relevant that language survives only as traces, and that most members of the ethnic group cannot speak it. More relevant is that the language of the shared music is a German that first becomes relevant for both ethnic communities in the repertories sung in North America— the Burgenlanders never communicated in the High German of

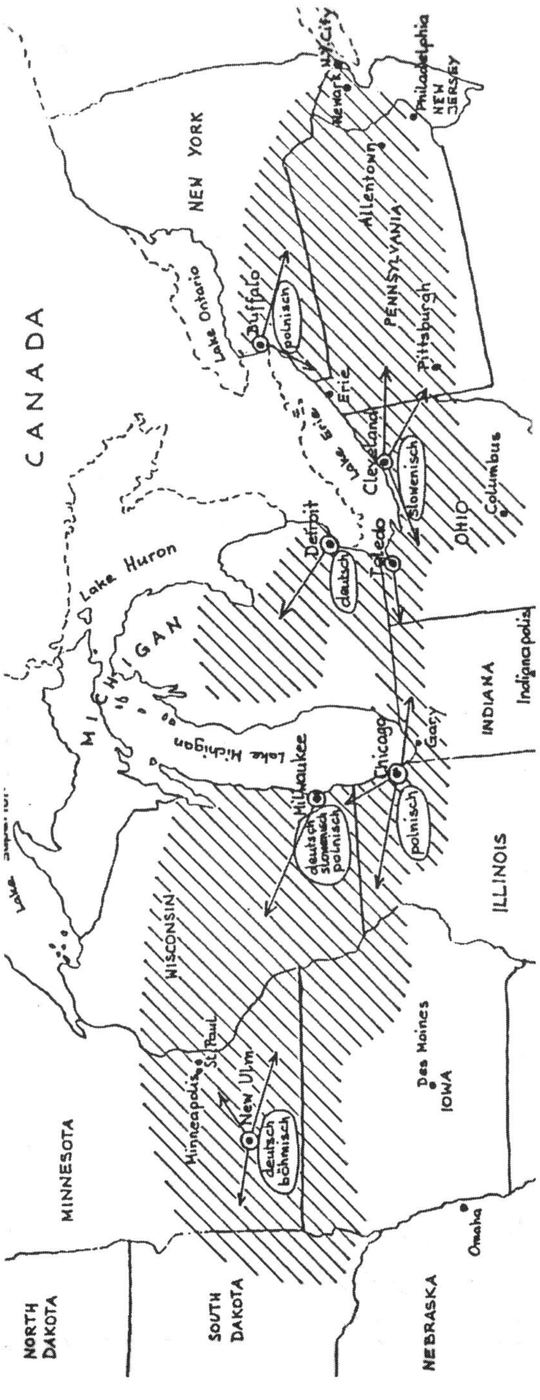

Figure 14. The Polka Belt, map by Franziska Stockhammer-Pietsch.

Figure 15. Eddie Wagner Orchestra of Chicago playing at an Austrian picnic at the *Steirer Alm* (Styrian Mountain Meadow), August 1991.

the songs, and the German-Americans acquired it first through the songs. Dance repertories provide a common culture in similar ways. Alpine *Ländler* survive only in traces for Burgenlanders, and the *czárdás* provides an inflection of a larger multicultural border region rather than the marker of a specifically Hungarian dance.

In the music of the ethnic mainstream of North America, Burgenland- and German-Americans have moved closer together, but it would be impossible to say that the Burgenlanders have become *more* German-American. If there ever was a German hegemony in the ethnic music of North America—and this is a topic I have left to others writing for this volume—there is none at the beginning of the twenty-first century. Whereas one can speak of "Dutchman polkas" or "German old-time music," such distinctions of genre have long been loosened from Germanness. The operative distinctions are, instead, "polka" and "old-time music." The musics of German-Americans are far more American than German precisely because they have become ethnic musics.

Burgenland-Americans effectively recognized the phenomenon of the ethnic mainstream much earlier than the larger immigrant and ethnic groups. In this sense, they might well serve as a type of model that would allow scholars of ethnicity and ethnomusicologists to rethink the ways in which music mediates the relation between a small group and its cultural surroundings. The traditional model that persists even at the beginning of the twenty-first century, no doubt because of the new immigration to North America, is portrayed according to large groups (e.g., Asian- or Hispanic-Americans, or the South-Asian diaspora). Against the backdrop of the larger groups, the model for small groups is that of surviving, of clinging to those musical elements and practices that represent a quintessential uniqueness. For the Burgenland-Americans, the quintessentially Burgenland was not, however, something that could be measured and maintained as unique. Burgenland-Americans realized that the most effective way to distinguish their identity in the ethnic mainstream was not to swim against its currents, but rather to navigate them so that they enriched their musical culture along with the musical cultures of other ethnic Americans.

Bibliography

Baumgartner, Gerhard, Eva Müllner, and Rainer Münz, eds. *Identität und Lebenswelt: ethnische, religiöse und kulturelle Vielfalt im Burgenland*. Eisenstadt: Prugg, 1989.

Bohlman, Philip V. *The Study of Folk Music in the Modern World*. Bloomington: Indiana University Press, 1988.

________. "Fieldwork in the Ethnomusicological Past." In *Shadows in the Field: New Directions in Ethnomusicological Fieldwork*, edited by Gregory F. Barz and Timothy Cooley, 139–162. New York: Oxford University Press, 1997.

Deutsch, Walter, ed. *Dörfliche Tanzmusik im westpannonischen Raum: Vorträge des 17. Seminars für Volksmusikforschung, Eisenstadt 1988*. With the assistance of Rudolf Pietsch. Schriften zur Volksmusik, 15. Vienna: Verlag A. Schendel, 1990.

Dujmovits, Walter. *Die Amerikawanderung der Burgenländer*. Pinkafeld: Desch-Drexler, 1992.

Elwert, Georg. "Nationalismus und Ethnizität: Über die Bildung von Wir-Gruppen." *Kölner Zeitschrift für Soziologie und Sozialpsychologie* 41(1989):440–464.

Ernst, August. *Geschichte des Burgenlandes*. Vienna: Verlag für Geschichte und Politik, 1987.

Grame, Theodore C. *America's Ethnic Music*. Tarpon Springs, FL: Cultural Maintenance Associates, 1976.

Greene, Victor. *A Passion for Polka: Old-Time Ethnic Music in America*. Berkeley: University of California Press, 1992.

Hemetek, Ursula, ed. *Klangecho—Echoes of Sound: Die traditionelle Musik der Minderheiten*. Vienna: Böhlau Verlag, 1996. (Schriften zur Volksmusikforschung, 18)

Keil, Charles, Angeliki V. Keil, and Dick Blau. *Polka Happiness*. Philadelphia: Temple University Press, 1992.

Martschin, Hannes. "Die Burgenland-Amerikaner im Kontakt: Sprachverhalten und Kontaktphänomene in Pennsylvania." *Yearbook of German-American Studies* 28 (1993): 93–106.

Nettl, Bruno. *Folk and Traditional Music of the Western Continents*. 1st edn. Englewood Cliffs, NJ: Prentice Hall, 1965.

Nettl, Bruno, et. al. *Excursions in World Music*. 2nd edn. Saddle River, NJ: Prentice Hall, 1997.

Proulx, E. Annie. *Accordion Crimes*. New York: Scribner, 1996.

Spottswood, Richard K. *Ethnic Music on Records: A Discography of Ethnic Recordings Produced in the United States, 1893–1942*. 7 vols. Urbana: University of Illinois Press, 1990.

Discography

Burgenland. Vol. 1: *Tondokumente zur Volksmusik in Österreich*. RST–91557–2.

Burgenländische Volksmusik. SSM CD 020 124–2.

Yankovic, Frankie. LP K–TEL International NC 420, Vol. 1; A2.

Index

Song Index